Dan Corjescu

The Global Ape: Between Extinction and Transcendence

Dan Corjescu

THE GLOBAL APE: BETWEEN EXTINCTION AND TRANSCENDENCE

Bibliografische Information der Deutschen Nationalbibliothek
Die Deutsche Nationalbibliothek verzeichnet diese Publikation in der Deutschen Nationalbibliografie; detaillierte bibliografische Daten sind im Internet über http://dnb.d-nb.de abrufbar.

Bibliographic information published by the Deutsche Nationalbibliothek
Die Deutsche Nationalbibliothek lists this publication in the Deutsche Nationalbibliografie; detailed bibliographic data are available in the Internet at http://dnb.d-nb.de.

ISBN-13: 978-3-8382-1612-6
© *ibidem* Press, Stuttgart 2022
Alle Rechte vorbehalten

Das Werk einschließlich aller seiner Teile ist urheberrechtlich geschützt. Jede Verwertung außerhalb der engen Grenzen des Urheberrechtsgesetzes ist ohne Zustimmung des Verlages unzulässig und strafbar. Dies gilt insbesondere für Vervielfältigungen, Übersetzungen, Mikroverfilmungen und elektronische Speicherformen sowie die Einspeicherung und Verarbeitung in elektronischen Systemen.

All rights reserved. No part of this publication may be reproduced, stored in or introduced into a retrieval system, or transmitted, in any form, or by any means (electronic, mechanical, photocopying, recording or otherwise) without the prior written permission of the publisher. Any person who does any unauthorized act in relation to this publication may be liable to criminal prosecution and civil claims for damages.

Printed in the EU

To All Those Who Want Something Better

Table of Contents

Introduction: The Global Ape Between Extinction and Transcendence 9

Chapter One: The Fiery People 13
- 1. War-Nests 33
- 2. Great Chefs 34
- 3. Highly Emotional People 35
- 4. Mind Readers 37
- 5. Socialites 39
- 6. Cuddly Punishers 40
- 7. The Cultural Animal 44
- 8. Masters of Complexity 46

Chapter Two: Human Behavior, War, and The State 51

Chapter Three: Global Elements of Genocide: The Scholars Speak 77

Chapter Four: Enlightenment, Modernity, and Genocide Reconsidered 103

Chapter Five: War's Dialectic? 133

Chapter Six: All of Caesar's Men 145

Chapter Seven: The Evolution of Leadership and Social Dominance 153

Chapter Eight: The Babbling Ape 167

Chapter Nine: The Religious Ape: Homo Religiosus 181

Chapter Ten: The Shifting Sands of Science and Technology 203

Chapter Eleven: Moral and Unfree or On the Moral Graciousness of Fatalism 215

Chapter Twelve: The Global Ape: Between Transcendence and Extinction 237

Bibliography 245

Introduction: The Global Ape

Between Extinction and Transcendence

Human beings were global long before they were even fully human.

Our direct ancestor, *Homo Erectus,* was not only the longest surviving hominin group ever recorded, existing for over 1.5 million years, they were also the most geographically distributed starting out from Africa and then spreading into many parts of Asia.

What was *Homo Erectus* like? Well, firstly, he was in many ways very much like you and me. He possessed human like body proportions with shorter arms and longer legs relative to his torso. Behaviorally, he may well have been the first hominin to tame fire and to begin to use it for cooking. The consequences of these two particular technological breakthroughs and cultural practices were to prove enormous.

The taming and use of fire allowed us to live a life on the ground, protected from wild animals by day and by night. It probably led to, among other things, the gradual shedding of our hair, modern day sleep patterns, a growing sense of social community focused on the campfire, pair-bonding, and the ability to not only release more energy from food (meat) but to do it more easily gradually shrinking our entire digestive system which contributed to a significant increase in brain size as well as allowing for more time on our hands to do other things, like tool making and socializing.

I will be arguing in this book that *Homo Erectus* was the hominin who combined a complex suite of behavioral and cultural traits that eventually led to the human conquest of earth. The development of technologies such as stone implements and fire use; an ever broadening palette of personal and prosocial emotions such as empathy; the ability to read other conspecifics' minds; the growing social need to associate, learn from, and to be helped by others; the gradual process of self-domestication through social selection, and the increasing accumulation and use of material and symbolic culture; all this led to a complex emergent behavioral system that jump started human evolution and continues to this very day. Separately, each of these processes greatly contributed to the course of human evolution; taken together, however, they produced the "slow big bang" of the human revolution in individual cognition, social organization, and power over the environment. It is the story of the "human algorithm".

Thus, human evolution can be seen as a complex system of different behavioral parts that when intertwined produced several kinds of social-cultural-biological feed-back loops which complexly fed into each other leading to something more than its separate behavioral strands: the emergence of the Global Ape.

Yet, this story is not just a powerfully inspiring one, it is also powerfully ambivalent. Why?

The development of the "human algorithm" eventually allowed for spectacular cultural feats such as Shakespeare's plays, the scientific method, the UN, and the Moon Landings but it also helped to enable countless millennia of warfare, slavery, and genocide. The "human algorithm" bestowed upon us unprecedented power, but by itself, it does not tell us how to best make use of it. For this, we need to rely on our inventive powers allowing us to create "ethics" or "values" which constitutes one of the more unique cognitive revolutions of the Global Ape: the revolution of imagination based, in part, on the prior revolution of the human bio-cultural algorithm. If there ever was a sort of "human magic" to transform the world it lies here in our moral imagination.

It is precisely our power to imagine different ways of "being" and "doing" and assign relative values to them that hold out the promise for better ways of living both among ourselves, other species, and our environment. This revolutionary mental faculty allows for the creation of greater levels of social complexity by imagining such things as money, states, and religions to name but a few socio-cultural constructs. Our moral imagination is quite literally our magical doorway to other universes. Culturally based universes of synergetically shared values and practices. Whether we ultimately choose more democracy over more dictatorship, more cooperation over more conflict, and, even, more love over more hate is in large part up to our ability to imagine heaven or hell here on earth. Thus, we are ever the Global Ape suspended between the possibility of either self-extinction or self-transcendence. The choice between infinitely possible worlds is apparently still ours to make.

Chapter One: The Fiery People

*How selfish soever man may be supposed,
there are evidently some principles in his nature,
which interest him in the fortune of others,
and render their happiness necessary to him,
though he derives nothing from it,
except the pleasure of seeing it.
— Adam Smith*

*Yes! I know now whence I came!
Unsatiated like a flame
my glowing ember squanders me.
Light to all on which I seize,
ashen everything I leave:
Flame am I most certainly!
— Friedrich Nietzsche*

*I see it feelingly.
— Gloucester to Lear
SHAKESPEARE, King Lear, act 4, scene 6*

*People just ain't no good
I think that's well understood
You can see it everywhere you look
People just ain't no good
— Nick Cave and The Bad Seeds
Selfishness beats altruism within groups. Altruistic groups beat selfish
groups. Everything else is commentary.
— E.O. Wilson and David Sloan Wilson*

In part, this is a story about fire. The fire of the camp-light and of the human heart and mind.

On the ancient open African Savannah, the kinds of social organization that ancestral hominin groups were able to create and sustain were crucial. Social ties had to be strengthened if these groups were to continue to survive. Cooperation within these ancient groups had to be developed. If not, they could never have successfully surmounted the various threats from their novel environment. Wild predators such as big cats, natural disasters such as floods and droughts, and, not least, long term climate extremes exerted significant evolutionary pressure on them. As we shall see, these volatile conditions helped to contribute to the evolution of human emotions which was destined to play a crucial role in creating ever more complex forms of cooperation allowing for better survival strategies. From these ancient precarious beginnings, man was to emerge not only the most intelligent animal, not only the most emotional animal, but the most cooperative as well.

Philosophical discussions about the exact nature of the relationships between the emotions, reason/intelligence, and cooperation go back to at least antiquity and probably much earlier. It was Plato who famously divided the human soul into three parts: the appetites, reason, and self-regard (Thymos). The first two concepts present us with no particular interpretive problems for our purposes while the last one "Thymos" requires some further explanation.

Thymos is what we would call today "self-regard" or "self-esteem". It is the psychological manner in which we regard ourselves and expect others to value us. When we do something against our own feelings of self-regard, we feel shame. When others challenge, despise, or negatively contradict our inner notions of self-esteem, we generally feel anger and, as often as not, seek some form of redress from the offender, whether person, institution, or even entire polity or society. Indeed, when we insert "Thymos" into modern discussions of the nature and origins of cooperation, altruism, and identity politics, as Francis Fukuyama has recently done, we quickly begin to see just how perspicacious Plato was. (Fukuyama 2018)

While our appetites are of a more bodily nature (if susceptible to cultural and historical modification) and reason a servant of practical instrumentality, Thymos presents itself as a very social feeling.

Our Thymotic self cries out for the regard of the other. We must feel valued, honored, and, even, treasured by those around us. We crave other people's approbation as we fear their contempt. We demand to be recognized by others as we recognize ourselves. Our particular place in our social universe, regardless how small it might be in objective terms, means much to us. In fact, even in the not too distant past, avoiding the status of a social cipher was often a question of life and death.

Plato's gifted pupil, Aristotle, also divided up the human soul, but this time into only two parts: the appetites and reason. He famously equated the nature of being human with that of sociality: Man as a social being, ζῷον πολιτικόν. As it turned out, this way of interpreting human nature was to be more in tune with modern evolutionary narratives of human origins than even the later theories of the social contract theorists such as Hobbes, Locke, Hume, and Rousseau. To be sure, Man arose within social groups probably not unlike those of present-day Chimpanzees and Gorillas but not at all like today's solitary Orangutans. As far as we know today, man was never the shy, solitary, environmentally exemplary noble savage as famously depicted by Rousseau.

Turning our attention now to the direct inheritors of Grecian civilization and culture, we find the powerful voice of the Roman writer Lucretius and his superb poem *On The Nature of Things* which was destined to have a great influence on Renaissance and Enlightenment thinkers and far beyond. (Lucretius 2001)

Lucretius, being a disciple of the ancient Greek Atomist, Democritus, viewed the origins of mankind in a naturalistic light and, with much insight, recounted the rise of humanity through, first, the taming and then increasing social use of fire (particularly cooking) during which early time he says "neighbors in their eagerness neither to harm nor be harmed, began to form mutual pacts of friendship" as well as claiming "protection for their children and womenfolk, indicating by means of inarticulate cries and gestures that everyone ought to have compassion on the weak." And perhaps most extraordinary of all, Lucretius quickly came to the very logical conclusion that "although it was not possible for concord to be achieved universally, the great majority kept their compacts loyally. Otherwise, the human race would have been entirely extinguished at that early stage and could not have propagated and preserved itself to the present day." These remarkable insights were not only to be preserved in time, but were to be fully resurrected in the scientific garb of today's scholarly literature on human origins and development.

Fast forward nearly two thousand years and we now come to arguably the greatest philosophical poem ever written in the English language, a work that was to have a profound influence on Enlightenment thought generally and on Immanuel Kant specifically: An Essay on Man by Alexander Pope. (Pope 1994)

Suggestively, Pope writes that "to copy instinct was Reason's part". By this he might have meant that instincts preceded reason and that it followed the social paths that instinct had lain down before it. Further and towards the very end of the poem, Pope concludes that "true SELF-LOVE and SOCIAL are the same" and that "VIRTUE only makes our bliss below". These are striking thoughts which seem to suggest that our individual well-being is best served when we cooperate with others and that this kind of behavior will eventually ensure a state of affairs that will not only nurture ourselves but society in general. We realize ourselves best through helping others. This is not just a pious Christian thought but, as we shall see, the transformative social-cultural-evolutionary vehicle through which Mankind eventually conquered the whole of earth.

Almost at the same time as Pope, the eminent Scottish Enlightenment philosopher David Hume also had a few things to say about the relationship between reason and what he termed the "passions". For him "reason is, and ought only to be the slave of the passions, and can never pretend to any other office than to serve and obey them." For Hume, what we would today call the emotions determine the ultimate goals of our lives, what we value and how we conduct ourselves and with whom. Reason merely gets us there. It is a practical tool for the satisfying of anciently rooted affective desires. (Hume 1984)

Man's emotional development made him more social than all the other apes and, in time, better able to cooperate. The evolution of the metaphorical heart of man preceded the evolution of his mind.

According to the enfant terrible of the French Enlightenment, Jean-Jacques Rousseau, the lived feeling of what he termed pity was the aspect of the human heart which organized and governed human existence prior to civilization. As he put it in his famous Discourse on the Origin of Inequality "it is pity in which the state of nature takes the place of laws, morals and virtues, with the added advantage that no one there is tempted to disobey its gentle voice." Thus, according to Rousseau, early man lived by a code of compassion for his fellow man intending him no direct harm. It is the classical benign vision of both our early beginnings and the basics of our human nature. And it was to have a significant impact on thinkers, scholars, and revolutionaries of all kinds, regardless of whether it was ultimately faithful to what actually took place within the distant mists of our human origins. (Rousseau 1984)

Another philosopher of note, this time from nineteenth century Germany, also compellingly challenges us to contemplate various aspects of human cooperation. Arthur Schopenhauer in his delightful work entitled On the Basis of Morality firsts offers us a succinct moral prescription that rivals The Golden Rule: Harm no one; rather help all people as much as you can, Neminem laede; imo omnes, quantum potes, juva. This is a remarkable moral injunction that serves both to lessen the inevitable social friction between people and to proactively build ties of amity, cohesion, and cooperation contributing to the flourishing of society as a whole (Schopenhauer 2014)

The reverse of this moral formula is the very essence of malign egoism: Help no one; rather harm everyone that you can when it is to your advantage, Neminem juva, imo omnes, si forte conducit, laede. Such a moral maxim immediately conjures up images of some of the evilest villains of Shakespeare and some of the darker passages in Machiavelli. It is a recipe for social disaster and the dissolution of all positive group activity. It is the death of trust upon which all human societies are built. If adopted by a majority and then taken to its extreme, it would guarantee the extinction of the human race.

But Schopenhauer's meditations on egoism and cooperation do not end here. He goes on to talk about what he considers the great mystery of ethics, das große Mysterium der Ethik, which for him is compassion, das Mitleid, what we would today call empathy. As Schopenhauer framed the conundrum, it is the question of how "the Not-I to a certain extent becomes the I": das Nicht-Ich gewissermaßen zum Ich geworden. It continues to be an ongoing scientific puzzle to this very day. In its modern form, it is known to some as the Riddle of Altruism, which the great Sociobiologist E. O. Wilson would come to call "the central unresolved issue in evolutionary theory".

Schopenhauer, like many philosophers before him, was certain that egoism was the leitmotif of human behavior. Yet he was keenly aware of empirical evidence which strongly seemed to suggest the contrary. Pure selfless acts were not fictions of the philosophical or religious imagination. They were real and Schopenhauer puzzled over them. In the Twentieth century, many thinkers sought to solve the dilemma by "uncovering" the suspected underlying selfish motives behind apparent altruistic acts through what would be called Kin Selection theory and Evolutionary Game theory. Others, particularly those who like E. O. Wilson and David Sloan Wilson (no relation) were staunch believers in what they called Group-Selection or Multi-level Selection theory believed that the selfless acts exhibited by humans were not only selfless in action but pure in motive, having been shaped by millions of years of inter-group conflict modified by natural selection. But here we are getting slightly ahead of our story.

For his part, Schopenhauer attempted to solve the riddle of egoistic man displaying selfless acts by saying that it was through our imagination, die Phantasie, that our inner state of compassion comes to be. We imagine the pain of the other person and make it our own. In a sense, we live the pain of the other as we imagine it to be, or as it would be for us. The happier we are in fact the more we feel the misfortune of the suffering other. For what it's worth, this is a good first proximate explanation. What it lacks, though, is an ultimate explanation. The why something should be so. Why is it that we have this power of imagination to place ourselves in the proverbial shoes of someone else? Today we would call this ability: A Theory of Mind (ToM).

Simply put ToM is the ability of people to intuit what other people are feeling, needing, wanting, intending, or believing. Without this ability human society would be impossible. Indeed, without ToM we would not be human. This ability "to read minds" seems to be, if not uniquely human, at least significantly more developed within humans when compared to all other animals. It would not be a stretch to say that it is a psychological characteristic which helps define what being human is. It is universal, necessary, and, yes, somewhat mysterious.

The strength and importance of compassion, empathy, Mitleid, in the lives of human beings did not escape Schopenhauer. He was convinced that it was an integral part of human nature transcending as he said all "dogmas, beliefs, myths, concepts, education, religion, and moral systems" and to be found in "all lands and times". We have it, because we are born with it. For Schopenhauer we are born Janus faced: as egoists and as altruists. For him, our compassionate psychological states and altruistic acts cannot be reduced to a more basic fundamental egoism such as is expressed in the common German saying "that the cleverest egoists are altruists". On this issue he was not a philosophical monist but rather a convinced dualist as regards human nature. For him it was an indisputable fact that we certainly think of ourselves and act according to our interests but that we also think of others too, not seldomly sacrificing our lives for them, even, at times, for complete strangers.

Following in Schopenhauer's footsteps more than a century later we encounter the American philosopher, Richard Taylor. (Taylor 1984) According to Taylor, man is a creature of passion, of will. He is not the rational animal of Aristotle. He is the passionate beast able to rationalize and achieve his will. As Taylor says:

> What is significant about man is that he wills certain ends. From one sunrise to the next, this is what gives his life meaning; indeed, it is the very expression of life itself. Human reason is employed almost exclusively in discerning the means whereby those ends, which are the product of the will, can be achieved. (Taylor 1984)

Taylor elaborating upon his voluntaristic philosophical project concerning good and evil logically states that "were it not for the need of men to get along together safely, no man would respect any principles of justice". This echoes Spinoza's earlier thought that "nothing is more of help to people than other people": Homini nihil utilius homine. The big question however is not only what natural and cultural forces of selection made this so, but what exactly kept it that way for so long?

In order to begin to answer these questions and others we must turn our attention now to the topics of Evolutionary Theory, Great Transitions in Evolution, Group Selection Theory, Science as a social and moral system, and the past misuses of Darwin's greatest idea.

Evolution as a theory was a revolutionary idea that had a venerable pedigree stretching all the way back to the ancient Greeks. However, in its Darwinian form, it offered itself up as a comprehensive theory of life's origins at a particular time in European historical and cultural development. It arrived at a time of aggressively competing nation-states, during the rapid development of the national-industrial economy, and amidst widespread popular ideologies of race, class, and gender.

The rise of nationalism combined with the intellectual misuse of Darwinian thought led to extreme interpretations of national origins, identity, and international competition which inevitably were to exert a material influence on world historical events most tragically in the form of the First World War. Similarly, the rise of free-trade doctrines and ideas of economic individualism were further radicalized when merged with Darwinian theory often arguing against the interests of the poor and the active amelioration of their economic and social conditions. As far as gender was concerned, Darwinism served to harden older more traditional forms of belief about the roles of women and men at home, in the workplace, in public life, and on the battlefield. As for race, the continuing misuse of Darwinian theory helped to exacerbate, often to a murderous degree, the various cultural, historical, and ethnic antagonisms between majority and minority groups within nations as well as encouraging the elimination of those persons deemed physically or mentally deviant. Indeed, when popular interpretations of Darwinism became united with then prevalent cultural ideologies of Honor and Blood, whether national, subnational, or individual; the twin threats of social injustice and international violence were to thereby fatefully increase their pernicious influence.

Thus, historically, Darwinian theory has been used negatively to support socially destructive viewpoints and practices. Social Darwinism, an ideological and methodological perversion of Darwinian theory, with its stark emphasis on the idea of the "survival of the fittest" was a naturalistic-sociological view of the proper aims of societal development that was successfully espoused for a time by Herbert Spencer in England and William Graham Sumner in the United States. It viewed society as a struggle for survival between the "less fit" (usually meaning the poor) and the "more fit" (usually meaning the elites), an idea which was used to argue against social support systems for the less fortunate. Additionally, other kinds of social eugenics (attempts to "improve" the human race through artificial selection) whether as governmental policy and/or serious intellectual pursuit were widespread and deemed respectable throughout the Western world prior to the Second World War. This often included authoritarian practices such as government mandated sterilization of the mentally challenged or otherwise physically sick. However, after the medical horrors perpetrated by the Nazis were revealed to the world, social eugenics quickly fell into general disrepute. It should be noted however that the causal relationship between Darwinian science and Hitler's worldview has been recently contested by scholars such as Robert Richards. (Richards 2013)

Despite this deplorable misuse of evolutionary theory to create execrable values and distinct dysgenic social policies by inflicting pain and suffering on the innocent, we should not confound the political, social, and cultural uses of a scientific theory with its ultimate explanatory value.

The great Scottish philosopher David Hume taught us long ago that you cannot logically jump from a statement of what "is" to a statement of what "ought" to be. This is his famous is/ought distinction. It was an idea that was latter elaborated by G.E. Moore as the "naturalistic fallacy". Here, Moore argues that the concept "Good" is not reducible to any "natural" quality such as "pleasantness" for instance. (Moore 2017)

Science can helpfully describe what "is" in fact but it cannot tell us what we "ought" to do with this knowledge. For example, if it were found out that a certain population of humans, call them "group A", carried a deadly gene that if left to freely spread would eventually lead to the extinction of the human race, science could not tell us what would be the appropriate social policies to adopt in such a harrowing case. Such task would necessarily be left to the politicians, ethicists, moralists, and philosophers to agonize over in, hopefully, wide open public debate.

Science is not in the business of morals creation except perhaps in one distinctive and important sense. The very practice, development, and maintenance of science as a social endeavor presupposes a strong belief in a particular value system. If we practice and support science it means that we *believe* in the value of the scientific method and the processes of rational thought associated with it. It is in this sense that *all* science is ultimately bathed in the values that were promulgated in the Enlightenment. Without these prior values serving as a moral support, science as a socially successful project could not even get started let alone develop. A society must believe in science in order for it to be successful. Thus, to repeat, science itself cannot give us values to live by even if, arguably, science itself is a value laden activity which directs and influences our modern technical society more than anything else. Initially, science needs to be believed in but once it gets started it cannot tell us what to do with its potentially world changing results.

Science is a specific kind of "fact producing machine" while man is the quintessential value creator and world interpreter among the animals. This is a theme which preoccupied philosophers and historians as diverse as Nietzsche, Burckhardt, Dilthey, Wittgenstein, and Gadamer. However, it could be cogently argued that an accumulation of new facts on a particular subject will certainly produce pressure on the mental processes leading to the effective application of a moral evaluation once taken. For instance, if science continues to produce substantial evidence that our economic activity on this planet is causing increasingly irreparable harm then people, being factually/evolutionary interested in their survival, will be necessarily constrained to take positive action rather than morally abstaining. In this way, it can be seen that even though science cannot create values it certainly can have a decisive and cumulative influence on which values and courses of action will ultimately be adopted by, in this case, our increasingly global society.

Encouragingly, during an age when many reveled in pseudo-Darwinian doctrines of nature "red in tooth and claw" there were some who even then well understood the distinction between the ethical world of value creation and the scientific world of the discovery of facts.

Two Victorian gentlemen come to mind here. The first was the Russian prince and notable anarchist Pyotr Alexeyevich Kropotkin who wrote the optimistic work Mutual Aid. (Kropotkin 2006) The other was the English Biologist and Anthropologist Thomas Henry Huxley popularly known as "Darwin's Bulldog" for his strong public advocacy of the then new theory. Huxley delivered a famous speech at the Sheldonian Theater in London on May 18th, 1893 entitled Evolution and Ethics. (Huxley 2009)

Kropotkin's book Mutual Aid forcefully argued that Darwinian theory teaches us cooperation and not conflict and competition; that it is not a struggle between life forms for existence and, ultimately, propagation. For him, the "fittest' were those who helped each other out. As he put it:

> we at once perceive that though there is an immense amount of warfare and extermination going on amidst various species, and especially amidst various classes of animals, there is, at the same time, as much, or perhaps even more, of mutual support, mutual aid, and mutual defence amidst animals belonging to the same species or, at least, to the same society.

It was this belief that led him to the idea that "sociability is as much a law of nature as mutual struggle." And much of the rest of the book is devoted to exhibiting historical and naturalistic examples of this, his fundamental thesis.

Kropotkin, following in the footsteps of Rousseau and others, was to have many imitators and followers in the twentieth and twenty-first centuries. Indeed, much of the present book will prove to be an intellectual exploration as to how right or wrong he ultimately might have been.

Huxley, too, in his speech Evolution and Ethics provides an uplifting vision. He strongly denies the conclusion, then prevalent, that evolution means the adopting of a "gladiatorial theory of existence". He contends that the ultimate direction of human society is guided by ethical choices based on careful, rational deliberation. He extols the force of human culture over human nature.

Indeed, he exhorts us to actively, consciously work against the "struggle for survival". In as much as we are able to do this, he argues, we will socially and morally progress. For him, then, the "struggle for survival" is not destiny, but an earlier natural fate that can and must be overcome through a successful combination of human decision making and moral evaluation.

As he stirringly put it all those years ago:

> Social progress means a checking of the cosmic process at every step and the substitution for it of another, which may be called the ethical process; the end of which is not the survival of those who may happen to be the fittest, in respect of the whole of the conditions which exist, but of those who are ethically the best.

Here, then, is a vision worthy of the world's quintessential cultural animal. The realization that we are able to superimpose another evolutionary layer on the natural world that of the ethical. It is our powers of moral evaluation and culture making that can, if we but will it, lead us towards new paths of social evolution independent of prior natural laws of selection and survival. Human culture can write another new chapter in the annals of evolution:

> The ethical progress of society depends, not on imitating the cosmic process, still less in running away from it, but in combating it. It may seem an audacious proposal thus to pit the microcosm against the macrocosm and

> to set man to subdue nature to his higher ends; but, I venture to think that the great intellectual difference between the ancient times with which we have been occupied and our day, lies in the solid foundation we have acquired for the hope that such an enterprise may meet with a certain measure of success …The history of civilization details the steps by which men have succeeded in building up an artificial world within the cosmos. Fragile reed, as he may be, man, as Pascal says, is a thinking reed: there lies within him a fund of energy, operating intelligently and so far akin to that which pervades the universe, that it is competent to influence and modify the cosmic process. In virtue of his intelligence, the dwarf bends the Titan to his will.

The "Titan" to which Huxley refers is, of course, the great discovery of Darwin, for some, perhaps the greatest discovery ever made by Man: the theory of natural selection. As the philosopher Daniel Dennett has put it:

> Let me lay my cards on the table. If I were to give an award for the single best idea anyone has ever had, I'd give it to Darwin, ahead of Newton and Einstein and everyone else. In a single stroke, the idea of evolution by natural selection unifies the realm of life, meaning, and purpose with the realm of space and time, cause and effect, mechanism and physical law. But it is not just a wonderful scientific idea. It is a dangerous idea. (Dennett 1996)

The "dangerous" idea itself was straightforward. Here, the evolutionary biologist David Sloan Wilson gives us a succinct summary:

> The theory is amazingly simple: 1) Individuals vary; 2) Their differences often have consequences for survival and reproduction; 3) Offspring resemble their parents. Given these three conditions, populations will change over time. Traits that contribute to survival and reproduction will become more common. Individuals will become well adapted to their environments. (Wilson 2019)

Daniel Dennett has interpreted the theory as an example of a mindless "algorithmic process". Individual organisms within a species vary. They compete for resources and mates. They are differentially successful at a) survival and b) the production of offspring. Those who are successful in reproduction pass on their genetic traits to the next generation which repeats the process. Over time, different traits will come to dominate depending, in part, on an ever-changing environment. As the environmental circumstances change, so too will the species. However, if environmental pressures are too abrupt in time or otherwise overwhelming the species may become extinct and the algorithm completely stops for that lineage. Indeed, it is a sobering thought that of almost all of the species that have ever lived on this planet the vast majority are no more. On this planet, the algorithm, itself, survives while the players are constantly changing.

This idea is both a biological philosophy of change and an elegant explanation for it. Although simple, it does not lack in aesthetic power. Darwin himself saw that:

> There is grandeur in this view of life, with its several powers, having been originally breathed by the Creator into a few forms or into one; and that, whilst this planet has gone cycling on according to the fixed law of gravity, from so simple a beginning endless forms most beautiful and most wonderful have been, and are being, evolved. (Darwin 2009)

Yet, if the theory is simple, elegant, aesthetically pleasing, and, above all, true why is it then "dangerous"? Again Dennett:

> Darwin's idea bear(s) an unmistakable likeness to universal acid: it eats through just about every traditional concept, and leaves in its wake a revolutionized world-view, with most of the old landmarks still recognizable, but transformed in fundamental ways.
> Darwin's idea had been born as an answer to questions in biology, but it threatened to leak out, offering answers — welcome or not — to questions in cosmology (going in one direction) and psychology (going in the other direction). If redesign could be a mindless, algorithmic process of evolution, why couldn't that whole process itself be the product of evolution, and so forth, all the way down? And if mindless evolution could account for the breathtakingly clever artifacts of the biosphere, how could the products of our own "real" minds be exempt from an evolutionary explanation? Darwin's idea thus also threatened to spread all the way up, dissolving the illusion of our own authorship, our own divine spark of creativity and understanding.
> Much of the controversy and anxiety that has enveloped Darwin's idea ever since can be understood as a series of failed campaigns in the struggle to contain Darwin's idea within some acceptably "safe" and merely partial revolution. Cede some or all of modern biology to Darwin, perhaps, but hold the line there! Keep Darwinian thinking out of cosmology, out of psychology, out of human culture, out of ethics, politics, and religion! (Dennett 1996)

As just mentioned by Dennett, among one of the most fascinating ways in which evolutionary theory has "crossed the line" is in its application to culture.

Culture-gene co-evolution otherwise known as dual inheritance theory attempts to explain how genes and culture interact through time.

What genetic and cultural evolution have in common is that both genes and cultures have variable traits that change their frequencies over time. The main difference is: what is transmitted. Genes "encode chemical messages to build proteins that ultimately enable form and function.". (Mukherjee 2016) Culture transmits learned behaviors and ideas. Another major difference between the two is the speed of transmission. Normally, genetic change is slow, or at least much slower than cultural change can be. Even if significant genetic change, under the right circumstances, could theoretically occur over the span of a few generations, significant cultural change can happen within the course of a single lifespan. One of the reasons for this is that cultural change can move "horizontally" through space from person to person, while genetic change is spatially and temporally sequential.

An oft used example illustrating the difference between the two methods of transmission is a hundred-year-old woman born in 1900 in East Berlin. She would have lived through a Wilhemine, Weimar, Nazi, Socialist, and a reunified Democratic Germany, all of which were culturally very different. Yet she, for the most part, would not have changed genetically.

Another interesting aspect of the theory is how culture and genes interact.

Perhaps the most significant illustrations available for this are the invention of cooking and the beginning of dairying.

Since we will talk in depth about the first one shortly, I will limit myself to talking about the second one for now.

Around 8K years ago, some human populations began raising cattle for milk. As a result, within these populations genetic traits for lactose digestion began to be strongly selected for. It was beneficial (in terms of enhanced survival and reproduction) for people to be able to drink milk into adulthood in these populations. This is a good example of how culture can influence genes.

In their controversial book *The 10,000 Year Explosion* Gregory Cochran and Henry Harpending explain how:

> human evolution has accelerated in the past 10,000 years, rather than slowing or stopping, and is now happening about 100 times faster than its long-term average over the 6 million years of our existence. The pace has been so rapid that humans have changed significantly in body and mind over recorded history. Sargon and Imhotepl were different from you genetically as well as culturally. (Cochran and Hapending 2010)

Ultimately, what is causing so much historically recent change are the selection pressures generated by Human Civilization itself. Human created culture and not the natural environment has become the main driver of genetic change in humans. This is an epochal change. A major transition in the history of evolution and life itself.

Interestingly, a common theme in the "major transitions of evolution" such as

> "the origin of life, of the genetic code, of cells, of sex, of multicellular organisms, of societies, and of language" is that they all share a common feature: "entities that were capable of independent replication before the transition can replicate as part of a larger whole after it". "As a result, "the constituent entities making up the higher-level units come to share a common fate, with selection pressures working on the higher rather than the lower level units." (Smith and Szathmáry 1998)

This is a characteristic example of a highly disputed idea within evolutionary theory known alternatively as "Group Selection Theory" or "Multi-Level Selection Theory". Some of the more notable proponents of this theory are E. O. Wilson, David Sloan Wilson and Elliot Sober among others. It is an influential minority view among evolutionary biologists, particularly as regards explanations for human biological and cultural evolution.

Darwin was the first to describe an early form of Multi-level Selection Theory in his book *The Descent of Man*:

> It must not be forgotten that although a high standard of morality gives but a slight or no advantage to each individual man and his children over other men of the same tribe, yet that an increase in the number of well-

endowed men and advancement in the standard of morality will certainly give an immense advantage to one tribe over another. There can be no doubt that a tribe including many members who, from possessing in a high degree the spirit of patriotism, fidelity, obedience, courage, and sympathy, were always ready to aid one another, and to sacrifice themselves for the common good, would be victorious over most other tribes; and this would be natural selection. At all times throughout the world tribes have supplanted other tribes; and as morality is one important element in their success, the standard of morality and the number of well-endowed men will thus everywhere tend to rise and increase. (Darwin 2011)

More recently this same idea has been re-expressed by E. O. Wilson and David Sloan Wilson as: "Selfishness beats altruism within groups. Altruistic groups beat selfish groups. Everything else is commentary."

Indeed,

> a number of writers have pointed out that multi-level selection may be of considerably greater importance among humans than among other animals given the advanced level of human cognitive and linguistic capabilities and consequent capacity to maintain group boundaries and to formulate general rules of behavior for large groups, and the resulting substantial influence of cultural inheritance on human behavior (Bowles and Gintis 2013)

And finally,

> Group selection is an important force in human evolution partly because cultural processes can create variation between groups, even when they are composed of large numbers of unrelated individuals. A new cultural "mutation" can quickly spread within a group, causing it to be very different from other groups and providing a decisive edge in direct or indirect between-group competition. (Wilson and Wilson 2007)

The most recent, dramatic example of group-selection at work is undoubtedly the "Columbian Exchange".

The Columbian Exchange refers to the exchange of culture and populations between the Old World and New. As is well known, it is a story of the displacement/eradication of one population by another. The Europeans supplanted the native populations of the New World through a mixture of premeditated violence and, for the most part, the unpremeditated spread of disease. They were able to do so because of their superior technology, internal organization, and ideology; all essential parts of culture. The end effect was, as Darwin wrote, the supplanting of one "tribe" by another.

Many scholars in line with Darwin believe that this was but the newest chapter in a long story of human groups supplanting/exterminating other human groups. And this grim story most likely extends to non-human groups such as the Neanderthals, although this is a topic that is hotly contested. Some believe that the Neanderthals died of "natural causes" due from either "extreme climate change", "low birth rates", "incest", or most recently "changes in the earth's magnetic field". (Davis 2021) While this point of view let's our ancestors off the hook, other scholars firmly believe that *Homo Sapiens* out-competed Neanderthals through either superior cognitive abilities, better technology, targeted warfare and overall better cultural transmission or a combination of all four. Perhaps we will never know for sure.

However, it may equally be true that in order for group-selection to work it does not necessarily require inter-group conflict. As the social psychologist Jonathan Haidt writes: "Group selection does not require war or violence. In general, groupishness is focused on improving the welfare of the in-group, not on harming an out-group." (Haidt 2013) While this might be an expression of Twenty-First Century wishful thinking on his part, we will explore his idea more fully once we get to the anthropological theories of Christopher Boehm.

Yet another factor potentially contributing to the plausibility of Group-Selection Theory is a controversial process known as the *Baldwin Effect*.

A subtle modification of the Darwinian theory of natural selection, first outlined almost exactly a century ago by the American psychologist James Mark Baldwin, "Baldwinian evolution", suggested that learning and behavioral flexibility can play a role in amplifying and biasing natural selection because these abilities enable individuals to modify the context of natural selection that affects their future kin. Behavioral flexibility enables organisms to move into niches that differ from those their ancestors occupied, with the consequence that succeeding generations will face a new set of selection pressures. For example, an ability to utilize resources from colder environments may initially be facilitated by seasonal migratory patterns, but if adaptation to this new niche becomes increasingly important, it will favor the preservation of any traits in subsequent generations that increase tolerance to cold, such as the deposition of subcutaneous fat, the growth of insulating hair, or the ability to hibernate during part of the year. In summary, Baldwin's theory explains how behaviors can affect evolution, but without the necessity of claiming that responses to environmental demands acquired during one's lifetime could be passed directly on to one's offspring (a discredited mechanism for evolutionary change proposed by the early nineteenth-century French naturalist Jean Baptiste Lamarck). Baldwin proposed that by temporarily adjusting behaviors or physiological responses during its lifespan in response to novel conditions, an animal could produce irreversible changes in the adaptive context of future generations. Though no new genetic change is immediately produced in the process, the change in conditions will alter which among the existing or subsequently modified genetic predispositions will be favored in the future ... In general, behavioral adaptations tend to precede and condition the major biological changes evident in human evolution because they are far more facile and responsive than genetic and morphological changes. (Deacon 1997)

Put in other words, social learning, behavioral changes, and cultural novelty can, if maintained and repeated through the generations, change the course of evolution. This idea has immediate major implications for how we theorize about human evolution. First, if true, it means that the introduction for example of a new tool, social rule, or group behavior, could, over the span of a few generations, favor the selection of new genetic traits. Thus, social learning, material invention, and intra-group imitation, in the human case, could have, in some instances, led to significant change in the human genome eventually transforming both our minds and our bodies. We have already mentioned an historical example of this in the cultural practice of dairying and its eventual genetic consequences. As Dennett has written: "A practice that is both learnable (with effort) and highly advantageous once learned can become more and more easily learned, can move gradually into the status of not needing to be learned at all." (Depew and Weber 2007)

How many other human traits that are now genetically encoded might have first begun with the learning of new ways of doing things? Even more provocatively, do species with ample behavioral plasticity "tend to evolve faster than those without it."? (Dennett 1992) And finally and perhaps most importantly, the Baldwin Effect allows us to believe that "organisms do not passively succumb to the severity of environmental judgment. Instead, they perceive, interpret, and act in the environment in ways that creatively and unpredictably change the whole setting for selection and evolution." (Hoffmeyer and Kull in Depew and Weber 2007)

Keeping our previous discussions of the theory of natural selection and the Baldwin effect in mind, we can now begin to piece together the mystery of human evolution by first introducing eight theories that, separately, have helped to explain it. I have nicknamed the eight theories as follows:

1) War-Nests

2) Great Chefs

3) Highly Emotional People

4) Mind Readers

5) Socialites

6) Cuddly Punishers

7) The Cultural Animal and, finally,

8) Masters of Complexity.

1. War-Nests

Our first theory comes to us from the work of E.O. Wilson and the theoretical biologist Samuel Bowles. (Wilson 2013)

In a nutshell, Wilson and Bowles argue that unlike modern-day chimpanzees, early hominins established campsites that served as defensible nests. With the taming of fire, this behavioral trend was reinforced. Both Wilson and Bowles argue that there was a high frequency of violent competition between "human nests". This violent multi-generational inter-group competition led to the selection of genetic traits that favored what Wilson terms "eusocial" behavior such as altruism and empathy leading to enhanced forms of intra-group cooperation. The key questions for this group-selection theory is whether or not violent competition between human groups based on territoriality and scarce resources is historically accurate and, if it was, if the frequency was high enough to significantly influence the evolution of human social behavior.

This theory suggests, among other things, that once a human group became collectively conscious of itself as a group or, in other words, saw itself as an organic whole, it became from that moment on an important bio-cultural selector for future human character traits and behaviors. It is exactly when a group becomes at least vaguely conscious of itself as a whole that we can say human culture as a significant evolutionary force was born. At that moment, when human members are seen as parts of a greater whole; punishments and rewards can be meted out in the name of and for the presumed good of the group.

In conclusion to his book *The Social Conquest of Earth* Wilson offers this suggestive vision:

> The dilemma of good and evil was created by multilevel selection, in which individual selection and group selection act together on the same individual but largely in opposition to each other. Individual selection is the result of competition for survival and reproduction among members of the same group. It shapes instincts in each member that are fundamentally selfish with reference to other members. In contrast, group selection consists of competition between societies, through both direct conflict and dif-

ferential competence in exploiting the environment. Group selection shapes instincts that tend to make individuals altruistic toward one another (but not toward members of other groups). Individual selection is responsible for much of what we call sin, while group selection is responsible for the greater part of virtue. Together they have created the conflict between the poorer and the better angels of our nature. (Wilson 2013)

2. Great Chefs

What I call the "Great Chefs" theory is based on the revolutionary/evolutionary consequences of the invention of cooking as described by the Anthropologist Richard Wrangham in his book *Catching Fire: How Cooking Made Us Human.* (Wrangham 2009)

According to Wrangham, cooking was the "big bang" that set off great changes in human evolution. First came the taming of fire and soon after, or even before, the probably accidental discovery of first dropping and then retrieving food from a source of extreme heat. Once food and in particular, meat, was being regularly processed by first pounding it and then cooking it a cascade of unintended evolutionary consequences occurred. As Wrangham writes: "Cooking increased the value of our food. It changed our bodies, our brains, our use of time, and our social lives."

The ancient hominin that started it all was probably *Homo Erectus* as early as 2mya. The advent of cooking by the world's first "great chef" led to a decrease in the size of our digestive system in terms of a smaller gut, jaws, teeth etc, an increase in digestive efficiency and a decrease in the time needed to complete the total digestive process (less chewing). As a result, we were able to obtain more energy more easily a fact which was very useful for unusually metabolically "hungry" brains such as ours. Cooking meat helped make our brains grow.

But having a permanent heat source at your disposal did a lot more for you than just cook your meat and veggies. A lighted campfire would have made living on the ground far easier. It would have allowed *Homo Erectus* to sleep on the ground, too. This probably led to a change in sleeping patterns. Arguably it also led to the gradual shedding of our body hair since now we didn't need it to keep warm. Most imaginatively however it might also have led to the sexual division of labor. As Wrangham sees it:

> when meat became an important part of the human diet, it was harder for females than males to obtain. Males with a surplus would have offered some to females, who would have appreciated the gift and returned the favor by gathering plant foods to share with males. The result was an incipient household ... Because females were smaller and physically weaker, they were vulnerable to bullying by domineering males who wanted food. Each female therefore obtained protection from other males' wheedling, scrounging, or bullying by forming a special friendship with her own particular male. Her bond with him protected her food from other males, and he also gave her meat. These bonds were so critical for the successful feeding of both sexes that they generated a particular kind of evolutionary psychology in our ancestors that shaped female male relationships and continues to affect us today. (Wrangham 2009)

Although the above quote certainly puts a new spin on the origins of the idea of a "candlelight dinner for two", it is not the most important takeaway from the Great Chef theory. Rather it is the multiple socially reinforcing effects of the advent of cooking which makes it so dramatically important:

> The newly delicious cooked diet led to their evolving smaller guts, bigger brains, bigger bodies, and reduced body hair; more running; more hunting; longer lives; calmer temperaments; and a new emphasis on bonding between females and males. (Wrangham 2009)

Quite an impressive recipe for any chef.

3. Highly Emotional People

In the popular TV/Film series *Star Trek,* Spock is a humanoid from the planet Vulcan that is purely rational having, for the most part, successfully suppressed all of his emotions (he is after all half-human). Is such a being possible? Not according to our latest understanding of how the emotions played a role in the evolution of cognition. (Evans 2010)

Basic emotions such as "Joy" "Distress" "Anger" "Fear" are "universal" and "hardwired" into the human brain. The so-called cognitive emotions such as "Love" "Guilt" "Shame" "Embarrassment" "Pride" "Envy" "Jealousy" "seem to have been designed by natural selection precisely to help our ancestors cope with an increasingly complex social environment...these emotions may be the cement that binds human society together". (Evans 2010) As the neuroscientist Antonio Damasio has emphasized in his work: "Natural selection made certain that feelings would become a permanent feature of mental states." (Damasio 2018)

Following Damasio's insights further, it seems that "cultural activity began and remains deeply embedded in feeling" and "feelings focused intelligence on certain goals, increased the reach of intelligence, and refined it in such a way that it resulted in a human cultural mind." And finally, Damasio's "simple idea" is "that feelings of pain and feelings of pleasure, from degrees of well-being to malaise and sickness, would have been the catalysts for the processes of questioning, understanding, and problem solving that most profoundly distinguish human minds from the minds of other living species. "

According to the sociologist of emotions Jonathan H. Turner:

> the brain cannot grow to the human measure and, hence, language and culture cannot emerge in the human measure without a prior rewiring of the hominin brain to be more emotional. For, without increasing social attachments and commitment to groups, which can only occur via emotions, the first hominins would not have survived, and thus, it is unlikely that the first Homo would have ever appeared....The emergence and survival of Homo required a dramatic expansion of emotional capacities, and the needed emotional turbocharger had to be built into and integrated with the still small neocortex before the larger brain and what it could bring (i.e., full language and robust systems of culture) could be dropped into the cranium of species of Homo that would emerge on the hominin line leading to humans. For what is now clear is that intelligence — storage of memories, complex cognitions, and rapid decision making — cannot exist without the evolution of a much larger palette of nuanced emotions. No organic intelligence among any species is possible without a larger palette of diverse emotions; for this reason, intelligent life forms are also highly emotional. (Turner 2020)

The initial evolutionary challenge which emotions helped to solve "was to convert weak-tie, non-group organizing primates into stronger-tie animals capable of forming more permanent groups with higher levels of solidarity than is evident among great apes today (and yesterday in the distant evolutionary past)." Thus, I interpret Turner as saying that the basic scaffolding of human emotions was selected *prior* to advanced cognitive/cultural abilities setting the stage for the support of those abilities down the line. Hence, right from the beginning "Reason" was indeed the "slave of the passions".

Indeed, Turner is so sure of his interpretation of the primary role played by the emotions in the development of higher-stage cognition that he sweepingly declares:

> Intelligence is manifest in enhanced capacities for memory storage, thinking, and decision making, and these capacities depend on emotional tags to cognitions, thoughts, and decisions. Such is the case for all intelligent life forms on earth (and I would suspect for allorganic life in the universe). Thus, the neocortex could not grow dramatically until the emotional palette of hominins had expanded, and dramatically so, perhaps close to the level of present-day humans. (Turner 2020)

If Turner is right, then Humans were "highly emotional people" long before they were "rational agents". The emotions, then, acting like magnets pulled rational development towards their own prior ends. Reason may have refined and even enlarged our emotional palette but it did not give rise to thinking as Plato and Kant had originally thought. Rather, it gave pretexts to rationalizations for actions first and fundamentally taken on an emotional level. Long before we became the brainiest animal, we had evolved to become the most highly emotional animal setting the developmental stage for cooperation, culture, language, and so much more. Unlike many other philosophers before him, it was Hegel who understood this relationship perfectly when he said: "Nothing great in the world has ever been accomplished without passion." Indeed, following Hamlet's lament, it would be difficult to find a person who in the end "is not passion's slave".

4. Mind Readers

Most of us possess an absolutely essential superpower: we can read minds. Using bodily, social, and linguistic cues we can read the intentions of others. We, each of us, have what is known as a Theory of Mind (ToM).

How did this special ability evolve? The world reknowned psychologist Michael Tomasello provides us with some tantalizing clues in his book *A Natural History of Human Morality*. (Tomasello 2018)

According to Tomasello, it all began with a change in environment/ecology. Environmental pressures "forced early humans to forage together with a partner or else starve."

> This new form of interdependence meant that early humans now extended their sense of sympathy beyond kin and friends to collaborative partners. To coordinate their collaborative activities cognitively, early humans evolved skills and motivations of joint intentionality, enabling them to form together with a partner a joint goal and to know things together with a partner in their personal common ground. (Tomasello 2018)

Quite simply, we needed to better understand each other's wants, needs, and intentions if we were to continue to survive out on the open Savannah. As Benjamin Franklin was to put it a few million years later: "We must, indeed, all *hang together* or, most assuredly, *we shall* all *hang separately*". The sentiment was not a new one.

A psychological corollary of being able to better read others intentions was the ability to be a good selector of partners with whom to work with and, by implication, to trust. This necessity formed the beginning of all morality and ethics. "Who can I work with effectively" really meant "Who can I trust". With the ability to read minds, the indissoluble link between trust and cooperation was born. It mattered greatly what your intentions were, your personal code of behavior towards others (morality), and the likelihood that your future cooperation would continue.

The ability to read minds led to better cooperation which led to enhanced survival and reproduction. Over time, we became better mind readers and better partners. It is easy to see how such abilities in combination with a broad emotional palette and increasing reasoning power would have knock on behavioral effects that slowly became genetically encoded. Cooperative mind readers became less and less solitary agents and more and more social representatives of their individual groups eventually creating the "super-organism" that some scholars have said is the true nature of modern-day human society. Two human-like creatures carrying a large animal carcass together a few million years ago led, over time, directly to the "Global Brain" of today's interconnected world.

5. Socialites

It is a truism to say that most people love to socialize. Today, more people socialize with greater numbers of people throughout the world than ever before. Social Networking Sites (SNS) like Facebook are the modern expression of Aristotle's definition of man as the social animal: ζῷον πολιτικόν.

A recent version of this fundamental Ancient Greek insight is Robin Dunbar's rather famous Social Brain Hypothesis. (Dunbar 2018)

Dunbar believes "that humans evolved large brains to enable them to live in large social groups." The idea is straightforward enough: Communal living required more cognitive power. But is it true?

Well, to start, lots of animals live in large groups and have small brains. Conversely, the Orangutan is an example of an ape with a large brain that is relatively solitary. From these examples alone, it doesn't seem like group living necessarily leads to brain expansion.

But before we dismiss this theory completely, it may prove useful to tinker with it a bit.

Perhaps when combined with a rich emotional life, mind-reading, fire-nests, and tool making sociality does matter. Thus, the original hypothesis would now read as The Social-Emotive-Intensional-Technological Brain Hypothesis. This means that Dunbar was perhaps partially right after all: communal living is a necessary but not a sufficient condition for the modern development of the Global Ape.

6. Cuddly Punishers

The following theory is actually a combination of two theories. The first one is known as auto-domestication theory (the cuddly part) and the second one as social selection theory (the punisher part).

Auto-domestication theory describes just what it says: how humans self-domesticated over time.

Domesticated animals share many physiological and psychological traits in common. Among these are the retention of neotenic (juvenile) traits which often give adult domesticated animals their "cuddly" appearance as well as the tendency to conserve childlike curiosity, playfulness, and trust. Also, domestication often results in better social skills and greater dependency on others while reducing brain size, levels of reactive aggression, decreased sexual dimorphism (the size difference between the sexes) and "enhanced sensibilities to social and emotional cues." (Benitez-Burraco 2020) Humans exhibit all of these traits.

An interesting and ongoing experiment started by the Russian scientist Dimitri Belyaev in the 1950s eventually showed that after only a few generations of selective breeding you can turn a Siberian Silver Fox into a Dog (well, almost). These foxes eventually displayed many of the behavioral and physiological traits of domesticated dogs including their trust of and dependency on humans. The experiment suggests just how fast evolution, under the right conditions, could lead to a more docile, cooperative creature. (Dugatkin 2017) Indeed, it has been hypothesized that one explanation for why Bonobos differ so markedly in behavior from their near cousins the chimpanzees could be the result of auto-domestication. It is a hypothesis that was developed by Richard Wrangham and his student Brain Hare in their joint article entitled: The Self-Domestication Hypothesis: Evolution of Bonobo Psychology Is Due to Selection against Aggression. (Hare 2012)

Hare and Wrangham argue that

> "by the luck of the draw, the bonobo lineage ... ended up with a huge advantage when it came to procuring food. Their territory boasted higher-

quality plant foods. And what's more, they faced less competition for food. There were no gorillas where bonobos lived and so, unlike chimpanzees, they did not have to compete with their larger primate cousins for food. In this world of relative plenty, with little competition over food, play, cooperation, and tolerance of others were advantageous. Bonobos who played during free time and cooperated with one another to obtain food, shelter, new friends, and sexual partners when play time was over, fared better than aggressive intolerant types. This selection for tameness led to changes in their bodies and behavior that are strikingly similar to the changes in the foxes." (Dugatkin 2017)

But what, if anything, does auto-domestication have to do with human beings? Enter the anthropologist Christopher Boehm with his social selection theory. *Enter the punishers.*

Boehm believes that early proto-humans gradually evolved away from a chimp like social dominance hierarchy with a despotic Alpha male on top towards more egalitarian social systems. As proto-human group-living became more egalitarian, members of the group were increasingly wary of aggressive, despotic individuals who wished to take control of the group. When such individuals arose, Boehm supposes, subordinate coalitions (of males probably) either exiled or executed the offender. This process of social policing and punishment for tyrannical minded offenders is called reverse dominance hierarchy. (Boehm 2001)

Over time, overly aggressive uncooperative individuals were eliminated from the group unable to pass their genes on to the next generation. In this way, proto-humans unconsciously self-selected themselves to become more docile and cooperative, they self-domesticated.

This theory helps to explain why humans exhibit many of the physical/psychological traits associated with other domesticated animals. It also seeks to explain why modern-day hunter-gatherers are largely egalitarian, explaining, like Rousseau, the reemergence of despotic hierarchies as a result of the advent of agriculture and more complex cultures and societies based on the extraction of surplus value from hierarchically inferior classes. It also has the added advantage that it does not need to postulate an environment where frequent inter-group violence was the norm to explain the development of cooperative behaviors within groups.

While I do not doubt that it is highly plausible that early human groups physically eliminated troublesome individuals in their midst I am not at all sure if we can assume that the rest of the theory is not entirely open to question.

For instance, extant hunter-gatherer groups are alleged to be relatively egalitarian. How could we otherwise interpret this oft-repeated ethnographic assumption?

I think we can interpret the observable egalitarianism of extant hunter-gatherer communities in at least three ways: that it is 1) a true reflection of how ancient hunter-gatherers lived or 2) a relatively recent social development or 3) a remnant of just one of many ancient group social organizational strategies that became less and less practiced over time resulting in marginalization.

Another difficulty with the theory arises I think depending on your theoretical positions regarding the question of the relative frequency of inter-group competitive violence. Since it is notoriously difficult to definitively "prove" or "disprove" whether ancient hunter-gatherers were engaged in primitive warfare, scholars positions on this issue often boil down to whether or not they are of the "Hobbesian" or "Rousseauian" persuasion; in other words whether they believe ancient man was constrained by uncertainty, scarcity, and aggressive tendencies to engage in repeated inter-group conflict or whether he was relatively peaceful and rarely concerned with his neighbors.

Put picturesquely, do you believe that the famous ancient walls of Jericho were built to keep someone (homicidal outsiders) or something (mud) out as Frans de Waal has recently suggested? (de Waal 2010)

Taking a tentative position on the issue, I'm somewhat skeptical that humans lived for millennia within relatively acephalous egalitarian group structures. I say this partly on grounds of historical logic, partly on a plausible imaginative scenario rooted in that logic and, most importantly, the theorized role and importance that primitive warfare played in human development by many, if certainly not all, prominent scholars in the field. (Keeley 1997) (Le Blanc 2004) (Gat 2008) (Pinker 2011) (Morris 2014) (MacMillan 2020)

Engaging in a bit of speculation based on those scholars who believe warfare to have been a major activity of pre-historical man, I would imagine that just because extant hunter-gatherer groups are egalitarian, it does not follow that 10K, 20K, 50K years ago that that was also the case. It could well be that one of the reasons modern day hunter-gatherer groups remained hunter-gatherer groups far longer than other groups is precisely because they were stubbornly egalitarian for far longer and not led by more dominant leaders in a hierarchically based militarized group. For me, the question hinges upon the hypothesized conditions surrounding pre-historical inter-group conflict: which group would have been more successful in repeated battle? An egalitarian group imbued with an egalitarian ethos or a hierarchically-militarized based group led by a highly dominant leader? If it was the latter, then it would make sense that egalitarian groups would be gradually pushed to the margins of the inhabitable world. This, of course, presupposes that inter-group warfare was fairly common and that it had a significant, perhaps the most significant impact on hunter-gatherer groups' internal organization. Thus, if this hypothesis were able somehow to be verified or backed up empirically, one would expect to find ancient successful hunter-gatherer groups with strong leaders commanding a primitive but effective militarized hierarchy based on relative status earned in repeated battle. Clearly, Boehm's version of events is far more palatable to modern sensibilities, however if only because of this one should be careful that we are not projecting the desires and fears of our own time back into the past. This is a risk which each generation of scholars inevitably runs most of the time.

Thus, if intergroup violence was ubiquitous in the past (and much evidence produced by reputable scholars says it was), it is hard to see how strongly egalitarian groups could have out competed strongly hierarchical (militarized) strong leader-led groups. Certainly, people love to share meat and other resources equitably, but they desire to stay alive when attacked or threatened even more. In a sense this reflects the old adage that "domestic policy can hurt you, foreign policy can kill you".

Were we domesticated by war? If so, how? Or was the story more complicated than that, being the result of a mixture of intra-group punishment for uncooperative members and the rewarding of cooperative members particularly in times of inter-group conflict? If the latter, then prosocial behaviors could conceivably have been doubly selected for both from within the group and from without probably accelerating the process significantly. If true, intra-group social selection for cooperative traits could indeed have served not one but two unconscious purposes, one negative the other positive: 1) to strengthen internal group cohesion by the elimination of troublesome members and 2) more fundamentally to protect the group's very existence through encouraging extreme altruistic acts of defense/offense when confronted with the ever-possible threat of inter-group conflict. A warrior who is willing to sacrifice his life unthinkingly for his group is exactly the kind of warrior you want in a situation of endemic uncertainty fraught with the potential of outside violence. In the end, we may never know for sure.

7. The Cultural Animal

If you dear reader are as WEIRD (Western, Educated, Industrial, Rich, and Democratic) as I am, do you think you could survive alone deep in the Amazon jungles or Arctic Tundra?

Many earlier, European explorers of various new environments, once stranded or shipwrecked, did not. However, the natives of these places, even when lost and alone, managed to live and go on if not exactly thrive. Why is that? It's probably not due to differences in innate intelligence between indigenous peoples and Europeans.

The answer of course is culture. Culture as a body of socially transmitted knowledge about oneself, one's environment, one's group explaining to us how to live and what to value and, oftentimes, why.

The evolutionary biologist Joseph Henrich in his book The Secret of Our Success explains that our oversized brains are not nearly enough to explain our success as a species. He goes on to spell out that:

> The key to understanding how humans evolved and why we are so different from other animals is to recognize that we are a cultural species. Probably over a million years ago, members of our evolutionary lineage began learning from each other in such a way that culture became cumulative. That is, hunting practices, tool-making skills, tracking know-how, and edible-plant knowledge began to improve and aggregate — by learning from others — so that one generation could build on and hone the skills and know-how gleaned from the previous generation. After several generations, this process produced a sufficiently large and complex toolkit of practices and techniques that individuals, relying only on their own ingenuity and personal experience, could not get anywhere close to figuring out over their lifetime. (Henrich 2015)

The advent of modern human language, agriculture, writing, printing, and science only accelerated this ancient process. More knowledge was accumulated, transmitted and shared with more and more people, until eventually, in the Twentieth Century, we could start speaking about a globally inherited culture. In a sense, all that we have learned and built could be labeled today as a UNESCO World Heritage Site.

For Henrich, genes and culture interact in an "autocatalytic process such that:

> This interaction between cultural and genetic evolution generated a process that can be described as autocatalytic, meaning that it produces the fuel that propels it. Once cultural information began to accumulate and produce cultural adaptations, the main selection pressure on genes revolved around improving our psychological abilities to acquire, store, process, and organize the array of fitness-enhancing skills and practices that became increasingly available in the minds of the others in one's group. As genetic evolution improved our brains and abilities for learning from others, cultural evolution spontaneously generated more and better cultural adaptations, which kept the pressure on for brains that were better at acquiring and storing this cultural information. This process will continue until halted by an external constraint. (Henrich 2015)

As the process continues over generations, the selection pressures only increase: the more culture accumulates, the greater the selection pressures on genes for making one an adept cultural learner with a bigger brain capable of harnessing the ever-upward-spiraling body of cultural information. (Henrich 2015)

Thus, as time goes by, there is a tendency for the accumulation of ever more things to learn putting pressure on learning abilities of all sorts and, arguably, general and specific kinds of intelligences. As a loose rule, "larger and more interconnected societies produce fancier technologies, larger toolkits, and more know-how". (Henrich 2015) If true, what are we to expect from a global society like ours that is nearly 8 billion strong and increasingly interconnected? Is our cultural best yet to come? Are we on the cusp of a cultural explosion?

8. Masters of Complexity

Our last theory is more of a meta-theory. It seeks to combine all the theories that we just talked about within a meta-theoretical discussion about complexity. (The following discussion is based on Holland 2014)

Complex systems "exhibit a distinctive property called emergence, roughly described by the common phrase 'the action of the whole is more than the sum of the actions of the parts." "Emergent behavior is an essential requirement for calling a system 'complex'.

Complex systems have the following four characteristics:

- *self-organization* into patterns, as occurs with flocks of birds or schools of fish
- chaotic behavior where small changes in initial conditions ('the flapping of a butterfly's wings in Argentina') produce large later changes ('a hurricane in the Caribbean')
- 'fat-tailed' behavior, where rare events (e.g., mass extinctions and market crashes) occur much more often than would be predicted by a normal (bell-curve) distribution
- adaptive interaction, where interacting agents (as in markets or the Prisoner's Dilemma) modify their strategies in diverse ways as experience *accumulates.*

I would suggest that the story of human evolution is the story of a complex system that exhibits all four of these characteristics. Furthermore, I would also suggest that our 7 prior theories are just some of the working parts of that system which when intertwined with each other explain the emergence of both individual human intelligence and the species' social conquest of Earth. Thus, it is perhaps more accurate to say that the Global Ape did not so much evolve, as arose as a sort of fortuitous computational design from a complex and directional bio-cultural system with emergent properties.

Conclusion

Now it's time to bring the various strands of this chapter together.

We start with a picture of extreme and rapid climate change which first forced our weakly-tied group-living ancestors out into the open Savannah. Before their stereoscopic color-sensitive eyes unfolded a strange, new landscape full of unexpected opportunities and deadly dangers. Presumably the first successful hominin groups in this new environment were the ones who could better navigate their territory through, in part, better group organization which meant stronger social-emotional ties. These stronger social ties were buttressed and evolved by the sub-cortical development of affective capacity: social emotions. While the emotional life of the early hominins evolved both socially and individually so too did their capacity to express intensionality regarding people and objects. These developments were strongly selected for by the volatile forces extant in the natural environment.

The next scene in this story has to do with the taming of fire, the building of campsites and cooking. Approximately a million years ago when according to our best guesses early hominins began to use fire for protection, warmth, and later (and most decisively) cooking significant cognitive and social changes began. First, the gradual taming of fire allowed these groups of early hominins to better protect themselves from other predators. This bought them time to devote themselves to other things like enhancing their social skills and bettering their primitive technologies. Secondly, when fire was actually able to be produced and fixed in one place it created the campsite, a social focal point, a nest. No eusocial animal can exist without such a nest. Living around the campsite resulted in a cascade of subsequent evolutionary events of primary importance.

The campsite allowed for the cooking of meat. This activity released vast amounts of previously untapped energy which impacted brain development through among other things the reduction of the human digestive system in size, user time, and a redistribution of caloric requirements relative to organs (hungry brains). The campsite (and cooking) also presumably gave rise to new social behaviors particularly as regarded their maintenance, serial creation, and, not least, who was to do the cooking and how for example.

A physically created social focal point such as the early campsite which provided caloric energy, warmth, and protection could easily be called a "home". Our first "fiery" home. By the firelight of the first campsites, early hominins not only ate but socialized (maybe even danced and made music). Indeed the campsite allowed for the creation of another level of sociality through the development of deeper and more broader social emotions which simultaneously enhanced early hominins' capacity for intensional mental states and behaviors leading to more social cohesion and group control.

Once the campsite as "fiery home" was created, group identity could be strengthened. With a more fortified group existence, positive rules, taboos, and social injunctions of all kinds could be (presumably non-verbally) instituted. Advanced language would not be necessary. Conceivably, much can be communicated through a mixture of gestures and vocalizations particularly for a hominin that was in the process of developing a theory of mind and the modes of intensionality that evolved co-terminously with it. In this way, the social group became an artificial selector for those social actions (such as the stealing of resources whether mates or food) which were punishable and others (such as bravery, honesty, sharing,) which were rewarded by reciprocal affections, social aid, or food (often most probably a combination of all three).

So, while intense inter-group conflict most certainly might have existed and may have served as an accelerator for group selection, intra-group conflict, arguably, played an analogous role. Once the group achieves consciousness of itself as an organic whole, it becomes a powerful artificial selector for pro-social behaviors. Thus, while the universal human tendencies to cheat, lie, steal, and kill certainly remained they were from now on to be forever in conflict with the social demands of one's own group as well as the mortal threats posed by other, competing foreign groups.

To recapitulate the main ideas: rapid and intense climate variation and harrowing environmental change came first and did not go away. The broadening and deepening of social emotions preceded advanced cognitive development and then continued to co-evolve alongside growing reasoning power. The taming of fire and the creation of campsites created the first home (and home cooking) and deepened group social consciousness and elaborated new behavioral practices. The threat of foreign groups or entities (whether animal or human or both) reinforced the prosocial tendencies already being socially selected for within the group. Thus, while Nietzsche was certainly at least partly right to poetically identify himself with a fiery flame this was only a small piece of the puzzle from whence the philosopher ultimately came from. Yet, even so and in more than just one sense, he was truly a direct descendant of the "fiery people" physically, emotionally, and culturally.

Chapter Two: Human Behavior, War, and The State

There is a great deal of human nature in people.
Man is the only animal that blushes, or needs to.
Everyone is a moon,
and has a dark side which he never shows to anybody.
Laws control the lesser man – Right conduct controls the greater one.
— Mark Twain

Does our Global Ape possess a hard-wired or malleable nature or something in between? Is he genetically preprogrammed for violence or is it more of an opportunistic behavior that is strategically chosen depending on the circumstances? And, finally, what is the nature of the political container (the State) within which he now lives?

Much has been written about human nature spanning opinions about its essential nature to its possible non-existence. In general, there seems to be three scholarly camps offering up their own version of the human predicament. The first camp we could label as "Hobbesian" which sees early man as essentially a brute enmeshed in a never-ending spiral of violence and counter violence. The second camp which we might call the "Rousseauian" argues vehemently for early man's inherent peaceable nature and harmonious relationship with nature. And finally, the third camp we might name after the American political scientist Robert Axelrod, as "Axelrodian" which posits human nature as an ever-changing mix of behavioral strategies both peaceable and violent reflecting apparently natural laws of cooperation to be found throughout the animal kingdom. (Hobbes 1982) (Rousseau 1984, 1988) (Axelrod 2006)

However, there is yet still another perspective which we might call "Hegelian" after the philosopher of the same name. (Hegel 1977) It is a unique perspective. It posits man as engaged in a dialectical struggle for personal recognition and ever-increasing freedom of action, thought, and belief. (Kojeve 1980) The Hegelian dialectic of Human History begins as a mythic struggle for power between an ultimately weaker and a stronger opponent resolving itself into a hardened social relationship between a lord and a bondsman. How this comes about is in a suspended violent struggle to the death. The individual who fears his death most, submits and becomes the Bondsman, while his opponent assumes the social position of Master or Lord. However, over time, their social situation is not stable. The bondsman, through work, becomes ever more conscious of his own power and through it his own inherent nature, while the Master increasingly craves "true" recognition. Eventually the bondsman, through dint of his labor, achieves recognition from his master and the relationship is thereby equalized. Both can now recognize each other for what they truly are: free individuals worthy of respect. Marx was later to transform this theory into a theory of "class struggle" which he believed was *the* algorithm for explaining human historical development. (Singer 2001)

In his later works, Hegel explored the idea that "war" was an essential form of social struggle which tested the unity of polities and kept them cohesive over the long term; this sounds very much like an early version of modern-day evolutionary theories of human development which stress the historical importance of warfare for human social evolution. (Hegel 1967) (Avineri 1974)

Many commentators from a wide range of scholarly fields have endeavored to show that man's propensity for violence is a natural outcome that can be traced back through his own evolutionary history and indeed much further back into the animal kingdom as a whole. (Peterson 2003) (Boyd 2012) We might characterize this way of thinking of human violence as "the naturalistic argument".

Philosophically this form of argumentation may have been stated most convincingly by the political philosopher Thomas Hobbes. Hobbes posited an initially murderous world mostly occupied by feuding for gain, safety, and or reputation. He laid out his argument in his immensely influential philosophical work *The Leviathan*. It should be pointed out however that, whether or not Hobbes thought humans were inherently "violent" remains ambiguous. What is clear though is that Hobbes thought that the *situation of uncertainty* in which early man found himself logically led to a spiraling behavior of violent preemptive strikes. According to Hobbes, without the credible threat of punishment from a recognized higher authority (A Leviathan) people would be trapped in what would later be called a "security dilemma" from which there could be no escape. In a world with no mutually respected central authority of some kind, a person could never be completely sure of the intentions of other people and so would have to always prepare for the worst possible outcome: various forms of violence directed towards his own person. Think of the movie franchise *Mad Max* and you would be close to the original condition of the human world as Hobbes imagined it.

A strikingly different interpretation on the same theme was offered by Jean-Jacques Rousseau who wrote of man as a timid and peaceful being living off the natural abundance of the land and in complete harmony with it. He explained this idyllic vision most fully in his *Discourse on the Origins and and Foundation of Inequality among Mankind* in 1755. For Rousseau, violence was a cultural product born of the rise of agriculture, private property, and the growing predominance of the state creating an uneasy class society dominated by culturally created forms of hypocrisy.

Turning our attention to the Twentieth century, scholars such as Desmond Morris and, especially, Konrad Lorentz viewed violence as a sort of threat display meant to communicate the possibility of aggression rather than as a prelude to actual physical violence. (Lorenz 1974) (Morris 1999) However, this view of violence as display/bluff promulgated in the 1960s has since become discredited.

New research has shown that intraspecific killing is the norm and the main cause of animal mortality. The suggestion of course is that man is not unique in killing his own kind. A major book on the subject has been Lawrence Keeley's *War Before Civilization* where he demolishes the doctrine that pre-state societies were peaceful and that warfare was a relatively late cultural invention. (Keeley 1997)

Following the ideas of Keeley and others, quarrels were rife among hunter-gatherers resulting in much higher homicide rates than are to be found in any modern industrial society. And it was precisely here, that issues concerning territoriality were found to be central as to some of the causes of pre-state endemic violence.

A crucial example for this line of argumentation has been the historical case of Tasmania. Arguably the most technologically primitive and isolated society ever found by Europeans; the Tasmanians were totally independent of any cultural contact for 10,000 years and were still found engaging in lethal/genocidal warfare among themselves — and the list of hunter-gatherers occupied by similar activities has not been short. The main conclusion from this point of view is that our hunter-gatherer ancestors suffered extremely high rates of killing — far surpassing that of today's industrialized societies and at least equaling those of the first half of the "bloody" twentieth century. (Gat 2008)

Yet it gets even worse; for it has been suggested that intraspecific fighting has been endemic to our species for millions of years.

If one accepts this line of argumentation then the sad fact appears that over millions of years, man's natural state was one of fear and apprehension from violent death. A fear that was all too often realized.

Philosophically, Sigmund Freud explored such thoughts in his dual vision of man as a being possessed of two almost overwhelming drives which he termed "Eros" and "Thanatos", or the sexual drive or death/destructive instinct respectively. (Freud 1990) For Freud, man seemed driven by these two drives and was caught between either their suppression or fulfillment even within the confines of modern-day life.

However, luckily for us, there is at least one other way of interpreting this potentially bloody and, at first glance, self-defeating cycle of violence and counter-violence and that is to see it as one of many possible strategies of behavior depending on the given social, economic, political, cultural circumstances. This way of looking at violence suggests that even if humans have the unquestioned capacity to commit horrific violence upon one another they will only show this side of themselves when the circumstances are "propitious" for their use.

But before we turn to a further analysis of this situational claim, we should in all fairness state that the modern converse of the vision of man as the "killer ape" still exists and is, perhaps not surprisingly, similar to Rousseau's statement of it nearly three centuries ago.

Scholars such as Douglas P. Fry, John Horgan, and Oliver Richmond who support this thesis claim, like Rousseau before them, that man's existence was essentially sparsely nomadic and thus not particularly marked by frequent encounters with others or the practice of warfare. (Horgan 2014) (Richmond 2014) (Fry 2015) Going slightly further than this, Franz de Waal sees us as possible descendants of a "gentle chimpanzee" much like the modern-day Bonobo. (de Waal 2006) Be that as it may, and the latest evidence is contradictory on this point, these modern day Rousseauists emphasize the cooperative, non-violent nature of the Global Ape.

The underlying drive or emotion behind various levels and forms of our highly beneficial propensity for cooperating, according to the new Rousseauists, is our mental capacity for empathy. This manifests itself in various ways from empathizing with different species, such as a stranded whale, to soldiers loathe to kill the enemy. This type of scholarly literature seeks to act as an optimistic corrective against the opposite view of man's inherently violent disposition.

Yet, however noble this scholarly project undoubtedly is, it should be noted that this school of thought, in the end, just shifts man's alleged violent nature, as did Rousseau, from our ape-like ancestors and hunter-gatherers to the start of the agricultural revolution and the rise of states, such as is famously and gorily depicted in ancient works such as the Old Testament. So, importantly, *both* schools of thought are saying that extreme violence such as genocide *predated modernity by thousands of years, if not necessarily millions.*

Fundamentally for their thesis, this scholarly literature of the "peaceful ape" contends that proponents of the pessimistic view of human nature have seriously misread the archaeological and anthropological evidence. Be that as it may, and it is a controversial claim, I am nonetheless inclined to a third alternative way of viewing human nature in both its historical and current context.

This third view or "Axelrodian" viewpoint derives as its name suggests from Robert Axelrod and his deservedly famous book *The Evolution of Cooperation*. But before we begin with Axelrod and his intellectual descendants, I would like to discuss some of the relevant profound insights by the celebrated American intellectual, Francis Fukuyama, taken from his two-volume Magnum Opus: *The Origins of Political Order*. (Fukuyama 2019)

Fukuyama reminds us that there never was a *solitary* human nature. That there never was a *lone individual*. This way of thinking Fukuyama labels as the *Hobbesian Fallacy* which he explains is the propensity to believe that there was an original human nature in isolation. Rather, as backed up by an impressive cross-disciplinary font of knowledge, Fukuyama asserts what is by now the main line of argumentation of this book that man has always been a social animal, as Aristotle taught us so long ago. It was in sociality that human nature within the context of hominin groups evolved. There never was a state of "man against man" just as there never was a "noble solitary savage". Man was always a group creature, born into a group and, more often than not, died within that same group. The only thing that has changed over time is the size and complexity of that grouping: from hunter-gatherers, to chiefdoms, to early city-states, to empires, and finally, and most recently, national states.

What Fukuyama ultimately offers us is nothing less than "the recovery of human nature by modern biology". Basing himself on primatology, population genetics, archaeology, social anthropology, and evolutionary biology he eventually introduces us to the twin concepts of kin selection and reciprocal altruism.

But before introducing these two central concepts for human behavior, Fukuyama criticizes Hobbes, Rousseau, and Locke, on one very important point: the historical primordiality of individualism.

As Fukuyama explains in a crucial excerpt:

> We might label this the Hobbesian fallacy: the idea that human beings were primordially individualistic and that they entered into society at a later stage in their development only as a result of a rational calculation that social cooperation was the best way for them to achieve their individual ends. This premise of primordial individualism underpins the understanding of rights contained in the American Declaration of Independence and thus of the democratic political community that springs from it. This premise also underlies contemporary neoclassical economics, which builds its models on the assumption that human beings are rational beings who want to maximize their individual utility or incomes. But it is in fact individualism and not sociability that developed over the course of human history. That individualism seems today like a solid core of our economic and political behavior is only because we have developed institutions that override our more naturally communal instincts. Aristotle was more correct than these early modern liberal theorists when he said that human beings were political by nature. So while an individualistic understanding of human motivation may help to explain the activities of commodity traders and libertarian activists in present-day America, it is not the most helpful way to understand the early evolution of human politics. (Fukuyama 2019)

And he further states that:

> there was never a period in human evolution when human beings existed as isolated individuals; the primate precursors of the human species had already developed extensive social, and indeed political, skills; and the human brain is hardwired with faculties that facilitate many forms of social cooperation. The state of nature might be characterized as a state of war, since violence was endemic, but the violence was not perpetrated by individuals so much as by tightly bonded social groups. Human beings do

not enter into society and political life as a result of conscious, rational decision. Communal organization comes to them naturally, though the specific ways they cooperate are shaped by environment, ideas, and culture. Indeed, the most basic forms of cooperation predate the emergence of human beings by millions of years. Biologists have identified two natural sources of cooperative behavior: kin selection and reciprocal altruism. (Fukuyama 2019)

The short definition of kin selection (otherwise known as inclusive fitness) as developed by William Hamilton and later picked up and developed by Robert Axelrod is that individuals of any sexually reproducing species will behave altruistically toward kin in proportion to the number of genes they share. (Segerstrale 2013) Thus the example of nepotism is not only a socially but a biologically grounded reality. The desire to pass resources on to kin is one of the most enduring constants in human societies. (Fukuyama 2019)

The second concept, social cooperation/reciprocal altruism, depends on an individual's ability to solve what game theorists label repeated prisoner's dilemma games. In these games, individuals potentially benefit by being able to work together, but they can often benefit more if they let other individuals do the cooperating and free-ride off of their efforts. In the 1980s, the political scientist Robert Axelrod staged a tournament of computer programs that mechanically implemented strategies for solving repeated prisoner's dilemma games. The winning strategy was called tit-for-tat, in which a player reciprocated cooperation if the other player had cooperated in an earlier game but refused to cooperate with a player who had failed to cooperate previously. Axelrod demonstrated that a form of morality could evolve spontaneously as rational decision makers interact with one another over time, even though motivated in the first instance by nothing more than self-interest. (Axelrod 2006)

Turning to the natural world vampire bats and baboons have been observed feeding and protecting offspring within a colony not their own, while in some cases like cleaner fish and the fish they clean, bonds of reciprocity exist between completely different species. The interactions between dogs and human beings suggest a similar set of evolved behaviors on the part of both species.

Interestingly, many evolutionary biologists have speculated that the human brain grew as rapidly as it did for a similar reason: to be able to cooperate and compete with other human beings within the context of groups of humans, not solitary ones. The psychologist Nicolas Humphrey and the biologist Richard Alexander have separately suggested that human beings in effect entered into an arms race with one another, the winners of which were those groups that could create more complex forms of social organization based on new cognitive abilities to interpret each other's behavior. (Humphrey 1976) (Alexander 1979)

Game theory, as indicated earlier, suggests

> that individuals who interact with one another repeatedly tend to gravitate toward cooperation with those who have shown themselves to be honest and reliable, and shun those who have behaved opportunistically. But to do this effectively, they have to be able to remember each other's past behavior and to anticipate likely future behavior based on an interpretation of other people's motives. This isn't so easy to accomplish, since it is the appearance of honesty and not honesty itself that is the marker of a potential collaborator. That is, I will agree to work with you if you seem to be honest based on experience. But if you have deliberately built up a fund of trust in the past, you can put yourself in a position to take even greater advantage of me in the future. So, while self-interest propels individuals to cooperate in social groups, it also creates incentives for cheating, deceiving, and other forms of behavior that undermine social solidarity.
> The Golden Rule mandating that you treat others as you want them to treat you is simply a variation of the tit-for-tat strategy, one that emphasizes benefits rather than the harm side to human interaction. The Christian principle (Turn the Other Cheek) of returning a favor for a harm is in this respect highly unusual and, one might note, more often than not unimplemented in Christian societies. No known society approves returning a harm for a favor as a general moral rule within the group, other than within an idealized Christian society. (Fukuyama 2019)

Inclusive fitness/kin selection, and reciprocal altruism "are default modes of sociability. All human beings gravitate toward the favoring of kin and friends with whom they have exchanged favors unless strongly incentivized to do otherwise. Human beings have a capacity for abstraction and theory that generates mental models of causality, and a further tendency to posit causation based on invisible or transcendental forces. This is the basis of religious belief, which acts as a critical source of social cohesion. Humans also have a proclivity for norm following that is grounded in the emotions rather than in reason, and consequently a tendency to invest mental models and the rules that flow from them with intrinsic worth. Human beings desire intersubjective recognition, either of their own worth, or of the worth of their gods, laws, customs, and ways of life. Recognition when granted becomes the basis of legitimacy, and legitimacy then permits the exercise of political authority. These natural characteristics are the basis for the evolution of increasingly complex forms of social organization." (Fukuyama 2019)

As mentioned earlier, Hobbes is famous for his assertion that the state of nature was a state of war of "every man against every man." Rousseau, by contrast, argued explicitly that Hobbes was wrong, that primitive human beings were peaceful and isolated, and that violence developed only at a later stage when society had begun to corrupt human morals. Hobbes is perhaps far closer to the truth, albeit with the important qualification that violence took place not between isolated individuals but between competing social groups.

Violence can be interpreted as a harmful social activity engaged in by groups of males and sometimes females. The vulnerability of both apes and humans to violence by their fellow conspecifics in turn drives the need for greater social cooperation within separate groups.

Could all this mean that the real driver of state formation is violence or the threat of violence, making the social contract an efficient rather than a final cause?

There have been many theories trying to explain the origins of early state societies. One of the earliest was called: *The State as a Hydraulic-Engineering Project*. A variant of the social contract theory, this is Karl Wittfogel's "hydraulic" theory of the state. "Wittfogel, a former Marxist turned anticommunist, expanded on Marx's theory of the Asiatic mode of production, providing an economic explanation for the emergence of dictatorships outside the West. He argued that the rise of the state in Mesopotamia, Egypt, China, and Mexico was driven by the need for large-scale irrigation, which could be managed only by a centralized bureaucratic state." (Fukuyama 2019)

However,

> "perhaps a major weakness in explanations that are primarily economic in nature concerning state formation is to leave out the role that violence plays. Take the following point into consideration, the transition from tribal society to state society involves huge losses in freedom and equality. It is hard to imagine societies giving these two things up even for the potentially large gains of irrigation. The stakes have to be much higher and could be much more readily explained by the threat to life itself posed by organized violence." (Fukuyama 2019)
>
> "We know that virtually all human societies have engaged in violence, particularly at the tribal level. Hierarchy and the future outlines of a state could have begun to emerge when one tribal segment conquered another one and took control of its territory. The requirements of maintaining political control over the conquered tribe led the conquerors to establish some sort of centralized repressive institutions, which evolved into an administrative bureaucracy of a primitive state. Especially if the tribal groups differ linguistically or ethnically, it is likely that the victor would establish a relationship of dominance over the vanquished, and that class stratification would become entrenched." (Fukuyama 2019)

The anthropologist Robert Carneiro has noted "that although warfare may be a universal and necessary condition for state formation, it is not a sufficient one. He argues that it is only when increases in productivity take place within a geographically circumscribed area like a river valley, or when other hostile tribes effectively circumscribe another tribe's territory, that it is possible to explain the emergence of hierarchical states. In uncircumscribed, low-population-density situations, weaker tribes or individuals can simply run away. But in places like the Nile valley, bounded by deserts and the ocean, or in the mountain valleys of Peru, that were bounded by deserts, jungles, and high mountains, this option didn't exist. Circumscription would also explain why higher productivity led to greater population density, since people didn't have the option of moving away. The tribes of the New Guinea highlands have agriculture and live in circumscribed valleys, so those factors alone cannot explain the rise of states. Absolute scale might also be important. Mesopotamia, the Nile valley, and the Valley of Mexico were all relatively large agricultural areas that were nonetheless circumscribed by mountains, deserts, and oceans. Larger and more concentrated military formations can be raised, and can project their power over larger areas, particularly if they have domesticated horses or camels. So, it was not just circumscription, but also the size and accessibility of the area being circumscribed, that determined whether a state would form. Circumscription would help early state builders in another way as well, by protecting them from external enemies outside the river valley or island while ever-larger forces were being marshaled." (Carneiro 2010) (Fukuyama 2019)

> "It also seems extremely likely that religious ideas were critical to early state formation, since they could effectively legitimate the transition to hierarchy and loss of freedom enjoyed by tribal societies. A possible composite factor for such an outcome could have been the rise of charismatic, religious-political leaders. Max Weber famously distinguished what he called charismatic authority from either its traditional or modern-rational variants. The Greek word charisma means "touched by God"; a charismatic leader asserts authority not because he is elected by his fellow tribesmen for leadership ability but because he is believed to be a designee of God." (Fukuyama 2019)

To a much larger degree "than economic benefit, religious authority could explain why a relatively free tribal people would be willing to make a permanent delegation of authority to a single individual and that individual's kin group. Conceivably, such a leader can then use that authority to create a relatively centralized hierarchical military structure that can conquer recalcitrant tribes as well as ensure domestic peace and security, which then, itself, reinforces the leader's religious authority in a positive-feedback loop. One of the problems with this explanation is that you probably need a new form of religion, one that can overcome the inherent scale limitations of ancestor worship and other kinds of particularistic, local forms of worship." (Fukuyama 2019)

There is perhaps no clearer illustration of "the importance of religious ideas to state formations than the emergence of an Arab state under the Prophet Muhammad. The Arab tribes played an utterly marginal role in world history up and until that point in time; it was only Muhammad's charismatic authority that allowed them to unify and project their power throughout the Middle East and North Africa. The tribes had no economic base to speak of; they gained economic power through the interaction of religious ideas and military organization." (Fukuyama 2019)

What then explains pristine state formation? "We need the confluence of several factors. First, there needs to be a sufficient abundance of resources to permit the creation of surpluses above what is necessary for subsistence. This abundance can be natural: the Pacific Northwest was so full of game and fish that the hunter-gatherer-level societies existing there were able to generate chiefdoms, if not outright states. But more often than not relative abundance is made possible through technological advances like agriculture. Second, the absolute scale of the society has to be sufficiently large to permit the emergence of a rudimentary division of labor and a ruling elite. Third, that population needs to be physically constrained so that it increases in density when technological opportunities present themselves, and in order to make sure that subjects cannot run away when coerced. And finally, tribal groups have to be motivated to give up their freedom to the authority of a state. This can come about through the threat of physical extinction by other, increasingly well-organized groups. Or it can result from the charismatic authority of a religious-political leader (which could later become institutionalized: think Pharaohs here). Taken together, these appear to be plausible factors leading to the emergence of a state in places like the Nile valley." (Fukuyama 2019)

In the end, "there seems to never have been a complete solution to the problem of human violence. Human beings cooperate to compete, and they compete to cooperate. The birth of the Leviathan/State did not permanently solve the problem of violence; it simply moved it to a higher level. Instead of tribal segments fighting one another, it was now states that were the primary protagonists in increasingly large-scale wars. The first state to emerge could create a victor's peace but over time faced rivals as new states borrowing the same political techniques rose to challenge its predominance." (Fukuyama 2019)

A good example for this is "China's transition from a decentralized feudal state to a unified empire accomplished entirely through conquest. Virtually every modern state institution established around the same time can be linked directly or indirectly to the need to wage war. While war was not the only engine of state formation in China, it certainly was the major force behind the growth of the first modern states in Chinese history." (Fukuyama 2019)

Here we should perhaps pause for a moment to gather our thoughts and review what has been written up to now. Based on the ideas and research of others we have posited the idea that man is a social animal that evolved, over millions of years, in groups. These groups, more often than not, engaged in violence, even on the scale of genocide. Over time, recurring violent interactions and the occasional "cease fires" served to modify and, eventually through new technologies, expand the extent and power of these human groups. In time, particularly after the invention of agriculture, early state structures began to form. This socio-historical event did not eliminate violence but began to transform the manner of its expression. That is to say, that with the rise of the state there began a series of transformations concerning the quality and nature of violence. More often than not violence within states declined, while violence between states continued (although this too would eventually decline as we will see in later chapters). We will now explore these fruitful ideas by taking a look at three prominent scholars and their work: Norbert Elias, Peter Singer, and Steven Pinker. (Elias 2000) (Singer 2000) (Pinker 2011)

In his classic book *The Civilizing Process* Norbert Elias explained an important historical trend that purported to show that increasing political centralization coupled with a growing commercial infrastructure was sufficient to reverse trends in violent behavior. In a sense his was a reworking of Hobbes's Leviathan thesis which posited man's deliberate giving up of his freedom to a central authority in exchange for safety from other's potentially malign intentions. Additionally, Elias postulated that political centralization and an increase in "gentle commerce" led to a crucial psychological transformation of warriors into courtiers. This is interesting in that it posits a psychological change first, followed by the creation of new social roles. To sum up: Elias's theory of *The Civilizing Process* suggests that government administered justice/power can have unintended effects leading its citizens to internalize norms of self-restraint and quash their impulses for retribution rather than freely acting on them.

Thus, over time the consolidation of states and the growth of commerce changed the incentive structure of people's psychology. It inculcated an ethic of self-control that made continence and propriety second nature. A primitive culture of honor gave way to a culture of dignity where men were respected for controlling their impulses. Thus, at least in Europe, the Leviathan and gentle commerce were the twin drivers of the European Civilizing process according to Elias.

Yet within Elias's work is something more. Indeed, it is particularly relevant to the world in which we live in today. Elias's work spoke of the advancing differentiation of social functions. He also told the essential story of the monopolization of force which led to 1) violence becoming more calculable 2) a warrior culture transitioning to a courtier culture 3) a general inner pacification of society 4) the development of a court rationality that helped pave the way for the Enlightenment 5) the creation of a nascent middle class that sought to ape the nobility and finally, and perhaps most importantly, the provocative early suggestion that a monopoly of force on a global scale would lead to the ultimate pacification of the earth. It is in this last sense that we can perhaps speak about an "Elian Dialectic".

This historical fundamental change in personality structure due in part to the monopolization of force by the state meant that individuals needed less reason to resort to violence for self-defense. In addition, the growing interconnectedness of urban societies required individuals to increasingly attune their conduct to that of others and hence to moderate their behavior. Thus, the centralization of authority/force, urbanization, and commerce set up a positive feedback loop or dialectic that would relatively quickly, in historical terms, drive down the expression of violence. Of course, it wouldn't occur in a smooth straight line down but rather in a jagged saw fashion, but the trend was clear: man had entered a dialectic of restraint which is still going on today.

Yet for all that, it should be noted that rather than staking out a claim of something altogether new, a radical new human nature for example, Elias was saying something more subtle. Human nature had not changed but its points of emphasis had. It had restructured its payoff scheme in favor of empathy, an emotion that is arguably as old as blind hatred. And this thought leads us to our next thinker: Peter Singer.

Elias not only spoke of the historical development of self-control but of an overall increase in empathy, too. Peter Singer, in some ways echoing Elias, talks about an ever-expanding circle of empathy over historical time. In short, he says, that over the course of history people have enlarged the scope of beings whose interests they value as they value their own. A good causal candidate behind the inflation of the "empathy circle" is the expansion of literacy. In a sense, Singer's version of a semi-conscious "upward" historical movement is similar to Hegel's assertion that the history of man is the progressive semi-conscious movement of peoples towards an ever-greater free recognition of each other as equals deserving of respect. An historical movement which had its apogee, according to Hegel, with the outbreak of the French and to a lesser extent American revolution. For Hegel, then, the years

1776 and 1789 marked the "End of History" at least in terms of mankind's necessary self-awareness of the rational principles required for successful and long-lasting political self-organization. No further ideological progress would be possible, any such attempts would either be retrograde (the restoration of Monarchy) or utopic (Marxism) and doomed from the start to ultimate failure.

Be that as it may, morality, for Singer, has an historical tendency. It begins first with the family extending then to a loosely knit tribe, further to a nation, then a coalition of nations, until it finally reaches out to the animal world. The roots of these changes can be found in biology, according to Singer. Like Aristotle, and more recently Fukuyama, Singer emphasizes the biological side of our sociality.

Singer, echoing Elias, says that as far as social life is concerned, it requires restraint — even among chimps. But crucially, it requires something more. And that something more is altruism. A trait as ancient as the hominin line itself, according to Singer.

Again, like Fukuyama, Singer goes into a fundamental description of kin selection and reciprocal altruism and comes to some of the same conclusions as he did. First, that there is a genetically based tendency to help one's relatives. Second, and once again in line with some of Fukuyama's thinking, hostility to outsiders is a very common trait among humans as well as non-humans. And thirdly, picking up Darwin's observation, the difference between man and the higher animals is one of degree and not of kind.

For Singer, then, human ethics has its origins in evolved patterns of behavior among social animals. This leads him to the observation that though kinship is the most basic and widespread bond between human beings, the bond of reciprocity is almost as universal (this is similar to Axelrod's "Tit for Tat" strategies).

Basing his remarks on the research of renowned anthropologists such as Edvard Westermarck, Marcel Mauss, and Claude Levi-Strauss, Singer finds man's penchant for reciprocity to be overwhelming and universal. This led, according to Singer, to a human psychological development that was profoundly attuned to possible cheating and ways to detect it.

Singer hypothesizes that there were biological benefits to having a genuine concern for others in that others would cooperate with you on a variety of goals from food gathering to mating. Thus, there arose an evolutionary advantage to having genuine concern for others. A good example would be hunting, where having altruistic companions would prove more beneficial to all rather than a loose collection of self-interested partners.

More controversially, Singer posits the existence of group altruism, alongside kin altruism and reciprocal altruism, predating some of the very same thoughts then recently expounded by the famed evolutionary biologist E. O. Wilson. (Wilson 2013) Singer is also sensitive to the flip side of group altruism and that is overt hostility to members of different, neighboring tribes. Thus, aggression and altruism are inbuilt possibilities in the repertoire that is human behavior, similar to the mixed strategies as laid out in *The Evolution of Cooperation* by Axelrod as discussed earlier.

Provocatively, Singer goes on to say that our mammalian nature is "the true reason for the universal rights movement". (Singer 2011) And furthermore, "to ignore biology is to ignore one possible source of knowledge relevant to ethical decisions." (Singer 2011) Both statements are philosophically fundamental, if not without their problems.

Aside from admitting the universal existence in human nature of aggressive and altruistic impulses, Singer points to, like Aristotle before him, man's singular use of his faculty of reason to define him and his future trajectory. As Singer famously put it: "Beginning to reason is like stepping onto an escalator that leads upwards and out of sight. Once we take the first step, the distance to be traveled is independent of our will and we cannot know in advance where we shall end" (Neo-Hegelians might dispute this last point). (Singer 2011)

But like Hegel, Singer too believes that reason is inherently expansionist and that it ultimately seeks universal application.

Thus ethics, for Singer, evolved out of our social instincts and our capacity to reason. And again, like Hegel, Singer points to a discernible trend in ethics/moral thought in which ethics first inhabits a group and then is able to adjudicate between groups; ever expanding to include more and more clusters of disparate individuals. In his view then, society is rapidly moving towards the direction of more general moral valuations encompassing ever more people eventually evolving into a single unit of humanity.

In support of his view that wider valuations in the long run attract more support than the narrower as a general tendency he recalls the case of Plato. In Plato's day an argument encompassing all of mankind would have been absurd, but nevertheless Plato made a crucial step towards universality by considering the welfare of all Greeks and not just the Athenians. (Singer 2011) A progressive move discussed by Hegel himself in his "Philosophy of History". (Hegel 2004)

And once again like Hegel, Singer pays significant tribute to the "brotherhood of man" along with their ideas of liberty and equality as espoused by the French Revolution; ideas which at their root are the expansion of the ancient mammalian drive towards empathy.

However, unlike Hegel, Singer goes beyond the famous German philosopher and calls for a solid embrace of the animal kingdom by human reason. All beings with the capacity for pleasure and pain should be included, according to Singer, and we should actively try to decrease the net total of the animal world's pain as well as increase their net pleasure. One might view this as a sort of "Hegelian ecologism".

Fully aware of the loftiness of his proposals, Singer asks if man is constitutionally able to adopt a universal standpoint of pure reason? The Singerian answer unsurprisingly is that he is. And the basis for it is once again biology. Controversially and in direct opposition to the theses laid out by the famed British Zoologist, Richard Dawkins, in his widely influential book *The Selfish Gene*; Singer believes that genes promoting strictly selfish behavior, at least in humans, would be less likely to survive than genes which do not. (Dawkins 2006) This is, even today, a thoroughly radical position to take up, one which has been recently seconded by the father of Sociobiology E. O. Wilson. (Wilson 2013)

Yet, Dawkins and Singer are of one voice on one crucial point: they both believe that the application of reason can thwart the millions of years of evolution which our genes represent. Singer offers the example of contraception, where the primal sex drive itself is stymied by reason's cunning. Thus, we can enjoy ourselves without the natural consequences. (Singer 2011)

Ultimately, Singer views sociobiology as providing a new basis for the understanding of ethics. Here ethics is seen as a mode of human reasoning which develops within a group context building on more limited biologically based forms of altruism. Yet at least one caveat does remain and that is the "naturalistic fallacy". Simply stated, discovering that some form of behavior has a biological basis does not, in itself, justify that kind of behavior.

Singer, then, reaches for a moral imperative when he says "I ought to do what is in the interests of all, impartially considered." (Singer 2011) This philosophical statement is immediately problematic of course when we simply consider how is it that we know what actually is in the interests of all concerned and how can we exercise that knowledge impartially? Singer gives no solid answer to this rather Kantian formulation.

We now turn to a more contemporary interpretation (2011) of the relationships between human nature, war, and the state as rigorously expounded by Steven Pinker in his acclaimed (not by everybody of course!) book *The Better Angels of Our Nature*.

It should be stated right up front that Pinker's book can and should be viewed as a continuation of Elias's and Singer's work with some important updates.

Pinker names and analyzes no less than six trends which he tries to unify holistically.

Trend number one he calls the Pacification Process which in effect echoes in part Elias's thesis that the rise of states led to a decline in violent deaths within this enlarged human group.

Trend number two is a direct nod to Elias and is called, as it was by Elias, the Civilizing Process and talks about exactly the same things: the rise of central authority, urbanization, and commerce.

Trend number three is linked to the Age of Reason and the Enlightenment and has to do with the first organized movements to abolish socially sanctioned forms of violence such as despotism, slavery, dueling, judicial torture, superstitious killing, sadistic punishment, cruelty to animals and the first systemic stirrings of pacifism. He calls this trend the Humanitarian Revolution.

The fourth major trend takes place after the end of World War II. It represents the historical fact that the great powers have not directly fought each other on the battlefield. He calls this ongoing "cease fire" The Long Peace.

Linked to the fourth major trend is what he calls the New Peace and has to do with the significant decline in conflicts of all kinds since 1989.

The final trend is also linked historically to trends three, four, and five and is called the Rights Revolutions and has to do with the explosion of litigation concerning ethnic minorities, women, children, homosexuals, and animals. It is the most recent evolution of the human rights discourse.

Pinker, like Elias and Singer before him, more or less views changes in human behavior as culturally driven. However, Pinker lets down his guard once and provides a provocative suggestion that over time some human populations have undergone a change in their genome leading to more pacifistic natures. His reasoning is simple and has been given some backing by the hugely controversial recent (2015) book by Nicholas Wade *A Troublesome Inheritance: Genes, Race, and Human History*.

Both men carry out an analogy with the animal kingdom where it has been shown that within a surprisingly few number of generations the character and or natural disposition of animals can be changed through selective breeding. Of course, neither men are saying that certain human populations have been consciously bred. What they are suggesting is that certain ways of behavior have been, during the last few hundred years, exhibiting selective pressure through cultural changes in the environment. It is to be sure a provocative and incendiary thought, but it is also one that should not be totally rejected out of hand. It requires further research and serious discussion.

Getting back to more mainstream ideas, Pinker picks out significant social trends that have had, according to him, a marked impact on recent human behavior even though rooted ultimately in ancient hominin group behavior.

He focuses on the Leviathan (like Hobbes and Elias) in that a judiciary with a monopoly on the legitimate use of force, can defuse the temptation of exploitative attack, inhibit "the impulse for revenge, and circumvent the self-serving biases that make all parties believe they are on the side of the angels." (Pinker 2011) He also (like Adam Smith, David Hume, and many others before him) pinpoints Commerce as a positive-sum game in which everybody can win; as technological progress allows "the exchange of goods and ideas over longer distances and among larger groups of trading partners, other people become more valuable alive than dead, and they are less likely to become targets of demonization and dehumanization." (Pinker 2011) He also sees Feminization as the process in which cultures have increasingly respected the interests and values of women. "Since violence is largely a male pastime, cultures that empower women tend to move away from the glorification of violence and are less likely to breed dangerous subcultures of rootless young men." (Pinker 2011) The forces of Cosmopolitanism are yet another trend encompassing literacy, mobility, and mass media prompting people to take the perspective of people unlike themselves and to expand their circle of sympathy to embrace them. And finally (like Aristotle, Hegel, and more recently Singer) Pinker sees an intensifying application of knowledge and rationality to human affairs — the escalator of reason — forcing people to recognize "the futility of cycles of violence, to ramp down the privileging of their own interests over others', and to reframe violence as a problem to be solved rather than a contest to be won." (Pinker 2011)

The Leviathan, Commerce, Feminization, Cosmopolitanism, and the "Escalator of Reason" are mostly, if not all, recent trends. For Pinker, not surprisingly, the past is a distinctively horrific place where the Hobbesian struggle was commonplace. Violence of all kinds was rampant including genocide. The past was a place where a person had a high chance of coming to bodily harm. Such statements of course are backed up by a plethora of scholarly research in a myriad of fields of knowledge. The scholarly literature on the subject is as vast as it is depressing.

Even our most ancient and revered books and traditions such as the Old Testament and the Homeric sagas are filled with gory tales of total war/genocide. The archaeological record backs up their bloody narratives. Truly one would not be wholly out of line to say that the Old Testament in particular is one long celebration of violence. Even the very first distinctly human tale of Cain and Able when the world, allegedly, had but four people in it comes out to a rate of a 25 percent chance for an early, violent death. A rate which interestingly enough coincides more or less with that of recently documented hunter-gatherer societies.

Yet, importantly, Pinker (as well as others) have pointed to the essentially strategic nature of violence. Organisms have evolved to deploy violence only in circumstances where the expected benefits outweigh the expected costs. That subtle point is especially true of intelligent species, whose large brains make them sensitive to the expected benefits and costs in a particular situation, rather than just to the odds averaged over evolutionary time. Thus, violence becomes a more attractive proposition the lower the risk of heavy costs to oneself. Therefore, the principle of deadly violence in nature is fighting against weakness, only at highly favorable odds — asymmetrical fighting. (Gat 2008)

Throughout history considerable intraspecific killing did take place, but it was carried out against the weak and defenseless who could not fight back effectively. Thus, deadly fighting was normally asymmetrical, with the casualties overwhelmingly concentrated on the receiving end. Therefore, "if humans can be caught unarmed, they are at a tremendous disadvantage and are extremely vulnerable. Humans therefore became quintessential first-strike creatures." (Gat 2008)

This and other considerations lead Pinker (among many other scholars) to the counter-intuitive conclusion that modern wars, despite their massive death tolls, have a much less lethal demographic effect overall than did pre-state fighting. Even the dreadful figures from cataclysmic events such as the World Wars fall short of those for primitive societies. Thus, contrary to a popular viewpoint, it was the distant and not so distant past that was murderous, rather than modernity itself.

For this school of thought, the human state of nature is revealed to be fundamentally no different from the state of nature in general. Killing in nature is normally done against the defenseless, when the odds are heavily tilted in the attacker's favor and little risk is involved. Thus, contrary to much wishful thinking, it was probably not the advent of agriculture or civilization that inaugurated periods of intense warfare.

Indeed, it is only in the past thirty years or so that scholars with no political ax to grind (or so they allege), such as Lawrence Keeley, Steven LeBlanc, Azar Gat, and Johan van der Dennen, began to compile systematic reviews of the frequency of and damage caused by fighting in large ethnographic samples of nonstate peoples. (Pinker 2011) And perhaps most gruesome of all, forensic archaeology has recently shown that cannibalism was widespread in human prehistory. (Pinker 2011, see Schutt 2018 for more in-depth analysis of this natural phenomenon)

Conclusion

We have seen that man is a social animal who throughout his evolutionary history has lived in groups. For most of that history, violence between groups and, indeed, within groups was common. Genocide, the most extreme case, was not unheard of.

This has led some scholars to believe that the further back one reaches into the human past the bloodier it gets. Paradoxically, this has led some scholars to some optimistic reasoning.

Among these thoughts is that, contrary to a very popular school of thought, it is not modernity that is the wellspring of violence but the ancient past. Modernity, in contrast, has set into motion a variety of long-term trends that have had a strong tendency in restraining violence of all kinds. The growth and refinement of the state/Leviathan, "gentle commerce", urbanization, cosmopolitanism, feminization, and the growth and use of reason have greatly contributed to the discouragement of violence. Demographically our ancient past was more like an Armageddon rather than our near future will likely turn out to be. And sadly, it seems that that aspect of human violence in its most horrific form, the act of genocide, predated modernity by at least thousands and perhaps even millions of years. Thus, our Global Ape can be viewed as an ancient serial murderer who, under the right social, cultural, and historical circumstances, can restrain his darkest impulses and slowly emerge into the light.

Chapter Three: Global Elements of Genocide: The Scholars Speak

*We are not going to leave a single one of them alive,
down to the babies in their mothers' wombs — not even they must live.
The whole people must be wiped out
of existence, and none be left to think of them and shed a tear
– Agamemnon*

*The blind and bloody soldier with foul hand
Defile the locks of your shrill-shrieking daughters;
Your fathers taken by the silver beards,
And their most reverend heads dashed to the walls;
Your naked infants spitted upon pikes...
– King Harry in Shakespeare's Henry V*

*Thank God that now, during wartime,
we have a whole series of opportunities
that would be closed off to us in peacetime
– Joseph Goebbels*

In the long history of the Global Ape perhaps nothing is so heinous as his propensity to commit genocide.

In this chapter, I will argue through the careful and extensive use of scholarly quotations that genocide is ancient, relatively frequent, and is unleashed by war.

Genocide is old. It is at least as old as some of our oldest texts such as the Old Testament and the Homeric Epics. As a behavioral practice, it has been historically recorded for the Assyrians, Athenians, Romans, and Mongols to name but a few. Genocide like war, then, is historically ancient. Yet what exactly is genocide and what are its preconditions.

To start with I should like to list some of the most famous scholarly definitions of Genocide taken from Adam Jones' *Genocide a Comprehensive Introduction*: (Jones 2017)

Peter Drost (1959)
Genocide is the deliberate destruction of physical life of individual human beings by reason of their membership of any human collectivity as such.

Leo Kuper (1981)
I shall follow the definition of genocide given in the [UN] Convention. This is not to say that I agree with the definition. On the contrary, I believe a major omission to be in the exclusion of political groups from the list of groups protected. In the contemporary world, political differences are at the very least as significant a basis for massacre and annihilation as racial, national, ethnic or religious differences. Then too, the genocides against racial, national, ethnic or religious groups are generally a consequence of, or intimately related to, political conflict. However, I do not think it helpful to create new definitions of genocide, when there is an internationally recognized definition and a Genocide Convention which might become the basis for some effective action, however limited the underlying conception. But since it would vitiate the analysis to exclude political groups, I shall refer freely ... to liquidating or exterminatory actions against them.

Yehuda Bauer (1984)
n.b. Bauer distinguishes between "genocide" and "holocaust":
"[Genocide is] the planned destruction, since the mid-nineteenth century, of a racial, national, or ethnic group as such, by the following means: (a) selective mass murder of elites or parts of the population; (b) elimination of national (racial, ethnic) culture and religious life with the intent of 'denationalization'; (c) enslavement, with the same intent; (d) destruction of national (racial, ethnic) economic life, with the same intent; (e) biological decimation through the kidnapping of children, or the prevention of normal family life, with the same intent ... [Holocaust is] the planned physical annihilation, for ideological or pseudo-religious reasons, of all the members of a national, ethnic, or racial group.

Isidor Wallimann and Michael N. Dobkowski (1987)
Genocide is the deliberate, organized destruction, in whole or in large part, of racial or ethnic groups by a government or its agents. It can involve not only mass murder, but also forced deportation (ethnic cleansing), systematic rape, and economic and biological subjugation.

Frank Chalk and Kurt Jonassohn (1990)
Genocide is a form of one-sided mass killing in which a state or other authority intends to destroy a group, as that group and membership in it are defined by the perpetrator.

Steven T. Katz (1994)
[Genocide is] the actualization of the intent, however successfully carried out, to murder in its totality any national, ethnic, racial, religious, political,

social, gender or economic group, as these groups are defined by the perpetrator, by whatever means.

Donald Bloxham (2009)
[Genocide is] the physical destruction of a large portion of a group in a limited or unlimited territory with the intention of destroying that group's collective existence.

As can be seen from the quotes above, definitions have varied over time but some elements have remained constant such as the basic *intent* to destroy in whole or in part the biological and cultural basis of a population group over a given (not necessarily contiguous) territory.

Although we have strongly insinuated that genocide in the words of the sociologist Leo Kuper "is ancient" we are interested, too, in what ways the coming of modernity transformed it qualitatively. So, for the rest of this chapter, we will turn our critical eye primarily towards the 19th, 20th, and 21st centuries.

Let us start first with the sorrowful story of the Herero and the Nama peoples.

The Herero and the Nama were peoples living in South-West Africa at the turn of the twentieth century under German control. Between 1904 and 1907 during the so-called "Herero Wars" these two peoples went nearly extinct.

During this conflict the German authorities waged a war of extermination complete with concentration camps and doctors who were encouraged to carry out gruesome experiments for so called racial-biological research. "Sample skulls were even sent back to Germany for further research. Incredibly, female prisoners were forced to scrape the skulls clean with glass shards." (Ferguson 2012)

For many observers, such as the philosopher Hannah Arendt and the historian Niall Ferguson the Herero and Nama experience of genocide was, in a profound way, the fertile intellectual breeding ground for the most infamous genocide that was yet to come: the Holocaust. (Arendt 1973) (Ferguson 2012)

Ferguson writes:

> For the many ex-colonial soldiers who joined the ranks of the Nazi Party — their old uniforms provided the SA with their first brown shirts — it was entirely natural that the theories born in the concentration camps of Africa should be carried over to the Nazi 'colonization' of Eastern Europe and the murderous racial policies that produced the Holocaust. It was no mere coincidence that the Reichsmarschall in charge of the Luftwaffe was the son of the Reichskommissar of South-West Africa. It was no coincidence that Hans Grimm, the author of People without Space (1926), had spent fourteen years in southern Africa. (Ferguson 2012)

In short, a major thesis concerning the rise of modern genocide as opposed to those genocides carried out in antiquity and before is that the art of modern annihilation was learned in colonial conflicts before being transported back to the European mainland in a sort of culturally lethal "boomerang effect".

Most disturbingly, even "liberal" states such as the United States have committed genocide against indigenous and colonial populations: we need here only mention the West African Slave Trade and the annihilation of the American Indian.

Yet it is "striking that a few individuals who would play important roles in the SS or in the academic and planning institutions with close ties to the SS had had direct experience in the German colonies and functioned as mentors — literary, scientific, professional — to the younger generation of Nazi officials." (Weitz 2015)

In addition, it "appears that the only early-twentieth-century imperial power that officially banned intermarriage between colonists and nonwhites, including those of mixed blood, was Germany." (Fredrickson 2002)

The view of "colonial rule as a lengthy and problematic apprenticeship for civilized modernity can be viewed as functionally racist to the degree that it justified denying civil and political rights to indigenous populations for the foreseeable future. But insofar as those relatively few individuals who assimilated Western civilization could actually gain such rights, the racist aspect was attenuated. Colonial policies that allowed for a kind of emancipation through assimilation, as the French in particular tended to do, were highly ethnocentric, but not, strictly speaking, racist. It was also the case that extreme racists could be anti-imperialists on the grounds that little or no good could come out of close contact with the inferior breeds inhabiting Africa and Asia, or from the effort to settle tropical environments for which Caucasians were naturally ill adapted. The principal English and French advocates of biological racism in the mid-nineteenth century — Robert Knox and Arthur de Gobineau — were both highly skeptical about the virtues of overseas imperialism." (Fredrickson 2002)

It is "tempting to see the genocidal brutality of the German officials and settlers in South-West Africa as reflective of a peculiar mind-set that would later sanction the annihilation of European Jewry. Perhaps Hannah Arendt was right, at least in the German case, when she postulated that the seeds of totalitarianism were sown during the colonial experience in Africa." (Fredrickson 2002)

For some observers then, the revolutionary social logic of modernity was inherently colonial. In a way we are talking about a "Sonderweg" of the West.

Also, we should not forget that beginning with the fifteenth-century open sea explorations of the Portuguese and Spanish, European imperialists began a process whereby newly "discovered" lands were conquered and colonized and the indigenous people living within them enslaved, exploited, and murdered. Tens of millions of indigenous peoples perished in the years that followed.

This historical fact helps to make clear that the Nazi mass murder of the Jews was not a total break with what had gone before but was instead a radical version of experiences that have taken place throughout modern history, especially within the confines of European overseas colonies.

At this point it might be enlightening to quote Aimé Césaire:

> Yes, it would be worthwhile to study clinically, in detail, the steps taken by Hitler and to reveal to the very distinguished, very humanistic, very Christian bourgeois of the twentieth century that without his being aware of it, he has a Hitler inside him, that Hitler inhabits him, that Hitler is his demon, that if he rails against him, he is being inconsistent and that, at bottom, what he cannot forgive Hitler for is not crime in itself, the crime

> against man, it is not the humiliation of man as such, it is the crime against the white man, the humiliation of the white man, and the fact that he applied to Europe colonialist procedures which until then had been reserved exclusively for the Arabs of Algeria, the coolies of India, and the blacks of Africa. (Stone 2010)

Indeed, in the last decade, the "claim that colonialism can tell us something important about the origins of the Holocaust has inspired a large historiography that now constitutes a major analytical challenge to established explanations because it adds to our store of long-term explanations for the Holocaust." (Stone 2010)

Does this mean that a 'new Sonderweg' is creeping into the historiography, a special German path 'from Africa to Auschwitz'? It might well be.

Importantly "the many definitions of genocide that were cited earlier sound like a definition of colonialism, with its stress on the interaction of two distinct groups and the imposition of the pattern of life of the oppressor on to that of the oppressed." (Stone 2010)

To what extent then does the concept of "colonial genocide" help us to understand the Holocaust? This is a crucial question that merits more attention.

Here, it should also be noted that "historians have begun to talk of 'colonization' as regards eastern Europe. They place the Nazi 'colonization' project in direct comparison with earlier European overseas practices, noting only that this time they applied to the creation of a continental empire in Europe." (Stone 2010)

In this sense Aimé Césaire is once again on point when he provocatively argues that " the Holocaust ... visited upon the peoples of Europe the violence that colonial powers had routinely inflicted on the "natives" all over the world for nearly five hundred years". (Stone 2010)

Adding to this idea Robert Gellately notes:

> The mentality of the [Nazi] conquerors and the intellectuals who supported them reminds one of late nineteenth-century imperialists in Africa. (Cited in Stone 2010)

Christopher Browning has also contributed significantly to this important discussion:

> Hitler's belief in the need for German Lebensraum implied that the Nazis would construct an empire in eastern Europe analogous to what other European imperial powers had constructed overseas. Not surprisingly, this also meant that the Nazi regime stood ready to impose on conquered populations in Europe, especially Slavs in the east, the methods of rule and policies of population decimation that Europeans had hitherto inflicted only on conquered populations overseas. (Cited in Stone 2010)

Lower adds:

> that although the Jews were not typical of the 'colonial other' — because they were feared more than despised — the Nazis 'viewed them as natives in the classical colonial sense and as pernicious colonizers of supposed ancestral German land. The Jew thereby incarnated both the native other and the colonizing other, combining contempt and fear in a lethal cocktail. (Cited in Stone 2010)

And perhaps most decisively is this quote from Adolf Hitler himself:

> The struggle for hegemony in the world is decided for Europe by the possession of Russian territory; it makes Europe the place in the world most secure from blockade ... The Slavic peoples on the other hand are not destined for their own life ... The Russian territory is our India and, just as the English rule India with a handful of people, so will we govern this, our colonial territory. We will supply the Ukrainians with headscarves, glass chains as jewelry, and whatever else colonial peoples like. (Cited in Stone 2010)

This and other quotes tend to confirm the idea that the Nazi occupation of 'the East' can meaningfully be conceptualized as a colonial project, taking colonialism as the imposition of one group's pattern of life on another's.

Starting with "the paradigm-shifting work of Susanne Zantop, who showed that the German colonial imagination long preceded and outlasted any formal imperial structures, historians have looked beyond a narrowly focused imperial history to show that ideas and fantasies of empire — an 'intellectual colonialism' — penetrated deeply into German culture and society in every sphere, from advertising to sexuality to science." (Stone 2010) Thus it could be said that the Holocaust had to be first imagined as an inverted utopian project before anything else.

Once again it should not be forgotten that "Hannah Arendt claimed, in her classic *The Origins of Totalitarianism*, that colonialism provided the building blocks for fascism in Europe, and scholars have recently begun testing this so-called 'boomerang thesis' empirically." (Stone 2010)

In broad terms, "the underlying structural similarities between German colonialism and Nazism are 'race and space', racism and the conception of 'living space'." (Stone 2010) State-perpetrated colonial genocide thus constitutes an important precedent for Nazi genocide. More important,

> "Zimmerer notes that colonialism made a deep impression on German cultural life in general, especially through the press, films, monuments, lecture tours, exhibitions, and literature. The novels of Karl May are only the most obvious examples." (Stone 2010)

However, it should be noted that "National Socialism and the German war of annihilation constituted a break with European traditions of colonialism rather than a continuation." "A closer look at colonialism helps us to understand how genocidal fantasies were developed and radicalized." (Stone 2010)

Fantastically enough, "the Nazis regarded Germans as an indigenous people who had been colonized by Jews who were undermining German national identity. The Nazis then thought of themselves as a national liberation movement. Interestingly, while the Holocaust can thus be seen as part of the history of antisemitism, to be sure, it can at the same time be trans-nationally contextualized in terms of "both the political emotions common in central European nationalisms since the nineteenth century, and later anticolonial movements." (Stone 2010)

The European contact with "exotic colonial 'others' in previously unknown parts of the world strengthened the belief in an alleged European/'white' superiority, and often resulted in the treatment of the 'other' as an inherently inferior form of life." (Kallis 2009)

If one looks closely at the history of the Belgian Congo and also that of other parts of Africa, you eventually notice something striking. "If you were to ask most Americans or Europeans what were the great totalitarian systems of the twentieth century, almost all would be likely to say: Communism and Fascism. However, there was a third totalitarian system — European colonialism — the latter imposed in its deadliest form in Africa. Each of the three systems asserted the right to control its subjects' lives; each was buttressed by an elaborate ideology; each perverted language in an Orwellian way; and each caused tens of millions of deaths." (Berghahn 2006)

Returning now from where we first started, "Herero men, armed or unarmed, who fell into German hands were murdered without further ado. What differed from nineteenth-century conventional European warfare was that women and children were also summarily shot, often after abuse and torture. Those responsible for such actions appreciated that fundamental human norms were being violated and therefore tried to justify their actions. A white farmer who had shot a woman because she had stolen one of his sheep was asked by a judge why he felt it necessary to use lethal force. He replied: "Should we simply subject ourselves to theft?" His defense attorney then used the term "vermin" that, however ominous as a harbinger of the racism that was to come, was not unusual for this time and related to the proliferating biological perceptions of human society. Planted in the mind of an ordinary white settler of European background, it was used to justify exploitation and murder." (Berghahn 2006)

Tilman Dedering has compared "the behavior of the colonial troops to that of the Wehrmacht in eastern Europe during World War II." (Cited in Berghahn 2006)

The Germans "approached South-West Africa initially with attitudes that were rooted in the social unrest of contemporary Europe. Later the methods used to treat human beings practiced in the colonies ricocheted back into the motherland." (Berghahn 2006)

While the practices of Europeans in their colonies was of the utmost importance as to the future practices of genocide, they do not explain all of the modern instances of genocide, for example those in Cambodia and Rwanda. In order to understand modern genocide more fully, then, we should turn to a broader discussion of racism and, later, utopianism.

Not only was a racial world view fundamental to the Third Reich (one which was rooted in a particular conception of human biology) but it was a singularly successful 'meme' that had replicated itself all over the world by the start of the twentieth-century. It would have repercussions throughout that century right until the end, especially in Rwanda.

Yet it was a combination of factors that was to prove decisive in modern genocide. "Ideologies of race and nation, revolutionary regimes with vast Utopian ambitions, and last but not least in importance, moments of crisis generated by war and domestic upheaval all taken together were to fuel the genocidal rage of the twentieth-century. They should be taken as warning signs for the future." (Weitz 2015)

Even the Soviet Union was not immune to such an outcome in its history.

Although the multiple 'genocides' that are often attributed to Stalinist rule are usually labeled 'politicides' we should not be fooled as to their practical equivalencies.

> "Anyone associated with the accused, families, colleagues, and friends, also became ensnared in the whirlwind of terror. It was as if the accused bore an infectious disease. In this fashion, the soviet regime came very, very close to racializing even political opponents, to rooting particular behaviors and ways of thinking in a kind of permanent identity shared by all individual members of the group. The vicious rhetoric used in the purge trials demonstrates this ominous tendency. A. Ia. Vyshinsky, prosecutor at the Zinoviev Kamenev trial, infamously shouted, "I demand that these dogs gone mad should be shot — every one of them!" The utter, complete condemnation of the accused, their placement in a category of "other," certainly less than human, is also evident in the animal metaphors used, the

charge that "alien elements" were "dogs," "reptiles," or "predatory beasts," or even worse, "vermin" and "lice." " (Weitz 2015)

Under Stalin, "the Soviet regime condemned entire generations of particular nationalities, not on the basis of what they actually did (despite official propaganda that they had engaged in treason), but on the basis of who they were. That is a racial logic at work." (Weitz 2015) So much then for 'objective socialism'.

The Soviets "had no extermination camps on the order of Auschwitz. Yet millions died in the waves of population purges, sometimes by direct killings, more often by neglect. The rigors of transport were killers, the bodies of the deceased unceremoniously discarded along the way." (Weitz 2015)

Yet "population purges were a central feature of Soviet life until the mid-1950s. These purges were entwined with the obsessive drive to categorize every member of the population, to determine their class, national, and political affiliations. On the basis of such extensive information, the regime hoped to determine its allies and its enemies among the population. It sought to use the information to form people into good Soviet citizens. But those whose attachments to older ways were considered too profound or whose association with co-nationals beyond Soviet borders made them immediately suspect had to be removed from society by deportations and executions. The drive to reshape the behavior, the thought patterns, and the very composition of the population was an intrinsic aspect of Soviet socialist modernity, the effort to create "a quintessential enlightenment utopia" that would result in a "conflict free, harmonious body. This social engineering drive was not unique to the Soviet Union, but under Stalin it became particularly systematic and virulent, precisely because of the system's totalizing claims and the absence of the legal and cultural limits imposed upon the state in liberal regimes." (Weitz 2015)

"The Soviet regime, to be sure, exercised a war against society, as Nicolas Werth depicts the history of the Soviet Union. Yet this war encompassed a very substantial segment of society as its perpetrators, the people who followed orders to repress the Cossacks, expropriate the peasants, purge party members, and deport the Chechens and Tatars. Though the orders came from the central state, their execution involved the participation of hundreds of thousands, probably millions, of Soviet citizens." (Weitz 2015)

At this point we should remember that The UN Convention, again, defines genocides as "acts committed with the intent to destroy, in whole or in part, a national, ethnical, racial, or religious group." The specific actions can range from deliberate killings to causing "serious bodily or mental harm to members of the group" or "inflicting on the group conditions of life calculated to bring about its physical destruction in whole or in part." (Weitz 2015) Thus whether or not we call the practices of the Stalinist regime 'politicidal' or not, they definitely meet the standards of genocide as agreed upon today.

We should not lose sight of the important fact that in many of these regimes now under discussion whether Nazi, Soviet, Rwandan, Cambodian, or Ottoman mass murder would become "routine, a part of everyday life, an act of professional responsibility, and of loyalty to race, nation, and, oftentimes, leader." (Weitz 2015)

While "a few individuals occasionally shrank from the exercise of violence, and some later claimed guilty consciences, many perpetrators, it seems, either simply followed orders or found intoxicating their complete power over the victims, their unlimited ability to violate the integrity of another's body." (Weitz 2015)

And what was the wellspring of modern mass murder? The state. The modern example of Cambodia is instructive as well as widespread.

Like the other perpetrators and movements being discussed here, "the Khmer Rouge venerated the state as the agent that would create the future society. It was their state that depopulated the cities and collectivized the countryside, creating the conditions for communism. The state would also protect the revolution from perceived enemies who were alleged to constantly threaten it. Like the Soviet state, the DK state would be a dictatorship of the proletariat, dispensing revolutionary justice to enemies and reeducating those who could still be saved. The state's reach would be total." (Weitz 2015)

The state was also "the agency that would reshape individuals, developing their class consciousness and making them into Khmer communists. The destruction of private property was understood as the first step in this process, because however small the plot of land might be, possession of private property inevitably results in individualist, capitalist ways of thinking, while collective property ineluctably leads to socialist consciousness." (Weitz 2015)

Ultimately, "the Khmer Rouge, like the Soviets and Nazis and, as we shall see, Serb nationalists, came to define politics by *Being*." (Weitz 2015)

Democratic Kampuchea "was a twentieth-century dictatorship, one that mobilized substantial segments of the population." (Weitz 2015)

They could "act out their brutalities with no fears of legal or any other kind of sanction, since there were no limits upon party power. Like the Nazi camp guards who ran over the bodies of Roma and Sinti children or the Lithuanian auxiliaries who clubbed Jews to death in the market square, some Cambodian men became enthralled with the total power they exercised." (Weitz 2015)

"Only rarely did the Khmer Rouge carry out killings in public. Usually, they took their victims away quietly, often at night. The next day they would not be there. Yet people certainly knew about the disappearances, just as Germans knew about euthanasia and the Holocaust, and Soviet citizens knew about the deportations, internments, and killings of all sorts of regime victims." (Weitz 2015) "If any singular idea captures the essence of the Khmer Rouge revolution, it was homogeneity — the effort to create a population purged of difference, whether of class, education, political affiliation, ethnicity, or race." (Weitz 2015)

"Everything about Democratic Kampuchea — the organization of the party-state, collectivization, purges, the racialization of nationalities — followed in the tracks of communist practices." (Weitz 2015)

It should also be mentioned that as with the other cases discussed here, "Serb nationalists, and their counterparts among Croats, Slovenes, and, finally, Muslims, sought to "fix" identities, to establish clearly and cleanly who was a member of what group. Only when that knowledge was firmly established could the state then determine those who deserved the rights and privileges conferred by membership in the nation, and those who had to be driven out and killed. In many instances, it proved quite easy to distinguish, for example, Muslims from Serbs in villages in northern Bosnia or Croats from Serbs in Krajina and Slavonia." (Weitz 2015)

Hence it is the modern state when linked to the ideologies of nation and race that has been the source of modern genocides.

At this point we should perhaps unveil The 1948 United Nations Convention on the Prevention and Punishment of the Crime of Genocide as: "any of the following acts committed with intent to destroy, in whole or in part, a national, ethnical, racial, or religious group, as such: (a) killing members of the group; (b) causing serious bodily or mental harm to members of the group; (c) deliberately inflicting on the group conditions of life calculated to bring about its physical destruction in whole or in part; (d) imposing measures intended to prevent births within the group; and (e) forcibly transferring children of the group to another group." (Roth 2005)

Another provocative question for us is: Has the tradition of philosophizing in the West served *"to foster a mode of thinking that gives subtle encouragement to genocide?"* (Roth 2005) Is it as Levinas contends that Western philosophy "is nothing less than an *egology?"* (Roth 2005) In our genocidal world, philosophy, now understood as "bearing witness to the face of the other calling me to account, can serve to ward off the temptation to ignore the injunction "Thou shalt not kill." " (Roth 2005)

Similar to all the other historical experiences discussed here, "the Hutu extremists believed that the Tutsi were a different race and that they had come from elsewhere to invade Rwanda. Hutu Power taught that the Tutsi were different, that they were lazy; that they did not want to work the land, that they were outside human existence — vermin and subhuman. The effect of the Hutu Power radio, with its catchy nationalistic theme tunes and its racist jingles must never be underestimated. The broadcasts of *Radio-Télévision Libre des Milles Collines* (RTLM) were an integral part of the genocide plot and it was thanks to the propaganda that spewed over the airways that by April 1994 a large number of people in Rwanda had come to believe that the elimination of the Tutsi, or "cockroaches" as they were called, was a civic duty and that it was necessary work to rid the country of them." (Roth 2005)

In the utmost profound way, it could be said that "it was Hitler who finally gave racism a bad name. The moral revulsion of people throughout the world against what the Nazis did, reinforced by scientific studies undermining racist genetics (or eugenics), served to discredit the scientific racism that had been respectable and influential in the United States and Europe before the Second World War." (Fredrickson 2002)

Interestingly, it is the dominant view among scholars who have studied conceptions of difference in the ancient world that "no concept truly equivalent to that of "race" can be detected in the thought of the Greeks, Romans, and early Christians." (Fredrickson 2002)

Nonetheless there was an undeniable tendency to consider the Jews who had not converted when Christ was among them as a corporate group that bore a direct responsibility for the Crucifixion. "For the organization of Christianity," writes the French historian Leon Poliakov, "it was essential that the Jews be a criminally guilty people." In Matthew 27:25 Jews who called for the death of Christ cry out after the deed has been done: "His blood be upon us and our Children." The notion that Jews were collectively and hereditarily responsible for the worst possible human crime — deicide — created a powerful incentive for persecution." (Fredrickson 2002) "The scriptural passage most often quoted to associate Jews as a collectivity with Satan was Christ's denunciation of the Jews who rejected him: "You are of your father the devil, and your will is to do your father's desires" (John 8:44 RSV)." (Fredrickson 2002)

Importantly, "sixteenth- and seventeenth-century Spain is critical to the history of Western racism because its attitudes and practices served as a kind of segue between the religious intolerance of the Middle Ages and the naturalistic racism of the modern era." (Fredrickson 2002)

However, it was "the scientific thought of the Enlightenment that was to serve as a precondition for the growth of a modern racism based on physical typology." (Fredrickson 2002)

> "In 1735, the great Swedish naturalist Carl Linnaeus included humans as a species within the primate genus and then attempted to divide that species into varieties. Whatever their intentions, Linnaeus, Blumenbach, and other eighteenth-century ethnologists opened the way to a secular or scientific racism by considering human beings' part of the animal kingdom rather than viewing them in biblical terms as children of God endowed with spiritual capacities denied to other creatures." (Fredrickson 2002)

Much later in the nineteenth century, "fear of Jewish success became in the minds of pioneer racists like Wilhelm Marr, who coined the term "antisemitism" and founded the Anti-Semitic League, a settled conviction that Jews were well on their way to establishing their hegemony over those of pure German descent. Marr's book *The Victory of the Jews over the Germans*, published in 1879, was the first systematic presentation from a secular perspective of the view that Jews were corrupt by nature and not because of their beliefs. Marr was the earliest of many theorists who argued that Jews were innately evil and beyond redemption. In 1880, Karl Eugen Duhring published *The Jewish Question as a Problem of Racial Character*, a fuller and more sophisticated exposition of the new racist antisemitism. The time would come, Marr, Duhring, and others warned, when the German victims of Jewish aggression would strike back and punish the Jews for their diabolical conspiracies." (Fredrickson 2002)

On the other side of the Atlantic, "when the Supreme Court declared in the Dred Scott decision of 1857 that free blacks could not be citizens of the United States, because the framers of the Constitution had assumed that they had "no rights which the white man was bound to respect," the racist foundation of the American polity was laid bare. (Fredrickson 2002) "Antiblack racism peaked in the period between the end of Reconstruction and the First World War, the era that historian Rayford W. Logan has called the "nadir" of the African American experience." (Fredrickson 2002)

Let us continue our hopefully fruitful comparison of Wilhemine Germany and nineteenth century America.

> "It is one of the great commonplaces of modern German history that the fate of the Jews was linked to the fate of liberalism. Emancipation occurred at a time when Bismarck was allied with the center-left National Liberals. When he repudiated the Liberals in 1879 and associated himself with conservative and aristocratic political elements, the situation of the Jews immediately worsened and political antisemitism emerged for the first time. The rights of blacks were similarly dependent on one of the majority political parties or factions — the Radical Republicans — who had passed the Reconstruction Acts of 1867 and 1868, partly out of idealism and partly out of political calculation. (They hoped to use black votes to gain political leverage in the southern states.) Analogous to the way that the decline of liberalism in Germany had made Jews vulnerable to antisemitic assaults, the Republicans' failure to prevent the South from becoming solidly Democratic after 1876, along with a decline of the influence of the Radical element within the national party, exposed blacks to white supremacist terror and Jim Crow segregation. German liberalism and American Radical Republicanism were by no means identical. The former was more elitist and less committed to popular democracy than the latter. But if newly freed African Americans could think of themselves as fully enfranchised citizens of a democratic polity, German Jews had good reason to think of themselves as part of a new elite based on achievement rather than birth. By the early twentieth century, liberalism had lost much of its ideological influence in Germany and Austria leaving middle-class Jews without powerful political allies. In the United States, the Republicans had become a probusiness par-

ty with little further interest in the rights of blacks, while the Democrats appealed to a coalition of southern whites and northern working-class immigrants and were therefore even less friendly to black aspirations." (Fredrickson 2002)

"In both the United States and Germany, the eugenics movement, which began in England as a biological approach to class differences, was eventually applied to racial and ethnic groups. The belief that government intervention was required to weed out or neutralize inferior breeding stock could justify a variety of policies, including immigration restriction, prohibition of interracial marriage, the forced sterilization of undesirables, and ultimately the euthanasia of entire categories of people." (Fredrickson 2002)

In the German case, "it was *Völkisch* nationalism, more than evolutionary biology, that was at the core of the racist antisemitism that emerged in the 1870s and crystallized by the turn of the century. It would take the Nazis to synthesize effectively the kind of scientific racism that had not previously focused on the Jews in particular with the mainstream German antisemitism associated with *völkisch* antimodernism. It was the latter, as articulated by thinkers like Houston Stewart Chamberlain, that did most of the damage prior to the 1920s." (Fredrickson 2002)

"The crimes against humanity perpetrated by Germans in the twentieth century were rationalized as much by the idealization of themselves as by hatred of the Other." (Fredrickson 2002) It is an historical irony, to say the least, that "if African Americans were not modern enough, German Jews were too modern." (Fredrickson 2002)

Significantly, it should be noted, tying in with our thesis of colonialism and genocide, that it appears that the only early-twentieth-century imperial power that officially banned intermarriage between colonists and nonwhites, including those of mixed blood, was Germany. "Among the European colonies in Africa in the early twentieth century, only the German dependencies banned intermarriage between whites and nonwhites, including Christian "halfcastes."" (Fredrickson 2002) These facts will link up with our discussion of a possible *sonderweg* of German history and the specific nature of Nazi racism.

An important aspect of genocidal fantasies is

> "the fear of sexual pollution or violation by the allegedly subhuman race. It is close to the heart of murderous or genocidal racism whenever and wherever it appears. In the racist imagination, blacks have been somewhat more likely than Jews to be viewed as violent sexual predators. The myth of the oversized black penis may be contrasted with the turn-of-the-century anti-semitic belief that the large Jewish nose signified a small penis, further truncated by circumcision. Such images raised questions about Jewish masculinity or virility." (Fredrickson 2002)

> "Nevertheless, the German fixation on the Jews clearly did not depend on large numbers:
> they made up only about 1 percent of the population when Hitler came to power." (Fredrickson 2002)

Of course, the outcome of the second world war did more than just seriously undermine racism, according to one celebrated observer it "pulled the rug out from under *all* claims to legitimacy that did not at least rhetorically embrace the universalistic spirit of the political Enlightenment." (Fredrickson 2002, the "observer" is Jurgen Habermas)

More than this, it also put an end to the eugenics movement,

> "which had enjoyed scientific respectability in the United States and Britain before the war, and did not survive the revelations of what the Nazis had done in its name. Not all eugenicists had been racists or even social conservatives, but the whole notion of using the state to improve the human gene pool was under a dark cloud for several decades after the war." (Fredrickson 2002)

In this, as in all our previous discussions in this chapter, we see the specter of the state. Its power and its hand in the most devastating and dark chapters of the twentieth century should never be forgotten.

Yet,

> "while xenophobia is an ancient and virtually universal phenomenon, racism, arguably, is a historical construction with a traceable career covering the period between the fourteenth century and the twenty first." (Fredrickson 2002)

As we have argued before, xenophobia like genocide is ancient, but at the same time had undergone changes during the premodern and modern periods. Like war, genocide changes its face over time.

Therefore, we should never forget how close racism is to genocide. It serves as a wellspring or as a main source for its practical formation. One could say that racism exists

> "when one ethnic group or historical collectivity dominates, excludes, or seeks to eliminate another on the basis of differences that it believes are hereditary and unalterable." (Fredrickson 2002)

The French philosopher Pierre-Andre Taguieff has even renamed racism/xenophobia 'heterophobia'. (Taguieff 1987)

Yet we should never forget that despite the horrors of the recent past;

> "empathy, curiosity, tolerance, dialogue, and co-operation are human traits that are as common as hostility and prejudice. Outsiders are not automatically feared or hated; they are as likely to be admired, found sexually attractive, to provoke ambivalence, or be envied. And nothing akin to the modern idea of race has been a human universal." (Rattansi 2007)

Up to now in this chapter we have discussed the possible links between colonialism and modern genocide, the state's role in the perpetrating of modern genocide, and racism's role in the ideological sustenance of modern genocide. It is now time to say a word or two about the role of Utopianism in genocides in the modern era.

Vast Utopian ambitions coupled with racist ideologies unified much of the mental landscape within which modern genocides occurred. Indeed, it underlined the key tension within genocidal regimes, the one between grand promises of the future and overwhelming, systematic political violence.

In almost all genocidal regimes, the drive for the creation of a "new man" and a "new woman" were prevalent.

National rebirth often through primordial rites of blood and fire were to guarantee the birth of the Utopian society.

It was radical Utopian thinking, often with roots in Nietzschean philosophy, that supported striving towards the "superman".
Ultimately, the nation became the focal point of all Utopian pursuits, for racial-anthropological purity and racial/hygienic health.

> "'Cleansing' thus became implicitly or explicitly a crucial part of the solution and the vehicle for a utopian future." (Kallis 2009)

Thus,

> "genocides will always need aggressive majorities mesmerized by utopias of wholeness and purity, imbued with allegedly justified hatred against some other group in their midst. But genocides only happen if a historical conjuncture renders, first, hatred and, then, violence to appear like a necessary and permissible step in an irresistibly positive, fulfilling direction. Intent and desire are not enough; the mass 'license' (whether derived directly from a leadership, assumed through precedents, or unfolding through a breakdown of order) to desire the abominable, do the unthinkable, and justify the otherwise unacceptable constitutes the critical mass of the genocidal chain reaction." (Kallis 2009)

As Omer Bartov has written:

> From the earliest records of human civilization to our own century, people have been fascinated by the notion of remaking humanity — molding individuals and societies in accordance with the laws of God or nature, history or science, into more perfect entities. But this quest for perfection has often been accompanied by an urge to unmake the present and erase the heritage of the past. Hence the path to Utopia is strewn with shattered edifices and mounds of corpses. Because by definition it must always remain a goal, Utopia engenders fantasies about a future whose imagined fabric draws heavily on myths about the past; fabricating a future earthly paradise is predicated on the imagery of a lost Garden of Eden. Such links between mythology and vision make for mechanisms of remembrance and prediction, fiction and representation, repression and categorization, which are at the core of humanity's self-perception and sense of identity. Materially nowhere, Utopia fills the mind; a site of infinite fantasy, it can also trigger limitless destruction. (Bartov 2000)

Robert Gellately goes on to further point out the key elements that the right and the left shared in the twentieth-century "scramble" for Utopia:

1. An ideological utopianism promoted the belief that the current regime could indeed create the perfect society that would be the end point of history.
2. That utopia necessitated population purges of one sort or another. Aside from carefully cultivated gender distinctions, utopia would be a leveled, homogenized society. Even when the exotica of cultural differences were celebrated, as in the Soviet Union — epic poetry, folk dances, food items — these lacked all substantive political significance.
3. The creation of utopia required massive popular mobilizations.
4. A breakdown of preexisting norms of behavior and a reworking of the rules of social interaction included the promotion of political violence as the method of progress toward utopia. (Gellately 2010)

This drive for a "perfect world" is something that was essential to the modernist narrative of the twentieth century and still has resonance today. Its genocidal potential should never be underestimated.

Finally, for this chapter, we should discuss as a somewhat practical matter the necessary condition of war for the carrying out of genocide.

As we have mentioned before, war and genocide have much in common. Indeed, while one can have war without strictly speaking committing genocide, the reverse, after much research, seems increasingly unlikely.

What then is the connection between war and genocide? At its most general war and the subsequent domestic upheaval that it causes opens the triple floodgates of "opportunity" "license" and "chaos". Simply put, everyday norms and taboos become easier to break. Violations of common human decency become the norm rather than the exception. For many scholars, then, war ranks as genocide's greatest single enabling factor.

> "War accustoms a society to violence. Large portions of the male population may be drawn into institutions, the prime purpose of which is to inflict violence. Much of the remaining population is cast in various productive and reproductive roles. Nearly all adults are therefore complicit in the war machine. The boundaries between legality and criminality erode. Psychological and social inhibitions diminish, often to be replaced by bloodlust." (Jones 2017)

> "War increases the quotient of fear and hatred in a society. "War creates a type of mass psychosis to which societies at peace cannot relate." Both soldiers and civilians live in dread of death. Propaganda emphasizes the "traitor within": "Know that the person whose throat you do not cut now will be the one who will cut yours," warned Hutu intellectual Ferdinand Nahimana before the outbreak of the Rwandan genocide against Tutsis and moderate Hutus in 1994. Fear fuels hatred of the one allegedly responsible for the fear, and dependence on the authority that pledges deliverance from the threat. The ideology of militarism inculcates "a condition of slavish docility" and "stolid passivity" throughout the militarized society. Societies grow more receptive to state vigilance and violence, as well as to suspensions of legal and constitutional safeguards. Dissidence threatens unity and stability, and provokes widespread loathing and repression." (Jones 2017)

> "War eases genocidal logistics. With the unified command of society and economy, it is easier to mobilize resources for genocide. State power is increasingly devoted to inflicting mass violence. (Indeed, the state itself, "evolving as it did within the crucible of endless rounds of combat, served initially as a more efficient apparatus to fight wars.") For example, the wartime marshaling of rail and freight infrastructure was essential to the "efficient" extermination of millions of Jews, and others, in the Nazi death camps. Much of that infrastructure was built and/or maintained by forced laborers captured as spoils, another regular phenomenon in wartime." (Jones 2017)

> "War provides a smokescreen for genocide. "That's war" becomes the excuse for extermination. Traditional sources of information, communication,

and denunciation are foreclosed or rigidly controlled. "Journalism is highly restricted, and military censorship prevents the investigation of reported atrocities. The minds of nations and of the international community are on other issues in time of war." (Jones 2017)
"War fuels intracommunal solidarity and inter-communal enmity. Many who experienced the wars of the twentieth century recalled them with mingled pain and pleasure. Few had ever before considered themselves citizens swept up in a common cause. Most soldiers experienced "a new kind of community held together by common danger and a common goal," which forged the most enduring friendships of their lives. In general, war "exaggerates nationalistic impulses as populations come together under outside threats ... During conflict group identities are strengthened as the gap between 'us' and 'them' is magnified, and individuals increasingly emphasize their solidarity with the threatened group." As psychologist David Barash put it succinctly: "In enmity, there is unity." "What is France if not as defined against England or Germany? What is Serbia if not as defined against Germany or Croatia?" Solidarity may coalesce around a dominant ethnicity within the society, prompting the anathematizing of Other-identified minorities." (Jones 2017)

"War stokes grievances and a desire for revenge. Large numbers of Serbs were spurred to support Slobodan Milosevic's ultranationalist option by the collective memory of genocide committed against Serbs during World War Two. Fewer Germans would have supported Hitler or the Nazis without an abiding sense of grievance generated by the 1919 Versailles Treaty. Cambodia's Khmer Rouge would have enjoyed less popular support if years of American bombing had not terrorized, enraged, and displaced much of the country's peasant population" (Jones 2017)
"Modern warfare, exacerbated by the spread of the technology of industrial slaughter from the late nineteenth century, has been a breeding ground for genocidal movements, even as it provides a cover for their crimes. The Young Turks, the Nazis, the Khmer Rouge, and others were all spawned in wartime atmospheres of crisis. The destabilization of entire societies through mass destruction, death, forced migration, and trauma opens up vast new possibilities for radical extremists not only to nurse paranoias about the enemy but also to project them on others, recruit supporters, seize power, and put their deadly goals into practice behind screens of war censorship and emergency military justification. Over the longer term, mass poverty, falling living standards, and rapid economic destabilization, including widespread land dispossession, have spread a similar sense of social crisis and often led to war, further encouraging simple solutions to complex socioeconomic problems. The targeting of easily visible, unarmed, and vulnerable victim groups follows." (Gellately 2010)

In the twentieth century, for some regimes (and for all genocidal regimes) "war became the substitute for democratic participation. Regimes encouraged the racially elect to pillage and purge, which made people complicit with the regime's policies." (Weitz 2015)

There can be no doubt that genocide developed at moments of

"severe crisis both domestically and internationally. Wars in particular created grave insecurities but also provided revolutionary elites with grand opportunities for asserting their powers and reshaping their populations." (Weitz 2015)

In particular,

"World War I created not only a culture of death but also a culture of killing — one that was often tied to the ideology of race and nation. It is no accident that one of the first modern campaigns of genocide, the late Ottoman Empire's slaughter of Armenians, occurred in the context of the war." (Weitz 2015)

"The reverberations of World War I are clearly evident here as well: the corollary of total war, with its model of complete state organization of society and mobilization for military victory, was found in the revolutionary regimes of the twentieth century, which sought an even greater level of societal organization and mobilization to purify the population." (Weitz 2015)

"The connection between genocides and extreme societal crisis is so critical because both war and revolution break standard codes of human interaction. Revolutions by definition overthrow the legal norms of a polity and, in the process, undermine existing legal and cultural constraints on human behavior." (Weitz 2015)

"The upheavals of revolution and war heighten the sense of insecurity, leading to calls for swift and forceful actions to remove those who are seen as dangers to the national cause or to the creation of the new society. At the same time, wars open up vistas of pleasure in the future and present great opportunities for vast restructurings of societies and populations. Wars and revolutions are by definition also violent acts; they create cultures of violence and killing. This was especially the case in the twentieth century because total war required the mobilization of entire societies in the enterprise of violence. The battlefields of World War I set standards of violence that revolutionary states sought to replicate in their deliberate purges of defined population groups." (Weitz 2015)

"Hence it was not accidental that the Armenian genocide occurred in the crisis setting of World War I; that the Soviet purge of nationalities began during the decade of the "great transformation," when the immense upheavals of crash industrialization and forced collectivization created social havoc, and then became still more extensive amid the cataclysm of the German invasion in World War II; that the systematic discrimination against Jews in the Third Reich escalated into genocide only in the context of total war; that in Democratic Kampuchea the purge of city dwellers and then mass killings of minority populations and anyone deemed hostile to the new society occurred amid the immense disruptions of traditional Cambodian society caused by the American bombings and the flush enthusiasms of revolutionary victory; and that the ethnic cleansings and genocides of Muslims in Bosnia and Kosovo occurred within a state order that had become extremely unstable, and in which wars of separation quickly escalated into violent purges of populations." (Weitz 2015)

Thus, as Lemkin long ago noted,

"war and genocide are almost always connected. The Ottomans killed more than 1 million Armenians during World War I, and the Germans exterminated 6 million Jews and 5 million Poles, Roma, homosexuals, political opponents, and others during World War II. Iraq later targeted its Kurdish minority during the Iran-Iraq war; Bosnian Serbs set out to destroy Muslims and Croats during a Balkan civil war; and Rwandan Hutu nationalists exterminated some 800,000 Tutsi while the Rwandan army also fought a more conventional civil war against a Tutsi rebel force." (Power 2002)

"If state formation, imperialism, war, and social revolution are genocide's "four horsemen," then war and genocide might be described as Siamese twins. The intimate bond between the two is evident from the twentieth century record alone. All three of the century's "classic" genocides — against Armenians in Turkey, Jews in Nazi-occupied Europe, and Tutsis in Rwanda — occurred within a context of civil and/or international war" (Jones 2017)

As Jacques Sémelin has said:

"War's special trick is to push to incandescence the imaginaire of fear ... It is "them" or "us." In the name of this security dilemma, everything becomes justifiable." (Quoted in Jones 2017)

Chapter Four: Enlightenment, Modernity, and Genocide Reconsidered

Terror and Civilization are inseparable
--Adorno

To talk of the twentieth-century atrocities is in one way misleading. It is a myth that barbarism is unique to the twentieth century: the whole of human history includes wars, massacres, and every kind of torture and cruelty: there are grounds for thinking that over much of the world the changes of the last hundred years or so have been towards a psychological climate more humane than at any previous time.
  – Jonathan Glover

The Holocaust did not emerge from the "spirit of science"
  – Dan Stone

So far, we have suggested that modern genocide, as opposed to ancient genocide, occurs under specific conditions. Among these conditions are a strong, mobilizing state, a state of war engendering an environment of extreme insecurity and brutalization, and a racialist-eliminationist ideology buttressed by utopist visions of a future society. These conditions, with the exception of war and its consequences, are indeed modern. However, they are a far cry from more universalist claims suggesting that the root of modern genocides lie within modernity itself and or the Enlightenment. Such claims have overemphasized a Weberian focus on rationality and bureaucracy, while totally overlooking what is perhaps the most important aspect of Enlightenment; political liberalism and the crucial conception of the rights of man which underpin it.

At the outset of our discussion, I would like to point to a trend in European intellectual thought that is nothing if not old. Almost a hundred and seventy years old to be exact. It usually goes under the name of "declinism". Its thesis has always been the

103

same: the immanent collapse of Western civilization. (Herman 2007)

The explanatory problem here is clear. According to the various thinkers which have represented this trend of thought for almost two centuries, the West is always living on borrowed time. And this despite the fact that during all that time science and technology, belief in democracy, the rights of the individual, the rule of law, as well as free-market capitalism and the private ownership of property have taken hold of more and more corners of the globe than ever before. Clearly then, over the course of nearly two centuries, Western ideas and institutions have not only not collapsed but have enjoyed an unprecedented global expansion.

For the representatives of Declinism, the state of modern/Western man is always the same: materialistic, devoid of spirituality, lacking in humane values. In a word, culturally and historically bankrupt. Such a view has often been termed "Cultural Pessimism".

Perhaps the greatest example of this particularly gloomy point of view of the modern predicament has been Oswald Spengler as espoused in his renowned work *The Decline of the West*. For Spengler, as for Nietzsche before him and Marcuse after him, modern man is a pathetic creature. One who is deteriorating, helpless, and on the verge of total collapse. An historical abortion. At best, he lives in contorted conceptual contradictions such as "democratic unfreedom" as Marcuse was to put it. For these thinkers and their ilk, modern man is of no use. He is merely a historical place holder for that which is to come. (Spengler 1991) (Marcuse 2013)

It is important to emphasize that much of Declinism and Cultural Pessimism took place in a very specific cultural/historical milieu: Modern Germany. Indeed, I will be arguing that there is a straight intellectual line to be drawn through Nietzsche, Burckhardt, Spengler, Husserl, Heidegger, Adorno, Marcuse and finally, even, Bauman. (Husserl 1970) (Heidegger 1977) (Bauman 2000) (Burckhardt 2012) What these thinkers have in common is that they were all directly or indirectly effected by the visions, pretensions, and predilections of a profound cultural pessimism that permeated the life, politics, and culture of modern Germany.

Yet, there was a larger European trans-Atlantic context too. Cultural pessimism and Declinism was a European wide phenomenon even if one of its central nodes and "meme" makers was in Germany. It cut across political creeds and ideologies. After all, figures such as Spengler and Heidegger turned, at least to a degree, towards Hitler while the disciples of the Frankfurt school were, at least nominally, adherents of Marxism.

Yet irrespective of country, era, or political persuasion all these thinkers were united in one shared belief. They believed that the capitalistic-bourgeois civilization of their own time was doomed to self-destruction. They forcefully, passionately rejected the course of Western civil society and all that usually goes with it: capitalism, commercialism, rationalism, the scientific method, and modern cultural and social attitudes. All this, they thought, were the products of an impending apocalypse. Modern Western man was, for them, a spectacular still-birth.

Interestingly, this apocalyptic frame of mind gave these types of thinkers a certain tendency to a peculiar kind of intellectual perversity which is still very much with us, at least within certain academic circles. So sure of their apocalyptic prophecies, the declinist or cultural pessimist always greets the "worst" as the "best". That is to say, that wars, depressions, conflicts of all kinds, and, of course, genocides are always greeted in a spirit of intellectual "Schadenfreude" which in effect says: "See, I told you so." Thus, every negative event, in their worldview, delegitimizes the modern world and its fundamental premises. The final destruction of modern civilization is always just a few years away. (For a good antidote to this way of thinking see Rosling 2018)

Perhaps we would not be too far off the mark if we said that the true father of all Declinism and Cultural Pessimism was Rousseau. It was he who argued that man's exit from nature was the original Fall and that all subsequent civilization was the true "bar-

barization". It is an idea that was to underline much of Western thought, particularly in twentieth-century cultural anthropology.

In stark contrast to Rousseau stands Hegel. Hegel believed that all History was a progress towards an inevitable goal which was Reason's own idea of freedom. Man and civil society in Hegel's view were progressing through stages in an inevitable upward spiral of self-understanding. Freedom was History's goal and thereby the ever greater self-empowering of man. It is no wonder then that the Frankfurt School was "compelled" to give Hegel up — he could not fit their world-view of decay that had revealed modernity and progress to be the 'true' harbingers of barbarity.

Another impetus to Cultural pessimism and Declinism was the traumatic experience of the French Revolution which seemed to drastically contradict some interpretations/expectations of the Enlightenment. After all, the French case started with terror and ended up in a dictatorship. For contemporaries, it was akin to the more modern moral shock of Auschwitz. In both cases, though, the interpretation was flawed. Universalistic conclusions were premature, a more reasoned opinion for what had happened would be more contingent and particularistic. In the French case, Tocqueville's *The Old Regime and the French Revolution* and for the German case Dahrendorf's *Society and Democracy in Germany* were clearer concerning the why and how of both historical catastrophes. In each of these two cases, it was not the entire "West" that was "sick" but the particular historical, cultural, and above all social constellations that pertained in each particular country that were paramount. After all, modernity took quite different paths in England, France, Germany, the US, and India for example. The question is why? Tocqueville's and Dahrendorf's classic texts go a long way to explaining the conundrum. (Tocqueville 2008) (Dahrendorf 1979)

Yet another cultural force that was to drive pessimistic and declinist analyses was the enduring legacy of Romanticism. Here was a cultural movement which idealized the past, doubted the present, and despaired of the future. Romanticism's pose was of man alienated from himself and his own time. In the nineteenth century it was fed not only by the experience of the French Revolution but also, crucially, by the failed revolutions of 1848. (Jones 1991) In a sense we could say that much of the spirit of pessimism was a product of frustrated political and social ambitions as quashed by quasi-feudal regimes all over Europe. In effect then, it was not modernism that was the problem, but a lack thereof: in particular a lack of true democratic political liberalism that was one of the deep systemic problems of both the nineteenth and the twentieth centuries.

This combination of what we could call a culture of "deep Romanticism" and a structural lack of political modernism or rationality of expression (the particularistic stalling of Hegel's historical "march of freedom through the world") was to prove a breeding ground for the next phase of cultural pessimism which was obsessed with all kinds of ideas concerning 'decline' and, now ominously, degeneracy. It was here that ideas of völkisch nationalism, neo-Gobinian vitalism, and racial eugenics were to thrive and expand. Importantly, although these ideas were born in the modern world and sometimes called upon modern terms and concepts, they were decidedly anti-modern and anti-Enlightenment in tone and meaning, often rabidly so.

Another crucial concept buttressing the general trend of declinism and cultural pessimism stemmed yet again from modern Germany. This time a crucial distinction was drawn between the forces of "Zivilisation" and "Kultur". The former was seen as superficial and materialistic, the latter as transcendent, organic and whole. It was mirrored in the concept of "Gemeinschaft" and "Gesellschaft" which offered a distinction between modern society's creation of an industrial, commercial civilization which supported "Zivilisation" and the farming, traditional village communities which were at the heart of "Kultur" and all that was allegedly vital in the "soul" of a nation. Clearly, a more potent protest against the forces of both technological or social progress could hardly be more prominent. Progress or "Zivilisation" was seen as soul-destroying, alienating, and just plain anti-life. This was a strain of thought that would lead in many directions, one of which was the Frankfurt's school classic anti-Enlightenment work entitled the *Dialectic of Enlightenment*. (Adorno 2016)

We should step back for a moment to discuss how Marxism fits into this intellectual tradition of pessimism and decay. Clearly, at least on the surface, Marxism is a progressive creed. True to its Hegelian roots it sees History as progressing through stages the culmination of which is the liberation of man through his mastering of the social and economic forces which had hitherto dominated him. It is a future gospel emphasizing man's ability to fully realize himself. On the other hand, there is not just a little pessimism in Marx's work. Similar to Nietzsche, Spengler, and others, Marx sees the current historical figure of the bourgeois as "historically" bankrupt and is not loathe to attack him both morally and spiritually, although a professed materialist. Similar to other authors already mentioned, the present situation, which is symbolized by the economic and social relations of capitalism is one of impending doom. It is a system racing to its apocalyptic climax. A furious and violent end which will herald the beginning of a new civilization based on entirely new relations yielding up a "new man" historically prepared for the "new society". Here progress and pessimism are epically mixed. Thus, it was to prove easy for later day Marxists to pick up on Marx's notes of pessimism, particularly after Marx's predictions stubbornly refused to come true. (The latest popular incarnation of this way of thought is Hardt and Negri's *Empire*) All this within a general culture of pessimism and Declinism, materially driven, as we said earlier, by the impotency or entire lack of appropriately modern political and social institutions; especially in a lopsidedly modern Germany as we shall see.

Another "Master of Suspicion" who was to have a crucial ideological role to play in many of the genocidal and violent acts of the twentieth century was certainly Friedrich Nietzsche. (Kee 2011) However, in all fairness to Nietzsche, it should be noted that the historical uses of his thought, particularly by way of Spengler, was an expurgated version as prepared by Nietzsche's sister and Wagner's wife. Nietzsche became the fountainhead of thought for racialist, völkisch pessimism of all kinds, as well as strident nationalism. An historical outcome which the original Nietzsche would probably have despised. Ultimately, though, his "will to power" became an idea used to justify all kinds of aggression both at home and abroad.

Yet it was to be Oswald Spengler who developed Nietzsche's ideas to their lethal climax. Spengler was an arch enemy of liberalism and the Enlightenment and longed for nothing more than for the "shopkeeper Zivilisation" to be torn asunder. He yearned for German "Kultur" to take the place of English/French 'decadent' "Zivilisation". He fantasized about a combination of the forces of "Kultur", military discipline, and Nietzschean 'Will to Power' that would give rise to new men to lead a new world. Again, whether Marxist or Fascist, much of modern continental European thought in the nineteenth century and especially in modern Germany was anything but rationalist and/or a proponent of anything close to Enlightenment thought. They were its ardent enemies. An intellectual reality which was to cost the world two-world wars.

At this point we should begin to emphasize what already has become somewhat apparent and that is that much of German and Continental European thought of the nineteenth and the first third of the twentieth century was in revolt against Enlightenment and, indeed, earlier Humanist values. A dark thread of Declinism, cultural pessimism, and apocalyptic utopianism runs through figures as diverse as Marx, Burckhardt, Nietzsche, Spengler, Adorno, Benjamin, Freud, Heidegger, Fromm, and Marcuse. German culture was a technologically advanced reactionary hot-house that was building its unstable violent potential for at least 70 years until it exploded. To say that it was the culmination of Enlightenment thought is at best a grave distortion, a case of self-willed blindness, a set of guilty delusions, and at worst a disingenuous intellectual absurdity. In the end, it was also to prove a self-made intellectual dead end.

Yet although we have mentioned Declinism, cultural pessimism, "deep romanticism", "Zivilisation" and "Kultur" and other trends and material situations there still is one item left to be discussed and that is the role of the German idea of "Bildung" and the social role of the universities and their professors. The German universities had always seen themselves as champions of "higher spiritual values" and "the cultivation of the intellect" a task which was to be fostered by the socially, and often politically, prestigious role of the professor. Modernity threatened all this. It also didn't help matters that in the concept of German "Bildung" all that was "merely" practical, technical, and utilitarian was socially denigrated. (Bruford 2010) And as for money making, that was an absolute moral scandal. People who were engaged in such things were looked down upon; that is to say that the new classes and pursuits that were being produced by modernity had no place in the temple of the German mind. Indeed, as we have seen, they were hotly contested. After all, the social prestige and power of a whole class (professors) and their educative mission (Ideology) was at stake.

It is worth reemphasizing that among the themes most precious to the cultural pessimists of the nineteenth and twentieth century was opposition to liberal/Enlightenment ideas such as limited government, human rights, and, especially, the free market. Thinkers, whether of the left or the right, were united in the idea that laissez-faire capitalism was a mortal threat to the very essence of man. In the words of Werner Sombart, it set up and perpetuated a world of "Lug und Trug" pandering to the basest instincts of man, finally locking him up in the souless "Iron Cage" of Max Weber's bureaucratic civilization. (Sombart 1913) (Weber 2002)

A central focus for the hatred of these thinkers was, not surprisingly, Great Britain and the United States. These two countries represented a situation of "negative freedom" of "live and let live" rather than endeavoring, in their view, to build a vibrant soulful community. Citing Werner Sombart again, the Anglo-Saxon world represented the playing field of the "trader" who approaches life with the question: "What can you give me?" while the German, presumably, more moral "hero" asks: "What can I give you?". (Herman 2007) Clearly, not only did German thinkers of this time have a very prejudiced and unclear view of what liberal civilization entailed and why; there was also little evidence of self-reflection/criticism on their part and not a little of self-agrandizing/self-conceptualization. Theirs was a world-view very much black and white, inflexible, reactionary, indeed, downright Manichean. It was to prove a serious historical miscalculation.

Crucially, the Germany of this time viewed herself as outside the mainstream of Western European values. No less a figure than the young novelist Thomas Mann viewed Germany's destiny as outside the trajectory of middle-class democracy. Such an outcome would, from his viewpoint, rob all that was best from Germany. (Herman 2007) Mann's people (Volk) had a special historical destiny set before it. Such messianic ideas had deep roots going back all the way to Herder, Fichte, and to a certain extent Hegel, too. Germany was to save the world form "the machine". (Herman 2007) If this was not an example of a stunning clarion call to defeat all that was modern in politics, society, and technology; I really don't know what else could be.

Popularized by Nietzsche, and through him all the way back to Heraclitus, with an added dose of Social Darwinism, the idea of "struggle" seized the imagination of the cultural/political elite of Germany and through them to the middle and working-classes. Mann spoke of Germany standing against the world-entente of civilization, Ernst Haeckel spoke of the immanent destruction of the weak by which he meant the bourgeois civilization of the West. (Herman 2007) "War as the father of all" was the Heraclitean fragment by which whole generations were taught to believe and idealize their world-historical mission. Within this cultural context, we should not be surprised at all that Hitler's most famous book was eventually to be entitled *My Struggle*; in this he was very much in the mainstream of the German thought of his time. Indeed, he was a 'natural' expression of it. The dark fruit of cultural pessimism and antagonistic reactionism had come to foully ripen.

Interestingly and not to be dismissed lightly, Britain herself produced an intellectual that was to have far ranging consequences for world-intellectual history via Lenin: J.A. Hobson. In his magnum opus, *Imperialism,* Hobson offered a particularly negative view of the British Empire and all other modern empires, too. (Hobson 2005) For Hobson, the British imperialist system was nothing more and nothing less than a system of capitalist exploitation of local natives deepening their poverty while bolstering armaments profits at home. Our task is not to take issue with the diagnosis but merely to present one particularly gloomy self-image of liberal British society at the turn of the century. It should also be noted that this particular line of argument was to have many resurgences and is still, in altered form, very much with us today particularly in the writings of Noam Chomsky. (Chomsky 2004)

Another equally important self-image of the state of liberal affairs at the turn of the twentieth-century was the idea that the British Empire was attempting to build, not unlike Alexander the Great's empire before it, a world-federation, an empire of man. Humanitarian and internationalist, this was an uplifting vision that saw Britain's role as one of amelioration of the common good rather than the ruthless exploitation of the many under its charge. This line of argument has had a resurgence lately in the works of the preeminently yet always fascinatingly provocative historian, Niall Ferguson. (Ferguson 2012) In our view both explanations contain some truth to them.

Within this general and deep context of cultural pessimism that we have been examining in the last couple of pages, now enters our first discussion of the Frankfurt School and its most notable work *The Dialectic of Enlightenment.*

The Frankfurt School, independent of its self-professed 'Marxism', was as much a product of its time and cultural environment as were their intellectual antagonists. Indeed, they shared many viewpoints despite their hatred for one another. Drinking deep from the well of the cultural pessimism that surrounded them, the Frankfurt School was against mass democracy as an aspect of true, political freedom; it was against technology and positivist science which they thought destroyed the human soul; it was against industrial capitalism which they viewed as the destroyer of "Gemeinschaft" and, finally, and seemingly most important for them, they were against the cultural products of modernity which they felt were the true signs of the end of the West and the emblems of man's enslavement to a "Zivilisation" of "Lug und Trug". These ideas were shared by the radical right. It is thus impossible not to see the theses of the Frankfurt School as a particular cultural product of a particular nation and era rather than a universalist prescription for "all" that is "wrong" with "Zivilisation" and the "West". There is more here of Nietzsche and of Spengler than there is of Marx, more even than their founders would have liked to admit.

More than this, German Marxism was in a state of despondency. Marxism had preached that the working-class were "the historically anointed" revolutionaries that would bring about a world communist movement that would finally and completely overthrow their oppressors. In Germany, and elsewhere, this did not happen. What did happen was that a significant portion of the Western working-class turned towards the radical right, and what was left of the communist movement became more and more slavish following the dictates of first, Lenin, and then Stalin. Historical certainty and a Marxian march through history seemed highly unlikely. This of course did not stop a cottage intellectual industry from springing up of "revisionist or post-Marxism" of which the Frankfurt School is one notable example, while Antonio Negri's and Michael Hardt's book *Empire* is but the latest fashionable example.

Like the many cultural pessimists before and since, the Frankfurt School saw the Western World as coming to an end, as a rotten and twisted example of "Zivilisation", as something (Nietzsche) that had to be "overcome". They never once thought that perhaps their viewpoint was being determined more from their specific cultural milieu rather than from inexorable, intrinsic, and universalistic principles. In short, they took a leap of cultural smugness; they mistook Germany for the world.

However, their sense of smugness went far deeper than this. As we mentioned, German culture had always encouraged German professors to consider themselves "exceptional" and to give them a leading role in society, politics, and culture. This leading role was increasingly put under pressure under the conditions of modernity. Yet the following statement which can only be called extraordinarily conceited and lacking in the slightest bit of self-awareness or true historical-cultural sense is revealing and it stems from the founder of the Frankfurt School, Max Horkheimer: "Under the conditions of late Capitalism, Truth has sought refuge among small groups of admirable men". (Cited in Herman 2007) Once again, there is much more of Nietzsche's and even Spengler's "Superman" here, then there is of Marx's proletariat. Not only were the members of the Frankfurt School inheritors of the pessimistic tradition they were also protagonists of the privileged position of the German professorate.

As for The Frankfurt School's use of Marxism, they turned to the then newly rediscovered manuscripts of the young Marx and enlisted them to explain modern cultural decline. They focused strongly on Marx's concept, borrowed from Hegel, of alienation. They combined it with the sociology of among others, Sombart, Durkheim, Simmel, and Weber. The root cause of Marxist alienation, Capitalism, was combined with German cultural criticism and Nietzsche.

As is well known, the Frankfurt School attributed the horrendous events of the 30's and 40's not to particular cultural and historical contingencies and anti-Enlightenment philosophies (as we are attempting to do here) but to an alleged universalist cause that congenitally inhered in liberal capitalism generally and in Enlightenment thinking in particular.

Similar to Spengler's "Faustian spirit of the West", the Frankfurt school attributed the catastrophe in Germany to an alleged Western spirit of absolute control and domination which drove Western civilization in particular through a totalitarian impulse towards total social-political-cultural negative integration. They did not see, or want to admit, that what had happened in Nazi Germany, was not happening in the traditionally liberal states of the West: France, England, and the US. The Frankfurt school focused far too much, in the spirit of Max Weber, on issues concerning bureaucratization, rationalization, and technology. Missing altogether the very essence of liberal and Enlightenment thinking which has to do with political liberalism and its underlying conception of human rights. But like other cultural pessimists before them, they obviously thought that the political traditions of the West had not much, if any merit. In this, their analysis falls far short of what is necessary and reveals their own blindness as to what actually occurred in their home country. A country without any real democrats with practical (and stable) governing experience on either the left or the right or among almost any of the social classes of the time.

Yet Horkheimer and Adorno went even further than just accuse modern day liberal capitalism and went back to the origins of Western Civilization where they alleged to have found the root cause of liberal bourgeois civilization's decline. They declared that the West suffered from a peculiar surfeit of rationality and reason. And that the Enlightenment was not about Reason at all, but concealed its real agenda which was preoccupied with the pursuit of power over nature and human beings. For them, there was a straight historical line connecting the ancient Greeks to the Nazis.

Focusing on the concept of alienation which as we have seen had deep roots in German culture, the Frankfurt School coupled this potent idea with the Marxist critique of capitalism and made it the scapegoat for man's alleged separation from both himself and nature. They drew a decidedly negative picture of the modern world, depicting it as obsessed with number, measurement, and the scientific method in general.

Thus, the chief rationale of the Enlightenment was a technological one which led to total domination and created the peculiar contradiction of a democratic-totalitarian society. Within this vision, science and technical progress are the twin horsemen of the cultural apocalypse for both Europe and the world. The Enlightenment is the deadly tool of those who would seek to completely annihilate the "other". There is no mention of the political and social aspect of the Enlightenment as represented by Thomas Paine or the American Federalists. The focus is on instrumental rationality.

However, on the face of it, it would be hard to justify such claims when Nazi-Germany was the self-professed enemy of all that Enlightenment thought represented offering, instead, a dark Wagnerian alternative view of Western culture and its future. At the very least it could be said, that the Nazis saw themselves as champions of "Kultur" and the negators of "Zivilisation". Such a view would have been dismissed by the Frankfurt School.

This neglect of the political by the Frankfurt school is characteristic. Rather than analyzing this crucial category of society, the Frankfurt school routinely dismissed it and rhetorically collapsed it within their cultural concerns. Yet, it was here, in the political that the fatal flaw in their analysis was to show itself.

Not surprisingly, as concerns the modern causes of genocide, the Frankfurt school was wide off the mark. As we have seen, the occurrence of Genocide is decidedly not a modern phenomenon. It is most definitely not an outcome of either modern society and, still less, Enlightenment thinking. Modern cases of genocide (but not all of them) do share some modernist traits such as a mobilizing state, an external condition of modern warfare, and a racialist-eliminationist, totalizing, utopist ideology. But the Frankfurt School dismissed Nazi-Ideology and the state of German society as irrelevant. Most absurdly of all, they seemed to strongly imply that antisemitism had no role to play in the events that took place between 1933 to 1945. Such thinking led them to construct crude analogies between German and American societies, analogies utterly deaf to the distinct political, social, and historical differences between them.

Interestingly, and not surprisingly, Frankfurt school rhetoric may well have owed more of a debt to German Expressionist thinking than to any Marxist based analysis. Again, their blindness to their own social-political-cultural roots makes their analysis function almost as an intellectual boomerang for much of the dysfunctionality and shortsightedness of German pre-war intellectual life and culture.

Almost obscenely, the Frankfurt School suggested that the Holocaust was nothing out of the ordinary since we, all of us in the West, were/are living a Holocaust of the Everyday. In their drive to discredit all of Western Civilization, these thinkers added nothing to our understanding of Genocide in general, or the Holocaust in particular.

On the human side however, it is immanently understandable why German intellectuals would seek to shift the blame for some of the worst calamities in Western history onto a general "system". If the whole was rotten, then surely a particular expression of it was not to blame. "All too human" and thus understandable, absolutely. But it does not excuse a serious intellectual disservice to generations to come.

Although not a central issue in our discussion, it is disturbing to note that the "radical left" seemed to inherit much from the earlier "radical right". Its heroes (with the exception of Marx) are the same: Nietzsche, Sorel, Heidegger, and Schopenhauer to name but a few. They are one in their fanatical disbelief in the possibility of social progress according to normative, historical Western models. They both reject the possibility of the autonomy of the individual, the possession of private property as a fundamental right, that science and technology serve to help mankind rather than hinder it, and that the individual pursuit of happiness is essentially a rational activity and not the source of immanent cultural decline and/or societal apocalypse. In this, as well as many other aspects, the radical left seems to mirror its arch enemy the radical right.

However, so as not to be misunderstood, one should point out that criticism of one's or any others society is an absolutely indispensable activity. Yet, it is a far cry to denounce parts of the whole as opposed to calling for the whole to be destroyed. Every system needs to be improved or altered since men and their times are always changing. Yet, not every evil is the result of deep-rooted systemic dysfunction.

Furthermore, this propensity of many nineteenth- and twentieth-century thinkers to view society as a whole was, ultimately, counter-productive. Thinking of a society as if it were an organism obfuscated the oftentimes discrete origins of problems. Indeed, the very idea of "crisis" whether of capitalism or imperialism owes much to this type of organicist thinking. Society was often seen as a body developing along deterministic rules and laws; everything then like culture and politics had to be tied to everything else rather than be analyzed separately and contingently.

Arguments, like those found in *The Dialectic of Enlightenment*, are still extremely popular in academia. They utilize sophisticated intellectual argumentation with powerful moral rhetoric. Nevertheless, they emphasize some aspects of modernity over others, obfuscating the historical record, particularly as regards the Holocaust. Outrageous historiographical distortions must be challenged, and the ethical imperative of challenging moral decay must be met.

One should never forget that it was an ideology of antisemitism and not the scientific method that was the driving force behind the Holocaust. Indeed, Nazi "science" as well as Soviet "science" under Stalin was more often than not pseudo-science hiding behind unscientific "historicist" concepts. Both these totalitarian societies attempt to ideologize scientific practice ended up in dismal failure and, even, arguably cost Germany the war (the attack on "Jewish" science).

Traditional science and "Nazi science" had very little to do with one another. The first was an uncompromising search for the truth, while the other was a willing handmaiden to falsehoods generated by political authority. It should be firmly stated that modern medicine and biology were not at the root of Nazi "science"; indeed, these modern tools have served to help the sick, elderly, handicapped, the genetically at risk, as well as triumph over malaria and cholera — to name but a handful of successes. (Menschenfreund 2010)

Another claim of the anti-Enlightenment school of thought is that bureaucracy and bureaucratization had much to do with the creation of the Holocaust. This is simply mistaking a tool with the tool user. Bureaucracy is an organizing tool. It does what the society within which it is embedded wants it to do. In the Nazi case, it helped organize mass murder. In many other cases it delivers social security checks and child support payments. (Stone 2010) Just as a knife can be used to slice butter, or slit a neighbor's throat; a tool's use depends on the motivations and outlook of the user. The really interesting question then is: why did bureaucracy function differently in the USA, United Kingdom, France, and Nazi Germany? The answer of course is that these nations operated on different political and social values. One was motivated by a murderous anti-Enlightenment ideology, while the others continued and developed the traditions of political liberalism and human rights.

Most recently, the renowned sociologist Zygmunt Bauman has followed in the footsteps of the Frankfurt school. His arguments are much the same, even identical. He blames the Holocaust on modernity and the ideas of the Enlightenment. (Bauman 2001) Science, bureaucratization, instrumental rationality, and an urge to organize and dominate are the ultimate reasons for the darkest outcome of the twentieth century. His arguments are by and large almost exactly the same as the Frankfurt school's before him and, not surprisingly, our counter-arguments are the same too.

Like the Frankfurt School, Bauman vastly underplays the role that the hatred of Jews and a comprehensive ideology of antisemitism played in the Holocaust. The unique character of German society under the Nazis with its murderous ideology drove the extermination process in spite of an instrumentally governed administrative system not because of it.

Indeed, the irrational lengths that the Nazi regime would go to fulfill its ideological mission are almost breathtaking. The extermination of the Jews was never either rational or economic from the point of view of the regime or their war effort. Their policy of extermination cost the regime precious time and economic and military resources that could have been far better used in the war effort. At the very least, the German economy suffered from the massive project of the elimination of the Jews and, in more general terms, the irrational world vision of the Nazis cost them the winning of the war. One might have to only ask what would have happened had the Nazis been an "ordinary" or "standard" national-dictatorial regime which not only employed but rewarded its German Jewish scientists for advances made in nuclear research? This historical counter-factual bears thinking about.

To further the point, Nazi ideology was not only irrational, it was fervently anti-rational. It hearkened back to a mythical pre-Christian past, adopted romantic ideas about nature and a way of life according to its mystical dictates, and most of all, similar to all cultural pessimism, it encouraged a messianic view that the end of the world was nigh and that a titanic struggle between "races" was at hand.

The Nazis had nothing but contempt for rationalism and despised the Enlightenment. They were at pains to emphasize the difference between a "Weltanschauung" or "World View" and a "Welt-an-Denken" or "Thinking about the world". (Menschenfreund 2010) In the first concept, the Nazis relished the idea of a direct and spontaneous experience of the world, while in the latter they denigrated the Western bourgeois penchant for reasoning and analyzing. For the Nazis there was no primacy of intellectual analysis only the glorious rush of direct action.

It should be recalled here that, generally, the "project of modernity' is linked to the Enlightenment and Immanuel Kant's injunction to "free one-self from self-incurred immaturity". (Kant 2001) Initially, Enlightenment stood against prejudice and the tyranny of ancient custom. It challenged authority of all sorts, particularly the universal church. It sought scientific progress, the rational investigation of society, politics, and ethics, all of which brought hope to large swathes of society that previously had none at least on this earth.

However, approximately a hundred years ago, the horrendous outbreak of the First World War helped to shatter this progressivist faith in a decisive way. The disappointment and despair of those times just after the "Great War" was echoed by thinkers and writers everywhere but perhaps nowhere more significantly than in Germany by Edmund Husserl in his *The Crisis of European Sciences and Transcendental Phenomenology*. Ideas that were to be developed by his most famous student, and later Nazi devotee, Martin Heidegger.

Yet the greater question of course is whether or not the project of modernity is truly a failure? Science cannot and should not replace faith, metaphysical yearning, and/or ethics. This is not its role. Any attempt to do so will run into all kinds of personal confusion and societal error. Despite this, science has a positive role to play in the development of mankind. Unquestionably, science has opened up new vistas undreamed of even 60 years ago. It has provided aid and comfort, and a modicum of protection and a rise of living standards for millions, something never imagined possible in the world before the introduction and institutionalization of the scientific method. Most importantly perhaps, it has provided mankind with its most successful tool to date in separating well-grounded theories from bunkum, delusions, fantasies, and fancies of all kinds — among which was "Nazi Science". How we use this powerful tool is up to us. As Sartre would put it; we can always choose to start something new. (Sartre 1993)

And then there is Rwanda. Rwanda is, in a way, the most recent "smoking gun" of our argument. The genocide in Rwanda is the most recent of the more serious genocides in modern history. It had very little to do with either instrumental rationality, bureaucracy, the scientific method, or Enlightenment ideas. The Rwandan genocide was for the most part carried out in close quarters with machetes. (Jones 2017) It is a most serious rebuttal to the Frankfurt school and all others, like Bauman, who feel that the modern world is to blame for all of its ills.

However, what Rwanda *is*, is a partial support of some of the necessary elements for modern genocide as outlined in chapter two. This genocide was carried out under conditions of a state of war and a general atmosphere of state emergency. Most importantly there was a racialist-climinationist ideology of Hutus against Tutsis that was strongly in play and that had been simmering for decades. The state mobilized and encouraged Hutu hatred and fear of Tutsis.

Without a doubt, the case of Rwanda is a serious blow to Modernity as being the ultimate culprit for genocide. In Rwanda, one million people were exterminated in twelve weeks. This is a rate of killing that exceeds by a wide margin the allegedly "modern" Nazi Holocaust. Not only is Rwanda more modern chronologically, it also was carried out by people using relatively primitive agricultural implements. No scientific or technical experts were involved. The killing was often face to face and public. No official policy of secrecy was implemented. No special or specific "distancing" strategies were used. What, however, was crucial was the Hutu's ideology of hate; just as Antisemitism was in the German case, as I have tried to argue.

We might take a moment now and step back and see where we have gone in our argument. We have argued that genocide is old, at least as old as war itself. We have also argued that some distinctions can be made between ancient occurrences of genocide and more modern ones. In recent genocides, a mobilizing state, a state of war/emergency, and racialist-eliminationist ideologies often coupled with utopist aspirations had a crucial role to play. Most recently we have categorically rejected the idea that the project of modernity, Enlightenment thought, and or science are the root causes for genocide's occurrence. Rather, we have suggested that cultural, social, historical, and perhaps most importantly, political variables, structures, and attitudes have had a much greater role to play as to whether or not genocide takes place. For the most part, we have used modern Germany as an example, tacitly sticking close to many critics' idea of German history as an example of a special historical path or *Sonderweg*. Some prominent members of this school of thought include the sociologist Ralf Dahrendorf, the historian Fritz Fischer (who coined the phrase), the political scientist Jeffery Herf and, to some extent, the philosopher Jurgen Habermas to name but a few. (Fischer 1961) (Herf 1986)

Yet despite all this we have only briefly touched upon what might indeed be the root cause of such specific outbreaks of group directed eliminationist violence and that question leads us to ancient predispositions in our genetic endowment.

W.D. Hamilton's notion of "inclusive fitness" might provide us here, with a preliminary answer. Simply put, inclusive fitness means that it is in the individual's global interest, from a genetic point of view, to protect those who are possibly genetically related to him or her. Such a disposition could go a long way to explaining man's ancient predilection for maintaining in/out groups and acting violently within this distinction. Yet, it should be emphasized, that although fear and hostility towards the "other" may have a biological basis that does not mean that it cannot be overcome by that quintessential (Aristotelian) element in man's nature: reason. It is an argument that was explored earlier in our discussion about Peter Singer's *The Expanding Circle* and something which he elaborated further upon in his book *A Darwinian Left*. (Singer 2000, 2001)

Nazism, as an ideology, certainly exploited this perhaps genetically ingrained sense of tribalism. As is well known, it focused on national, collectivist feeling particularly as regards alleged wrongs meted out to the German nation/people. It played on people's collective instinct mixing Social Darwinist, Nietzschean, and Völkisch strands of thought. In this it was anything but an inheritor of Enlightenment thought. It negated the universalistic in favor of the particularistic. It had not the slightest interest in the Rights of Man, indeed it was actively hostile to it. Men per se had no rights, not even the right to live. Only the "Nazi-Man", the "Superman" had the right to live, by right of superior force and calculated cruelty and not reason.

At this point, for the sake of additional clarity, we might bring up and modify George Orwell's famous essay on Gandhi. (Orwell 1971) Let us ask, as George Orwell did, would a Gandhi be possible in a Nazi controlled Europe/world? The answer of course was no. The difference between the British Empire and the Nazi "New World Order" was extreme. As Niall Ferguson has recently put it, the British Empire always had a "self-liquidating" character about it; for once its possessions acquired "the rule of law, liberal political institutions, a workable free-market, and a relatively impartial administrative bureaucracy it could not contradict its founding political principles for long and deny its charges that which they eventually so longed for: complete self-determination." (Ferguson 2012b) Such an outlook is based firmly, on basic Enlightenment principles particularly as expressed by Montesquieu, Spinoza, Locke, Hume, Smith, Paine, and the Federalists to name but a few. In stark contradiction to this tradition, we find the Nazi world view dividing the world up between "master" and "slave" nations; basing itself on notions of an inherited non-negotiable 'genetic' status.

Clearly, we have argued that it is untenable to lay the entire blame for modern genocides at the feet of modernity and/or Enlightenment thought. But does, as Dirk Moses asks, modernity bear at least some of the blame? In one specific sense, it might.

And that is the idea concerning the different historical paths different societies took to reach modernity from pre-modernity. This epochal journey also includes, I think importantly, the transformation and/or loss of traditional forms of moral authority, particularly in the form of religion. Yet despite this partial admission of modernity's "guilt", one again should emphasize that the crucial intervening variable in this journey from traditional to modern society were the political and social values and philosophical/moral contexts within which it was realized: liberal/non-liberal, individual/collective, democratic/authoritarian. Thus, for countries like Germany, Russia, and China the historical balance was tipped in favor of a transformation that proved to have a high cost in human life, while for countries like France, Great Britain and many of her former colonies the transformation was significantly less costly in terms of human life and was a journey collectively negotiated rather than unilaterally dictated from above.

At the risk of belaboring the point, one should pick up on Dan Stone's notable analysis of the Nazi genocide as an example of "transgressive" violence that had, at its roots, a lethal combination of "mystical" antisemitism, political conspiracy theories, and "fantasy" thinking. (Stone 2010) For Stone, this archetypal example of modern genocide had very little, if anything, to do with the logic of reason, Foucault's "Bio-power", or the "Dialectic of Enlightenment". For Stone, the historical tragedy of the Holocaust was a result of a culture saturated with racial fantasies.

Crucially, Stone goes on to say that modernity was the setting for genocide but not its driving force. Thus, in the German case, bureaucratic involvement may have been considerable and essential but it was not the primary locus from which the Holocaust was born. In the end, though, according to Stone and buttressing one of my main points, bureaucracy was placed at the service of the Nazi world view and not the other way around.

Unlike Bauman and the Frankfurt school before him, Stone focuses on historical and cultural contingencies in order to explain the Holocaust. Factors such as centuries of anti-Jewish hatred and short-term variables such as imperial rivalry, World War I, the Great Depression, and the general cultural atmosphere and structural problems of the inter-war years of the Weimar Republic come to the fore.

> "In the final analysis, no form of economic or any other kind of "rationality" can account for the destruction of the Jews. The immense trouble that the Nazi regime went through, during a time of existential crisis, to hunt down the Jews of Rhodes, Crete, and Southern France belie any kind of ends-means rationality, indeed it bespeaks of a vast and deep fanaticism." (Stone 2010)

To conclude, we may say, along with Stone, that the German case evinces the "trappings" of modernity: bureaucracy, organization, and technology but does not, thereby, account for the origin of the idea to murder the Jews.

Perhaps one of the more fruitful ways of interpreting Nazism and other genocidal movements is as a political religion. This way of understanding has a long and distinguished pedigree going back to such figures as Eric Voegelin, Carl Schmitt, Raymond Aron, and Jules Monnerot. It has recently been popularized by Emilio Gentile and Michael Burleigh.

Seen in this way, Nazism, but not only Nazism, can be seen as an ideology which gave new meaning to German society and culture. In the mix was national prestige, old fears of racial degeneration, international conspiracies, and the momentous rebirth of community. Yet the shared utopian goal of rebirth was key. The murder of the Jews was the requisite sacrifice for such.

Indeed, Nazism was not just an attempt to create a Nazi Empire in Europe. It was also not just an attempt to reorganize Europe along racial lines. Although it was all these things, it was something more. In the words of Yehuda Bauer, it was a "total rebellion against Western civilization". (Stone 2010)

It was the apogee of an ideology which idealized and attempted to realize the epitome of anti-rationalist thought of "thinking with the blood". (Stone 2010)

As we already mentioned, Emilio Gentile has repopularized fascism's interpretation as a political religion. Gentile sees fascism as a "sacralization of politics". (Gentile 1996) As a fusion between the political and the sacred producing an eschatological vision of salvation for the national community. Importantly, a political religion such as fascism seeks to displace traditional forms of faith. It tries to go beyond any kind of conflict of values, providing a solid and comfortable framework for rebirth and deliverance.

At this point we may offer our own thoughts, partly based on Hannah Arendt, that the cultural figure of the Jew stood at an important crossroads of modernity. The Jew became the countervailing figure in some of modernity's most historically wrenching transitions: nationalism, capitalism, and socialism. The figure of the "Jew" was made responsible for two of them (capitalism and socialism) and an enemy of the third (nationalism). Hence, then, are some newer ideological reasons for the explosive revitalization of ancient sources of antisemitism. The Jew became the dark figure lurking behind the forces of modernity while threatening national unity.

At the same time, as Hannah Arendt had argued, the rise of colonial/imperialist structures coincided with Darwinist discoveries that led, indirectly, to Social Darwinism making a pan-European atmosphere of "race-talk" and "race-thinking" more acceptable, and most importantly, conveniently useful as an ideological support. However, it should be noted that Aristotle had long ago argued for a distinction between those "naturally" born a "slave" and those born as a "master".

Although genocide is ancient, and modernity was not its ultimate cause, it was reformulated by humanity's transition from the pre-modern to the modern. A part of that transition took place under formal conditions of imperialism buttressed by the new ideology of social Darwinism.

Social Darwinism was certainly an influential line of thought in the European Age of Imperialism. It strongly implied that the natural "struggle for survival" was occurring at a national level between peoples and different races. It gave the nation-state a new and dangerous racial understanding of itself. This type of thinking cut across class and national lines. It was a European wide phenomenon. It was certainly a phase of European intellectual history, but not necessarily a "destiny". Social Darwinist thought did not doom Europe to become genocidal, indeed no such thing happened in Britain and/or France. Again, England's and France's continued adherence and belief in political liberalism as developed in the seventeenth and eighteenth centuries precluded such an outcome as would occur in Germany where Enlightenment thought, practice, and, especially, institutions were weaker. In a pluralistic society, there can be many competing beliefs, some of them pernicious, what there cannot be, at least not for long, is one uncontested undisputed paradigm. Modernity has gone through many phases, and most probably will go through many more. One of its historical phases, precipitated in part by Darwin's discoveries and their misapplication, we can now term "racialist" or perhaps more accurately, if somewhat exaggeratedly, as "The Age of Social Darwinism". It was a phase/era that was to find its dramatic end in 1945. As one observer put it, "Hitler gave racism a bad name".

In a sense, after the discoveries of Darwin, all of European society engaged in a bout of the "naturalistic fallacy" or an erroneous revival of Hume's "is-ought" problem. They simply interpreted the natural findings of Darwin as having a moral import. This was a conclusion that was not logically warranted. Indeed, it was much more of a "leap of faith" during an era in which the traditional religions and moral authorities were rapidly losing ground.

Social Darwinism thus became a "belief" or even a new gospel rather than a scientifically well-grounded theory. Apparently, at the time, no one thought to ask if something "is" such as "the survival of the fittest" whether or not that meant that it "must be"? In a sense, people made of the new discoveries an ersatz religion or new moral code, especially since the critical questioning of the old religions created an opening for a replacement. To those, and there were many, who adopted this outlook, it seemed the "modern" thing to believe at the time. After all, science too was given an almost sacral mantel at the time, something which it was always most unsuited to assume, as we have repeatedly emphasized.

In addition to this, Social Darwinism provided a dangerous critique of liberal thought and its institutions. (Menschenfreund 2010) The essential liberal idea of human equality came under attack from Social Darwinist ideas of biological inequality. There was a drive to construct society along more "natural" lines more suited to the "survival of the fittest". Thus, the pseudo-science of "negative eugenics" was born. It flew in the face, not only of political liberalism as such but also was in revolt against traditional forms of Christian morality, Renaissance Humanism, and any hint of sentimentalism, human decency, and kindness. In a word, it was an undermining and destabilizing element in European civilization from the start.

Yet, at a time of rapid technical and scientific advance and at the same time a growing body of critical work against traditional morality and religion (especially in the work of Nietzsche) it is not surprising that the initial instinct of European man would be to erect something new upon what seemed the solid edifice of science. After all, this was an Age of Progress that had yet to witness the trauma of two World Wars and a Holocaust. The general trend was towards a society of improvement and, in this small if misleading way, the Frankfurt school was correct.

However, as we have said before, the Frankfurt school was not very big on the idea of contingency in History which they tended to believe, in Hegelian fashion, unfolded as a total system according to general forces. Yet, although it cannot be proven, it would not be terribly off the mark to say that the unfortunate events in Germany may not have come to pass at all had it not been for the following historical events: World War One; Germany's Defeat; the Versailles Treaty; the rise of Hitler. Had any of the former been even slightly different, the Holocaust may not have occurred. However, on the other hand, many seasoned historians have argued that the outbreak of World War One was over determined since the military and political elites of Wilhelmine Germany were actively working for its outbreak to provide them (so they believed) preventive security from a perceived future Russian threat as well as possibly giving them an opening for a "place in the sun" among the world powers of the time. (Copeland 2000)

Yet there was also something ancient that died in the modern era and that was the culture of honor and the celebration of war that pervaded men's minds since at least the dawn of civilization and probably much before it. (Bowman 2007) The shock of World War One ended it in the democratic West, while the catastrophe of the Second World War did much to end it almost everywhere else. People, at least in the West, were never to look at violence, or the glorification of violence in the same ways again. That it took the harsh lessons of two world wars might have been unavoidable, such are the stubborn and slow ways of man, particularly in moral matters.

Much of what we have already said has not inconsiderable intellectual back up from the "modern conscience of Germany" the philosopher, Jurgen Habermas. Habermas, too, has argued that the German outcome was due to its not following the historical path of both France and England. (Gellately 2010) That German culture and society was too particularistic and only thinly universalist. That Germans were in the grip of viewing themselves as culturally and ethnically unique. And that all this led to a stunted, lopsided growth not allowing it to mature into a modern nation-state. Finally, we are also in agreement with him that in order to ensure that no other historical monstrosity occurs we must practice ever more cosmopolitanism, support constitutional patriotism, and endeavor to buttress such extraterritorial constructs as the European Union. In short, we must continue to be good liberal democrats in the traditional sense of the word embracing what is best in traditional Enlightenment thought.

Yet perhaps Jeffery Herf and Ralf Dahrendorf represent our thesis most adequately. Simply put, in modern Germany and elsewhere where genocide took place, the bourgeoisie, political liberalism, and strong Enlightenment beliefs were weak. While in England and France the state was associated with democracy and equality, in Germany it continued along illiberal and authoritarian paths. In Germany, rapid industrialization took place within "the inherited structures of the dynastic state of Prussia". (Herf 1986) A situation that gave little leeway for political and economic liberalism.

Thus, German society was only "partially", never "fully" enlightened. Horkheimer and Adorno overlooked this fact and projected Germany's problems into "dilemmas of modernity per se". Therefore, they wrongly blamed the totalizing strength of the Enlightenment when, actually, it was its relative weakness that was to blame. In the words of Jeffery Herf: "this unique combination of industrial development and a weak liberal tradition was the social background for reactionary modernism." (Herf 1986)

And once again Herf specifically on the *Dialectic of Enlightenment*:

> "Auschwitz was the Enlightenment's truth: reason as total domination. What is striking in rereading this now-classic work is how little, if any, space is allotted to the Enlightenment as a contributor to the liberal political tradition – political pluralism, parliaments, public discussion, the defense of individual liberty against the state - and how much the book focuses on scientific reason undermining universal normative claims to the good life. The book is also striking in how little it has to say about the fate of the Enlightenment in Germany, discussing it instead as if it were a uniform development throughout Europe and America. Its authors' clear intention was to suggest that Auschwitz presented the possible fate of the modern world as a whole. Modernity in general, not only German modernity, combined myth and reason. Enchantment and disenchantment exist side by side. Auschwitz, not the proletariat, is the specter that haunts the modern world ... Yet, in the end... Germany did not suffer from too much reason, too much liberalism, too much Enlightenment, but rather from not enough of any of them." (Herf 1986)

Chapter Five: War's Dialectic?

I know not with what weapons World War III will be fought, but World War IV will be fought with sticks and stones.
— Einstein

I against my brother; I and my brother against my cousin; I and my brother and my cousin against the world.
— Arab Proverb

Accursed be he that first invented war.
— Christopher Marlowe

"La guerra è diventata una faccenda di macchine," conclude, "e i soldati sono poco più che dei bravi meccanici."
— Alberto Moravia

Is war good for anything? At first thought, the question might sound absurd to many so any positive answer to such a question is sure to raise a few eyebrows.

Historian Margaret Macmillan has written:

> War raises fundamental questions about what it is to be human and about the essence of human society. Does war bring out the bestial side of human nature or the best? As with so much to do with war, we cannot agree. Is it an indelible part of human society, somehow woven in like an original sin from the time our ancestors first started organizing themselves into social groups? Our mark of Cain, a curse put on us which condemns us to repeated conflict? Or is such a view a dangerous self-fulfilling prophecy? Do changes in society bring new types of war or does war drive change in society? (MacMillan 2020)

Good questions all. We will try our best to answer some of them shortly.

To start with, one thing is perhaps indisputable: "We live in a world shaped by war, even if we do not always realize it". (MacMillan 2020)

If so, what are the fundamental causes of war? Again we turn to Macmillan:

> Perhaps war is the result of greed or competition for dwindling resources — for food, territory, sexual partners or slaves. Or are we shaped by biological ties and shared culture to value our own groups, whether clans or nations, and fear others? Like our cousins the chimpanzees, do we instinctively lash out when we feel threatened? Is war something we cannot help doing or is it something we have constructed through ideas or culture? (Macmillan 2020)

One thing is for sure though:

> One of the many paradoxes of war is that humans got good at it when they created organised societies. Indeed the two developments have evolved together. War — organised, purposeful violence between two political units — became more elaborate when we developed organised sedentary societies and it helped to make those societies more organised and powerful. (MacMillan 2020)

Here we see the first inklings of "War's Dialectic" as I've chosen to call it. As societies become more complexly organized, so does warfare. However, it is neither the sedentary nature of societies nor their complexity which is the direct cause of warfare as we shall see. Yet, when two or more organized societies go to war the experience often leaves at least one of the players more, and arguably better, organized than when they started.

A "second paradox of war: that growing state power and the emergence of bigger states — what Hobbes called Leviathan — are often the result of war but that in turn can produce peace." (MacMillan 2020) This suggests that when complex and sedentary societies play the game of war often enough there is a tendency for bigger units to emerge covering more territory and population under a stronger centralized state. A situation that, although its origins are warlike, produces more total peace in the long run.

When thinking about the "peace dividend" provided for by large states, ask yourself what kind of benefits did the British Empire and/or the American Empire ultimately bring to itself and the world? Were these Empires able to provide an essential modicum of stability and security to the world in terms of trade, peace, and progress? Does the world, when all is said and done, need a global policeman to hold it firmly in place? A Leviathan "to keep them all in awe"?

Another paradox that is hard to avoid is that War has often brought with it technical advancement. An existential clash to the death has a tendency to motivate a society to use all of its resources wisely and to sharpen its collective mind while stimulating the social imagination. This is not unlike Hegel's Master and Bondsman dialectic where the confrontation with death determines one's social being. Here, though, what is being determined is the relative ingenuity, strength of organization, and overall social health of a society. War tests all three of these characteristics starkly revealing any weaknesses. It is in this sense that Hegel thought war increased a society's relative strength by forcing it to face its inherent weaknesses resulting in beneficial reforms. Something that is often put off during times of peace.

War acts as a natural selector between societies. Those societies that are defeated in war are sometimes completely eliminated or, if they are not, their social patterns of organization are not spread widely or imitated by others. This explains, in part, why the world is today divided up into 200 or so states, why the majority of states have some sort of market economy, and why all states, even the most irrational one's, believe in and practice some sort of modern science. They do this, in part, because all these things have proven themselves in war. They work. They help you survive as a political unit, although they are not, by themselves, sufficient.

The story of Japan and China is instructive in this regard. In the nineteenth century China was a slow modernizer that was wary of new ideas from the West, while Japan embarked on a rapid program of modernization. The Chinese, for cultural and historical reasons, did not readily adopt the cultural-political "smart tricks" of the West leading, inevitably, to their prostration and subjugation while the Japanese successfully escaped this fate and went on to become Asia's first preeminent Global power. In the end, War has been the great arbiter for what works. It is merciless in its historical rationality.

This of course doesn't mean that it wouldn't be much more preferable if peaceful means were to take precedence as regards the transfer of technical, political, and cultural know-how. However, that's not how history, up until recently, unfolded.

Indeed, another "uncomfortable truth" about war is that it has arguably helped lead to the emancipation of women where "women in many societies gained access to careers, education and rights as a result of their participation in war." (MacMillan 2020) This suggests that war can have thoroughly positive social effects such as increasing social equality, stimulating reconstruction projects, and social benefits and gains of all kinds not the least of which would be the narrowing of the gap between rich and poor.

However:

> To say that war brings benefits and can help to build stronger, even fairer, societies is not to defend it. (MacMillan 2020)

> Of course, we would rather improve our world, help the weak and unfortunate, or have advances in science and technology in a state of peace. Yet finding the will and the resources to make great advances is harder in peacetime; it is all too easy to put off doing something about poverty, the opioid crisis or climate change until another day. War concentrates our attention and, like it or not, has done so throughout human history. (MacMillan 2020)

So to sum up Macmillan's contribution to our "Dialectic of War" we could say that 1) war helps to organize societies better 2) war can contribute to an increase in social spending and higher levels of social solidarity and equality 3) war has led to technological advancement in many fields, including medicine 4) most controversially war eliminates those social structures and cultural behaviors that are less functional/rational over the long run and 5) war has a tendency to create larger states (Leviathans) that cover more area and populations under the sway of an increasingly centralized and powerful state producing more peace and stability over the long run.

Following in Macmillan's footsteps, Ian Morris also seeks to directly answer the question: War What is It Good For? In his book by the same name.

According to Morris "war has been good for something: over the long run, it has made humanity safer and richer. War is hell, but — again, over the long run — the alternatives would have been worse." (Morris 2014) At first sight, this is certainly a startling claim.

He goes on to back it up though by first claiming that "by fighting wars, people have
created larger, more organized societies that have reduced the risk that their members will die violently." (Morris 2014) How exactly, then, has war made the world safer?

> beginning about ten thousand years ago in some parts of the world, then spreading across the planet, the winners of wars incorporated the losers into larger societies. The only way to make these larger societies work was for their rulers to develop stronger governments, and one of the first things these governments had to do, if they wanted to stay in power, was suppress violence within the society. (Morris 2014)

The startling end result of this process was "that rates of violent death fell by 90 percent between Stone Age times and the twentieth century." (Morris 2014) Unintentionally, war has bestowed the blessings of peace for an ever-wider swath of humanity. A counter-intuitive result to be sure.

Morris' second claim is historically descriptive rather than morally prescriptive when he says that "while war is the worst imaginable way to create larger, more peaceful societies, it is pretty much the only way humans have found." (Morris 2014) This statement can be easily fact checked and is, alas, not a "Just-So" story.

Morris' third claim is even more counter-intuitive than his prior ones. "The creation of a bigger society tends to make everyone, the descendants of victors and vanquished alike, better-off. The long-term pattern is again unmistakable. By creating larger societies, stronger governments, and greater security, war has enriched the world." (Morris 2014) Heady, controversial stuff!

His final claim looks positively towards the future:

> For millennia, war (over the long run) has created peace, and destruction has created wealth, but in our own age humanity has gotten so good at fighting — our weapons so destructive, our organizations so efficient — that war is beginning to make further war of this kind impossible. (Morris 2014)

This argument is interesting not least because it sets a limit or an end-point to our "Dialectic of War" much as Hegel once supposed that political ideological development had a definite historical conclusion. Trends come to an end. War has become so good at destruction that it no longer holds out the promise of any significant material pay off. If we want to increase our wealth and well-being today, global war will no longer help. Instead, we look to trade, science, and better internal governance and international cooperation to help better ourselves. Same goal, different means, other times.

However, I would allow myself the opportunity to tweak his End of War argument and say that it was technological development that ended war and not the project of war itself. I suspect that if our modern weapons of mass destruction were somehow magically rendered ineffective that we would soon be back to fighting massive global wars despite having built up complex international trade, political, and cultural networks. So it's not that war has put itself out of business, but rather it is an aspect of war that eventually laid it to rest: technology.

The answer to why I believe this to be so is to be found, in part, in Azar Gat's monumental work *War in Civilization*. (Gat 2008)

Gat attacks the question of why we ultimately fight rather convincingly.
First, he says,

> "intraspecific killing has been found to be the norm and one of the main causes of animal mortality." (Gat 2008)

Second:

> the evidence suggests that hunter-gatherers in their evolutionary natural environment and evolutionary natural way of life, shaped in humankind's evolutionary history over millions of years, widely engaged in fighting among themselves. In this sense, rather than being a late cultural 'invention', fighting would seem to be, if not 'natural', then certainly not 'unnatural' to humans. (Gat 2008)

Thirdly, and perhaps most importantly

> deadly aggression is a major, evolution-shaped, innate potential that, given the right conditions, has always been easily triggered. However, its occurrence and prevalence are subject to wide fluctuations, depending on the prominence of these conditions. (Gat 2008)

In the end, then, the ultimate reason for war is that it proved itself as a successful technique in the evolutionary struggle for survival.

If war furthered individuals' reproductive success rate over evolutionary time as Gat suggests what were its main triggers? Over what, principally, did we fight about?

> Resource competition is a prime cause of aggression, violence, and deadly violence in nature. The reason for this is that food, water, and, to a lesser degree, shelter against the elements are tremendous selection forces. (Gat 2008)

So, people fought over stuff, no wonder Marx envisioned Communism as a blessed state of plenty!

Sadly, one of the resources men fight to the death over (as so much of world literature reflects) are: women. Within many hunter-gatherer societies "the struggle for reproduction is about access to sexual partners of reproductive potential." (Gat 2008) Within many of these tribes "women-related quarrels, violence, so-called blood feuds, and homicide were rife, often as the principal category of violence." (Gat 2008) Throughout history women mattered and were beings that were worth fighting and dying for (Just ask Romeo).

Evolutionary pressures when applied to the human practice of war resulted, similarly if not exactly identically to other species, in a brutal human "algorithm of war": "kill the men, rape the women, and take the most young and beautiful as war trophies." (Gat 2008) Unfortunately, this algorithm makes perfect evolutionary sense. By killing the foreign men, you eliminate competitors for current resources and the future spreading of foreign genes, by raping the women you spread your own genes, and by capturing the young and beautiful you potentially enhance your own gene pool for the future. In this story, humans really show themselves to be "survival machines" hell bent on spreading their "selfish" "gangster" genes. (Dawkins 2006) It should come as no surprise then that Richard Dawkins implored us to "understand what our own selfish genes are up to, because we may then at least have the chance to upset their designs, something which no other species has ever aspired to." (Dawkins 2006) Amen to that.

Not surprisingly our "algorithm of war" also helped to deepen the sexual differences between men and women:

> In evolutionary terms, women specialized in child bearing and rearing and in foraging close to the home base, whereas men specialized in long-distance hunting and in the struggle to acquire and defend women and children, specializations that required, among other things, force and ferocity. Indeed, the difference was more than occupational. Not only did men compete for women both inside and outside the group, but, in case of a threat to the children, the father, although also highly significant for the children's provision, was more expendable than the mother in this respect. For this reason, as well, the men formed the group's main line of defence, while the women covered the children to the best of their abilities. Moreover,
> Palaeolithic men were of no use to the enemy. For them, the options were either running away or fighting to the finish. By contrast, women were themselves a resource in competition. They had better chances than the men did to survive the day by submitting, conforming, co-operating, and manipulating. Both the capabilities and evolutionary strategies of men
> and women, capabilities and strategies that were of course interconnected

and mutually reinforcing, made men much more predisposed to fighting than women. (Gat 2008)

In this sense, the constant threat of violence helped lead to developmental divergences between women and men. It not only shaped who we intrinsically are, it also significantly impacted the relationship between the sexes. The different social roles we adopted, different behaviors, and, most controversially, different minds leading to different expectations and desires.

In addition to Gat's stark illumination of war's ancient origins, he, like Morris, also offers us an explanation and a prediction for the decreasing likelihood of war in the future.

Arguing against *Democratic Peace Theory*, which believes world peace is being achieved through the spread of democratic ideals, institutions, and polities (an idea at least as old as Kant's *On Perpetual Peace*), Gat says "no" it is not democracy that is the root cause of the modern peace between democracies: rather it is their wealth.

Indeed,

> "what has been on the rise during the past couple of centuries, and accounts for the growth of democratic peace, has been not only liberal countries' level of democracy and liberalism, as proponents of the democratic peace theory believe, but also their wealth. Moreover, all these developments are not separate and distinct from each other but are closely intertwined. The idea that the growth of liberalism and democracy rested on the very tangible material developments of the age, such as advanced communications (both transportation and information technology), urbanization, increasing levels of literacy and education, and growing material well-being has been widely held since the nineteenth century and strongly endorsed by sociologists and political scientists. Democracy on a country scale and liberal societies emerged only in the nineteenth century, rather than in any earlier time in history, and have evolved ever since, not merely because they were suddenly recognized as good ideas; their growth has been underpinned by the revolutionary changes in the socioeconomic infrastructure during modernity." (Gat 2008)

Thus, the proximate cause for the current "long peace" between the great powers is their growing multiple stores of wealth, but the ultimate cause is the rise of our modern industrial-technical society based on the scientific method. This type of modern society has rapidly shifted the payoff matrix between the costs of war and the benefits of peace overwhelmingly favoring the latter.

While I find this explanation for the "long peace" somewhat convincing, I have a few questions for it. When do/did we reach enough material wealth to make large-scale war irrational? Were the European societies of the late nineteenth and early twentieth centuries either insufficiently wealthy or industrialized to explain the outbreak of the two world wars? Is our industrial-technical society a sufficient guarantor against future conflicts or could, conceivably, pernicious ideologies stir up old war-like demons? Will the economic and political rise of China be a peaceful one, unlike the twentieth century German case, or will it result in global conflict despite the shared economic interests of the two most likely participants in the case of war: The United States vs China?

Now to sum up Gat's contributions to our theory of "War's Dialectic": War is a social behavior that has deep roots in our evolutionary past. It survived (and thrived) as a practice because it enhanced the survival and reproduction of those who engaged in it. Resource and sexual competition were often the proximate triggers of war leading to an "Algorithm of war" where foreign men were eliminated, women raped, and the "young and the beautiful" were carried off as war trophies.

Except for Gat's "End of War" theory, this is pretty dark stuff wouldn't you say? That's exactly what thinkers like John Horgan believe. Horgan in his book *The End of War*, based in part on a famous essay by the celebrated anthropologist Margaret Mead, offers a competing story for war's origins and intrinsic nature. (Horgan 2014)

Horgan immediately stakes his claim against those who believe that war is an evolutionary adaptation: "We are not hardwired for war". (Although in all fairness that is emphatically *not* what theorists like Gat and others are saying: see the discussion above)

Following Margaret Mead's intellectual lead taken from her famed essay *Warfare is Only an Invention* Horgan forcefully argues that war is an invention like cooking. Once one community invents it, it necessarily forces other communities to adopt it if they wish to continue to compete and survive: "Militarism — the culture of war — is a meme that can infect any society." (Horgan 2014)

Once war is invented it successfully replicates its beliefs, institutions, and practices wherever it can. It expresses an inexorable cultural logic. The invention of a first strike capability means that all other societies must develop one if they are to survive. In effect, war is a killer meme.

The question that I have for Horgan is: if war is a "cultural invention" how can he be so sure that it wasn't invented by, let's say, *Homo Erectus*? Indeed, Horgan's argument relies heavily on the Rousseauist idea that it's all "civilization's fault" and that war is not in our nature. Thus, whether you eventually accept or reject his argument really depends on how old you think the logic and practice of warfare is? Is it found in the animal kingdom? Does it predate anatomically modern humans? Is the archaeological record sufficiently clear?

Perhaps even more important than these questions is your position on modern evolutionary theory and how it works. If you believe, as do many evolutionary biologists, that evolution is about the successful spreading of one's genes then the logic of warfare seems inescapable. If you deny this interpretation of evolution and follow the cooperative empathetic thoughts of Prince Kropotkin and more recently Frans de Waal, you will tend to deny the ancient status of warfare. (Kropotkin 2006) (de Waal 2006,2010) As of now, it seems the intellectual choice is still yours to make.

Conclusion

The "Dialectic of War" is simply the result of two or more combating social-political groups engaging in a repeated struggle to the death which leads, over time, to the unintended consequences of peace and prosperity through the physical enlargement of territory and increase in population, better overall organization and increased rationality, strong centralized states, social leveling and support, and the creation of increasingly complex economic, political, and cultural networks. The dialectic itself may come to an eventual end due to technological improvements that make war extremely unprofitable or through the accumulation of relative wealth made possible by an industrial-technical society that significantly favors the benefits of continued peace against the potential uncertain gains of engaging in war.

Chapter Six: All of Caesar's Men

A tyrant is the worst disease, and the cause of all others.
— William Blake

In his book *Totem and Taboo,* Freud speculated that in pre-history society was dominated by despotic fathers who exiled their male children so they could have unfettered sexual access to the females of their group. (Freud 2012) Although the male children both feared and respected their fathers, they nevertheless found their own sexually frustrating situation increasingly intolerable. In order to finally and unequivocally solve it, "bands of brothers" eventually found the courage to kill their fathers and take sexual possession of the females. In this story, the killing of the father is mankind's "original sin". From this act, society carries an ancient sense of collective guilt which is expressed in the "Oedipus Complex": the alleged universal subconscious desire of adolescent boys to sleep with their mothers.

Although no one really believes this Freudian Fable today, it has arguably been resurrected by the anthropologist Christopher Boehm albeit in a radically altered form as we shall see.

Before we recapitulate Boehm's theory in the hands of another anthropologist (Richard Wrangham) I'd like to turn our attention to a few salient remarks by the political philosopher Thomas Hobbes.

Hobbes famously stated in his classic work *Leviathan* that

1.1 NATURE hath made men so equal, in the faculties of the body, and mind; as that though there be found one man sometimes manifestly stronger in body, or of quicker mind than another; yet when all is reckoned together, the difference between man, and man, is not so considerable, as that one man can thereupon claim to himself any benefit, to which another may not pretend, as well as he. For as to the strength of body, the weakest has

1.2 strength enough to kill the strongest, either by secret machination, or by confederacy with others, that are in the same danger with himself
1.2 And as to the faculties of the mind ... I find yet a greater equality amongst men, than that of strength.
1.3 From this equality of ability, ariseth equality of hope in the attaining of our ends. And therefore, if any two men desire the same thing, which nevertheless they cannot both enjoy, they become enemies; and in the way to their end, (which is principally their own conservation, and sometimes their delectation only,) endeavor to destroy, or subdue one another. (Hobbes 1982)

In these famous passages Hobbes is expressing his fundamental belief that men are more or less similar in their physical and mental abilities. If this premise is true, then according to Hobbes, in a state of anarchy each man potentially has the power to take from another man whatever he chooses through a combination of stealth, guile, or surprise attack. In terms of sheer force, no man is better than another. In this physical sense, men are more or less completely equal. It is a vision of a supremely "dark" egalitarianism fraught with uncertainty and danger. But as the Roman poet Lucretius logically surmised earlier in our book, if things really had been this bad human beings would have never survived for very long.

Similarly, John Locke, Hobbes' intellectual successor, also postulated that early man lived under conditions of equality, but not nearly as dark. In Locke's mental model of a primeval world people found themselves equal "without subordination or subjection" in a state of "liberty" but not of unbridled "license". (Locke 2016) A far more preferable egalitarianism than Hobbes' to be sure.

Whether or not the anthropologist Christopher Boehm was unconsciously following the Lockean tradition, or, as he himself says, just trying to explain the ethnographic evidence for the egalitarian nature of extant Hunter-gatherer societies I do not know.

However, it is a tradition of thought that like Rousseau's has had a strong intellectual following in Anglo-Saxon society and culture (and increasingly not only there).

In earlier chapters we have talked about Boehm's social selection theory. The anthropologist Richard Wrangham refers to it as "the execution hypothesis":

> "The idea of the execution hypothesis is that during thousands of prehistorical generations, the victims of capital punishment were disproportionately those with a high propensity for reactive aggression. Killing or repression of such individuals is supposed to have happened so often that our species evolved a calmer, less aggressive temperament. Unfortunately to quantify the past rates of execution, or to calculate the Pleistocene selection pressures, is impossible. The concept that the domestication syndrome results from capital punishment is supported, however, by the human system of male egalitarianism, because the primate-style alpha males that are missing from human society are characteristically reactive aggressors...." (Wrangham 2019)

The question is: was the rate of killing group members who had a high tendency for reactive aggression sufficient to be a significant evolutionary force? (Wrangham 2019)

Simply put, unduly obstreperous troublemakers with an Alpha male complex were put to death by other group members. But there is still one more important facet to the theory. It is the idea of a Reverse Dominance Hierarchy "in which the rank and file rise up to collectively quash their self-appointed superiors". (van Vugt 2010) Whenever a would be alpha male would seek to despotically control the group, the group would seek ways to overthrow him by either exiling him or killing him outright. The key premise here is that ancient hunter-gatherers jealously guarded their societies from would be usurpers who sought to upset their egalitarian ways.

Earlier we pointed out potential flaws in this way of thinking such as its dependence on relative peaceful inter-group relations. A situation which many scholars find hard to believe ever truly existed. But for the moment, our concern is not with criticism but rather with the possible support of the theory and this from an unlikely source: Shakespeare.

More precisely from Shakespeare's play *Julius Caesar* and in particular some lines uttered by Cassius, one of the chief conspirators in the plot to assassinate Caesar. (Shakespeare 2009)

Now, throughout human history, Julius Caesar is definitely considered the epitome of an Alpha-male. Strong, self-assured, clever, and, most importantly, hungry for power over others. And this is exactly how Shakespeare portrays him: as an arrogant would-be tyrant.

Cassius, the play's chief conspirator hell bent on Caesar's physical elimination, would have none of this and seeks the aid of the noble and virtuous Brutus, Caesar's closest friend (of Et Tu fame), to plot to end this perceived threat to their freedom and, most importantly for our purposes, a restoration of their sense of social equality.

One of the minor characters in the play, Flavius, early on sets the urgent tone and the dramatic problem before themselves and we the spectators: "Who else would soar above the view of men and keep us all in servile fearfulness."? Translated into terms related to Boehm's theory, Flavius is saying: Caesar threatens our freedom and equality by his ambitions to become an Alpha-male. The suggestion of course is that something drastic must be done. And that, just as Boehm's theory predicts, is execution.

Cassius echoing ideas similar to Hobbes and to Locke about people's essential equality of ability complains:

> I cannot tell what you and other men
> Think of this life; but for my single self,
> I had as lief not be, as live to be
> In awe of such a thing as I myself.
> I was born free as Caesar, so were you.
> We both have fed as well, and we can both
> Endure the winter's cold as well as he.
> For once upon a raw and gusty day,
> The troubled Tiber chafing with her shores,
> Said Caesar to me 'Dar'st thou, Cassius, now
> Leap in with me into this angry flood,

> And swim to yonder point?' Upon the word,
> Accoutred as I was I plungèd in,
> And bade him follow. So indeed, he did.
> The torrent roared, and we did buffet it
> With lusty sinews, throwing it aside,
> And stemming it with hearts of controversy.
> But ere we could arrive the point proposed,
> Caesar cried 'Help me, Cassius, or I sink!'
> Ay, as Aeneas our great ancestor
> Did from the flames of Troy upon his shoulder
> The old Anchises bear, so from the waves of Tiber
> Did I the tired Caesar. And this man
> Is now become a god, and Cassius is
> A wretchèd creature, and must bend his body
> If Caesar carelessly but nod on him.
> He had a fever when he was in Spain,
> And when the fit was on him, I did mark
> How he did shake. 'Tis true, this god did shake.
> His coward lips did from their colour fly;
> And that same eye whose bend doth awe the world
> Did lose his lustre. I did hear him groan,
> Ay, and that tongue of his that bade the Romans
> Mark him and write his speeches in their books,
> 'Alas!' it cried, 'give me some drink, Titinius',
> As a sick girl. Ye gods, it doth amaze me
> A man of such a feeble temper should
> So get the start of the majestic world,
> And bear the palm alone

In a nutshell, Cassius is saying the same sort of things as Hobbes did. Caesar is but a man like me, both equal in ability and susceptible to the same sorts of dangers like, using his examples, sickness and drowning. There is no essential reason that he should become the supreme Alpha-male taking away our precious freedom. The sentiments here expressed do indeed seem like a fancy literary version of Boehm's anthropologically based theory. People don't want to be ruled unfairly. They want to maintain a situation of equality avoiding by force, if necessary, attempts at domination.

For the noble Brutus, arguably the great tragic hero of the play, the question is a simple one: "Shall Rome stand under one man's awe?". In Boehm's language: should we run the risk of being dominated by an Alpha-male?

Brutus eventually answers his own question with the bloody hands of a successful conspirator (executioner): "Ambition's debt is paid. As he was fortunate, I rejoice at it.
As he was valiant, I honour him. But as he was ambitious, I slew him. ... There are tears for his love, joy for his fortune, honour for his valour, and death for his ambition." Translated again into "Boehmese": Caesar was a brave and noteworthy man, but he threatened our unwritten social boundaries that safeguard our freedom and equality and for that he had to pay with his life.

But now that we have done with our short literary-anthropological exegesis, is it really true that these lines spoken by Cassius and Brutus strongly support the "execution hypothesis"?

At first glance, it might seem so, indeed that's what I initially thought myself. But when I reflected for a bit, I asked myself were Brutus and Cassius *really* interested in equality or freedom? For themselves, most definitely, but certainly not for those "senseless things" that made up the majority of Rome's population: the common people. In fact, I would go so far as to say that they were interested in maintaining their social groups despotic power over everybody else, something which Caesar did indeed threaten.

But wait you say: Romans weren't hunter-gatherers. That's true. But it doesn't take much imagination to suggest that ancient hunter-gatherers might have been similar to Romans in that a small but powerful coalition of alpha-males may have held sway over other members of their primitive groups. Despotism doesn't always have to be in the singular, it could just as easily have been in the plural. Especially if, as I have suggested earlier in the book, ancient hunter-gatherers were constantly subjected to extreme inter-group competition (war).

So, there you have it. Shakespeare looked good for Boehm for a while until we delved a bit deeper. Nevertheless, I think Boehm has a point. When we think of the whole gamut of human political history, we are confronted with a mind-boggling series of assassinations of powerful alpha-males playing the role of chiefs, generals, warlords, kings, tyrants, and despots of all kinds. However, as I just mentioned above, as often as not the freshly assassinated were soon replaced by other alpha-males or a coalition of alpha-males. But as Boehm himself openly admitted: "I make the major assumption that humans were egalitarian for thousands of generations before hierarchical societies began to appear." (Boehm 2001) Of course I am, myself, making the major assumption that, particularly under conditions of endemic warfare, alpha-male led groups or coalitions of alpha-males were of the utmost importance for group survival. In the end, it all boils down once again to what you believe about the nature and frequency of ancient inter-group conflict.

Chapter Seven: The Evolution of Leadership and Social Dominance

A leader is best when people barely know he exists,
when his work is done,
his aim fulfilled,
they will say: we did it ourselves
— Lao Tzu

Never alone
Did the king sigh, but with a general groan.
— From Shakespeare's Hamlet

Where there is no vision, the people perish.
— Proverbs 29:18

Do Global Apes need to be led? If so, by what kinds of leaders? Is leadership always necessary? Why do we live in Dominance Hierarchies and how has that shaped the evolution of our minds? The answers to these and other questions might hopefully be provided for by an examination of the *Evolutionary Leadership Theory* developed by the Dutch evolutionary psychologist Mark van Vugt in his book *Selected,* Jim Sidanius' *Social Dominance Theory* and Denise Cummins ideas about Dominance Hierarchies and the human mind. (Cummins 1996) (Sidanius 2001) (van Vugt 2010)

Van Vugt's main idea is that evolution created *both* leaders and followers because it was a social arrangement that provided significant survival and reproductive advantages for both. Indeed, the power relationship between "leaders" and "followers" is not restricted to humans alone. It's ubiquitous in the animal kingdom and most probably predated the rise of *Homo Sapiens* by millions of years. An important additional assumption of the book is that leadership is a human universal to be found in one form or another throughout the world.

There are many benefits to being a "leader". Vugt sums them up as the "three S's": salary, status, and sex. But really mostly sex. Because the first two "perks" significantly enhance the last one and evolution is all about spreading your genes. As Vugt says "political leaders have a long and ignoble history of polygamy and infidelity". (van Vugt 2010) Monica Lewinsky was no statistical outlier.

Besides reproductive success, were there other underlying causes for the rise of leaders and followers? Yes. Since humans are thought to have evolved in groups which competed with each other, groups that had effective leadership presumably did better than groups that didn't. This is our old friend "Group Selection Theory".

Good leaders helped their groups survive in a harsh competitive environment where the losers were not infrequently exterminated. Group competition meets genocide meets the necessity of leadership in the game of survival. This is yet another reason why I am skeptical about Boehm's assumption discussed in previous chapters that humans existed in a semi acephalous egalitarian society. It seems unlikely that in our hunter-gatherer past hierarchy and leadership (and strong leadership for that matter) would have been absent, especially under conditions of frequent intergroup conflict.

OK, then, while it's not too hard to see why someone would want to be a leader how do we explain why somebody would want to be a follower? This is Vugt's vision:

> (the) basic premise is this: at the dawn of human history, more than two million years ago, in the hostile environment of the African Savannah, there was safety in numbers. Individuals who possessed the cognitive capacity for followership thrived better than those lacking it. By 'cognitive capacity' we mean a set of inbuilt 'if-then' rules that pushed us to follow a person, or group, when we needed to. This followership brain enabled our ancestors to make quick automatic decisions about who to tail in certain situations — for example, 'if I am hungry, then follow the best hunter' or 'if my group is under attack, then follow the strongest person'. Those with a 'followership brain' — who instinctively understood they were safer with the crowd than going it alone — were more likely to survive until they

could reproduce, and so produced more kids than individuals who struck out on their own. If we make the reasonable assumption that behaviour and personality are at least partly heritable, then parents with brains wired for followership bore children with similarly wired brains. The followership brain thus spread through the generations, as herd-shunning individuals died out. And so the cognitive blueprint for followership became a common feature of the human brain. (van Vugt 2010)

Thus, if people became followers, it was, at least initially, in their interest to do so. They benefited, in reproductive terms, by following the "strongest" "smartest" "most charismatic" member of the group. By doing so, they managed to live another day and were able to beget and successfully raise their children.

But is there a special trait that makes a good leader? According to Vugt there is. It is the gift of "Charsima" which in ancient Greek means "a special divine power bestowed by God". It is the divine stuff from which great leaders are made of.

Any display of the "divine" gift of Charisma, through evolutionary conditioning, has immediate psychological, behavioral effects on us. We listen, we are moved, we follow. It is a social sign that our minds have been built to discern when deciding upon who should be our leader.

Today, we can break down Charisma into more manageable analyzable parts. For example, it has been shown that leaders tend to have high verbal IQ; they not only speak well but are able to use words to motivate those around them. Recall your high-school Shakespeare here and Shakespeare's ideal Leader, Henry V, and his immortal, stirring words to his men on the eve of the battle of Agincourt:

> And Crispin Crispian shall ne'er go by
> From this day to the ending of the world
> But we in it shall be rememberèd,
> We few, we happy few, we band of brothers.
> For he today that sheds his blood with me
> Shall be my brother; be he ne'er so vile,
> This day shall gentle his condition.
> And gentlemen in England now abed
> Shall think themselves accursed they were not here,

And hold their manhoods cheap whiles any speaks
That fought with us upon Saint Crispin's day.
(Shakespeare 2017)

Additional highly correlated leadership traits besides Charisma and High Verbal IQ are extraversion, as would be expected based on the babble effect (the most talkative person in a group is often seen as the leader). Leadership also correlates positively with openness to new experience (e.g., being creative and adventurous) and negatively with neuroticism — who would want to follow an emotionally unbalanced person? (van Vugt 2010)

And finally, to round off our list of positive attributes: generosity.

However, and historically unfortunately, these positive traits can serve to hide far darker ones: the so-called Dark Triad of Narcissism, Machiavellianism, and Psychopathy. (van Vugt 2010) Many would-be and actual leaders have displayed one or more of these dangerous characteristics. The narcissist is a person excessively concerned with himself and usually lacks empathy. The Machiavellian is an amoral manipulator and exploiter of others while the Psychopath is, well, a Psychopath: selfish and remorseless to an extreme. Adolf Hitler is probably the classical embodiment of all three.

Yet, what ultimately makes people follow leaders like Adolf Hitler? To many of his fellow Germans (and not only), he certainly seemed to speak impressively well and exhibit a high level of Charisma. These were certainly necessary leadership skills to be sure, according to Vugt's theory, but they were not sufficient in and of themselves. That's why Vugt adds the additional requirement of specific social situations which make people more prone to follow a leader (no matter how insane). People are more likely to follow a leader when "they (a) believe group unity is under threat, (b) don't know what to think or do, and (c) aspire to a leadership position". (van Vugt 2010) All of these social conditions were in play in the Germany of 1932/33. Indeed, Hitler's rise to power was due in large part to his consistent harping on the theme "Germany is in danger" from "socialists" "democrats" "intellectuals" "Bolsheviks" and "Jews". At the same time, the Weimar Republic was in the throes of the Great Depression with millions desperately scared and out of work, many of whom certainly felt that they did not "know what to think or do" and finally the strongly hierarchical nature of the Nazi party and movement held out the promise of future leadership positions to those who would blindly follow *Der Führer*.

However, there is a surefire way to stop insane leaders: assassination. History is littered with their desecrated dead bodies from Caligula to Nero to Mussolini to Ceausescu and many kings and chieftains in between. Even in hunter-gatherer societies the practice is not uncommon:

Leader assassinations have been documented by anthropologists in many primitive societies — it is not a contemporary phenomenon. For instance,

> "in Papua New Guinea a leader who seriously oversteps his prerogatives can face a death sentence from his own community — with his kin encouraged to carry it out (to avoid tit-for-tat killings between different families). With the spread of weaponry such as spears and knives, and later guns, it became easy for disgruntled followers to finish off a chief" (van Vugt 2010)

Yet perhaps most disturbing of all is that those men (and they are usually men) who score high on "the Dark Triad" are, on average, more reproductively successful. If true, then, nice guys *might not finish last but they certainly don't finish first* (in this metric at least). So it seems that it pays to be a bastard with the ladies (at least in the short term) and not only there but in business, politics, even, dare I say it, academia. Such nasty people are everywhere apparently, successful and dominant because, in part, highly adept at cloaking their dark side through a combination of charm and cunning.

Nevertheless, people know *exactly* what they want in their leaders and it's all good:

> "The GLOBE research programme — the Global Leadership and Organisational Behaviour Effectiveness research programme, based at Wharton

Business School at the University of Pennsylvania — studies perceptions of desirable and undesirable leadership attributes all over the world. In a study of 62 cultures, its academics uncovered a remarkable consistency in the way leaders were described. Examples of universally positive attributes are integrity — good leaders can be trusted; generosity — good leaders are helpful; fairness — good leaders are just and equitable; diplomatic — good leaders handle conflict well; decisiveness — good leaders make sound, timely judgements; intelligence and competence — good leaders contribute to the group's performance; and vision — good leaders can describe a desirable future. These leader prototypes closely match the perception of respected Big Men in traditional band societies. Big Men were able to exercise influence through their personal qualities rather than through a divine or inherited right to rule. In order to lead they needed to prove they were an asset, not a drag, to group living, helping it to survive and prosper (in terms of providing a safe, well-resourced environment in which to raise families)." (van Vugt 2010)

Some cheerful news for us good guys after all.

ELT was relatively straightforward. Unfortunately, the same cannot be said for Jim Sidanius' Social Dominance Theory. However, be that as it may, we will try to simply his theory without hopefully losing any of its power and relevance.

Social Dominance Theory's (SDT) basic assumption is that all human societies tend to be structured as systems of group-based social hierarchies. At the very minimum, this hierarchical social structure consists of one or a small number of dominant and hegemonic groups at the top and one or a number of subordinate groups at the bottom. (Sidanius 2001)

Importantly, according to Sidanius, this hierarchical social structure is not limited to humans: Considering only closely related primates in the hominoid clade, there are a number of other common and relevant features of social organization, including (a) the existence of closed social networks, or what might be called ingroups, (b) communal territoriality, (c) male domination of intergroup relations, (d) male domination of hostile and agonistic relations between groups, and (e) male domination of stalking, attacking, and killing of outgroup males. This list suggests that the hominoid clade appears to be predisposed toward an ingroup-centric, or ethnocentric, orientation in which the boundary maintenance toward outgroups is enforced largely by males. (Sidanius 2001)

In the human case, the social values which are being unevenly distributed within an hierarchical social system relate to what Sidanius calls positive/negative social value. Positive social value consists of things like political authority and power, good and plentiful food, splendid homes, the best available health care, wealth, and high social status (Sidanius 2001)

Negative social value is made up of such things as low power and social status, high-risk and low-status occupations, relatively poor health care, poor food, modest or miserable homes, and severe negative sanctions (e.g., prison and death sentences) (Sidanius 2001)

Not surprisingly, dominant social groups have more positive social value, while subordinate groups possess more negative social value.

Why this is so depends on the way hierarchical social systems are stratified.

Sidanius presents a three-fold scheme of stratification. He says that hierarchical social systems are stratified according to age (where older members dominate younger ones), sex (where males dominate females) and what he calls an "arbitrary set" system. This last one needs some further explanation.

> What Sidanius means by an "arbitrary set" is the following: "The arbitrary-set system is filled with socially constructed and highly salient groups based on characteristics such as clan, ethnicity, estate, nation, race, caste, social class, religious sect, regional grouping, or any other socially relevant group distinction that the human imagination is capable of constructing" (Sidanius 2001)

Now while the age and gender systems are certainly no strangers to very brutal forms of social control, the brutality associated with arbitrary-set systems very often far exceeds that of the other two systems in terms of intensity and scope.

For example,

"besides the infamous Holocaust, the twentieth century alone has witnessed at least seven major episodes of genocidal, arbitrary-set violence, including (a) the episodic massacres of the Kurds by Turkey in 1924, Iran in 1979, and Iraq in 1988, (b) Stalin's wholesale slaughter of the Kulaks in 1929, (c) the widespread massacre of the inhabitants of East Timor in the late 1990s, (d) the Khmer Rouge terror in the late 1970s, (e) ethnic cleansingof Muslims in Bosnia and other regions of the former Yugoslavia in the late 1990s, (f) the widespread killing of Kasaians in Zaire, and (g) the most recent massacres of Tutsis and Hutus in Rwanda and Burundi in the late 1990s. Furthermore, Gurr and Harff cataloged some 63 ethnic and armed conflicts around the world in 1993 alone.

These conflicts were not restricted to any particular part of the world, being found in Europe, the Middle East, North and Sub-Saharan Africa, Central, South, and East Asia, the Pacific Islands, and the Americas. This level of barbarism and blood lust is rarely, if ever, observed within the age and gender systems of social stratification." (Sidanius 2001)

However, Sidanius makes one exception as to those societies susceptible to "arbitrary-set systems: It is widely assumed that one major reason for the lack of arbitrary-set, group-based social hierarchy among hunter-gatherer societies is because such societies lack sufficient economic surplus. The technologies of food production and storage within hunter-gatherer societies do not permit long-term storage of food.

Similarly,

"because hunter-gatherer societies tend to be nomadic, people within such societies are not able to accumulate large amounts of other, nonedible forms of economic surplus such as animal skins, weapons, and armaments. This lack of economic surplus does not allow for the development of highly specialized social roles, such as professional armies, police, and other bureaucracies facilitating the formation of expropriative political authority. Because of the absence of military and "coercive specialists," all adult males within hunter-gatherer societies are essentially the military equals of all other adult males. Therefore, the extent to which political authority among adult males exists, this authority tends to be based on mutual agreement, persuasion, and consultation rather than coercion. Although hunter-gatherer societies are generally not completely egalitarian, when social and political hierarchy does exist among adult males, it tends to be based on the general skills and leadership capacities of particular individuals. As a result, this hierarchy tends not to be transgenerational or hereditary in nature."(Sidanius 2001)

While I am in general agreement with his qualification exempting modern day hunter-gatherers from "arbitrary-set" systems I am not so sanguine if that was the case with ancient hunter-gatherers as I have amply explained in the previous chapters, after all, Sidanius himself has pointed to the highly hierarchical social nature of our closest hominoid relatives, chimps.
Yet,

> "Even if attention is restricted to nonsubsistence societies, one is truly hard pressed to find a society anywhere in the world that does not have an arbitrary-set stratification system." (Sidanius 2001)

Although there are social dominance hierarchies throughout the world, as Sidanius rightly points out, they are not static. They are shaped by two countervailing forces which Sidanius terms 1) Hierarchy Enhancing (HE) social forces which maintain "ever higher levels of group-based social inequality" and 2) Hierarchy-attenuating (HA) forces, "producing greater levels of group-based social equality".

Examples of HA forces are everything from early Christian discourse, to the widespread sociopolitical discourse emanating from social democratic, socialist, and Marxist movements of the nineteenth century, to the civil and human rights activists of the middle and late twentieth century. However, for the most part, these counterdominance, or HA, tendencies within nonhunter-gatherer societies appear to function to moderate the degree of inequality. (Sidanius 2001)

Within this equilibrium of countervailing forces, between HE and HA, subordinate groups, according to Sidanius, both actively and passively seek to maintain the given system of social hierarchy *even if it is to their ultimate social detriment*. This suggests a solution as to why systems of group-based social hierarchy exhibit "remarkable degrees of resiliency, robustness, and stability." (Sidanius 2001)

Therefore, seen from this perspective,

> "social hierarchy is not maintained primarily by the oppressive behavior of dominants, but by the deferential and obsequious behavior of subordinates." (Sidanius 2001)

Although I am not sure to what extent this idea is empirically and historically true, it does mesh well with our previous discussion of ELT by Vugt. You may recall that Vugt believed *both* the mental disposition to be a follower *and leader* were evolutionarily selected for. If true, it would make sense that subordinate social groups would tend, for long periods, to follow whatever social groups had set themselves up in leadership positions, particularly if they had created persuasive Legitimizing Myths (LMs).

LMs "consist of attitudes, values, beliefs, stereotypes, and ideologies that provide moral and intellectual justification for the social practices that distribute social value within the social system." (Sidanius 2001) They make you believe how utterly fantastic you are or how utterly worthless. They are the ideological lens through which we view ourselves and others and our place in society. Sidanius' theory owes much to Marx, Mosca, Pareto, Gramsci, Durkheim, and Moscovici to name but a few intellectual predecessors.

There are many types of HE-LMs:

> including sexism and classical racism, the notions of the "white man's burden/' fate, and the doctrine of meritorious karma, Confucianism, negative stereotypes of subordinate groups, traditional forms of classism, the thesis of papal infallibility, nationalism, the Monroe Doctrine and the notion of manifest destiny, the thesis of the divine rights of kings, and speciesism (the idea that humans have the right to rule the planet and all living creatures on it)

> There are also more subtle, yet no less powerful examples of HE-LMs. In contemporary U.S. and Western cultures, among the most important of HE-LMs are the notions of individual responsibility, the Protestant work ethic, internal attributions of the misfortunes of the poor, and the set of ideas and assumptions collectively referred to as "political conservatism." What all these ideas and doctrines have in common is the notion that each individual occupies that position along the social status continuum that he or she has earned and therefore deserves. From these perspectives then,

particular configurations of the hierarchical social system are fair, legitimate, natural, and perhaps even inevitable. (Sidanius 2001)

Luckily there are some HA-LMs as well such as the Global Human Rights movement to name one prominent example.

Sidanius concludes his theoretical framework on this suggestive note:

> "Given the historical record of both human and hominoid social structure, it seems most reasonable to assume that hominoid social systems are predisposed to organize themselves within some range of group-based inequality. Furthermore, the historical record also seems to suggest that under normal circumstances and everything else being equal, the degree of this group-based social hierarchy will tend to stabilize around a given level that we can refer to as the point of hierarchical equilibrium. In broad terms, we suggest that this point is established at the fulcrum between HE forces and HA forces." (Sidanius 2001)

If we believe, at least partly, in what Sidanius has written then we are constrained to come to the conclusion that our Global Ape has for millions of years lived in social groups based on social dominance hierarchies and that some form of social inequality was universal in *all of these groups*. The good news however is that there are not only HE forces but HA forces as well which are always evolving and establishing new social equilibriums particularly in the last 100 years; if not everywhere in the world, then throughout an ever-increasing part of it. To what extent the ideal of social equality can be met seems to be a question that is tied to another one: to what extent can humans' in-born cognitive biases and social behaviors geared to form in-group/out-group distinctions be overcome by new laws, customs, democracy, and ideology? The answer is being formulated right now and will, presumably, be partly resolved in the not-too-distant future.

Another related topic to this is the question of what kind of influence did millions of years of social dominance hierarchies have on the human mind? It is a question which has intrigued the cognitive scientist Denise D. Cummins.

Cummins believes that our strong evolutionary based tendency to establish dominance hierarchies led to a "fortuitous result: great intelligence". How so?

According to Cummins:

> "The fundamental components of our reasoning architecture evolved in response to pressures to reason about dominance hierarchies, the social organization that characterizes most social mammals." (Thayer 2009)

According to Cummins, submissive individuals can detect, exploit, and circumvent the constraints of domination. If an animal can take what it wants by force, it is sure to dominate the available resources unless its subordinates are smart enough to outwit it. To survive, a subordinate must use other strategies: deception, guile, appeasement, bartering, alliance formation, or friendship. Thus, intelligence is particularly important to the survival of subordinates. "The evolution of mind emerges," Cummins writes, "as a strategic arms race in which the weaponry is ever-increasing mental capacity to represent and manipulate internal representations of the minds of others." (Thayer 2009)

This is surely an intriguing theory but I think it can only be part of the story. As we discussed in Chapter one, the emergence of human intelligence as we now know it was a confluence of processes that included, the taming of fire, tool manufacture and use, cooking, a rich palette of emotions, sociality and intentionality (to which ideas Cummins can be added), Culture making (of which the evolved capacity for language is an integral part) and presumed inter and intra group conflict and cooperation. So, while Cummins theory is interesting, it, ultimately, cannot stand alone.

In conclusion it seems the Global Ape's evolutionary propensity to divide themselves up into leaders and followers and social hierarchies based partly on this primordial division has to do with the outstanding question of the "social coordination" of a social species. Who decides? Who gets what and when? Where do we go from here? What is valuable for us and what is not? These are questions that an intelligent social species has to answer for itself among many others. There must be mechanisms that make these decisions both decisive, relatively fast, and efficient, particularly under uncertain environmental conditions both physical and social. Increasingly, since at least the Enlightenment, we have begun questioning the old ways of social division and submission but, nevertheless, they still seem firmly in place even in our most "advanced" social-democracies. Will leaders, followers, dominant and subordinate groups always make up our social landscape for as long as we are human? Or will we eventually hand over these tasks of social coordination to AI like beings and their "superior" algorithmic minds? And if we do so, would we not just have created a new leader, a new master potentially far more dominant than the worst in-groups and despots in history?

Chapter Eight: The Babbling Ape

Language is an art, like brewing or baking; but ...
it certainly is not a true instinct,
for every language has to be learnt. It differs, however, widely from all
ordinary arts, for man has an instinctive tendency to speak,
as we see in the babble of our young children;
whilst no child has an instinctive tendency to brew, bake, or write.
— Darwin

Man is a social animal
— Aristotle

The word is able to express the whole of human spirit.
— Hegel

You taught me language, and my profit on't / Is, I know how to curse
— Caliban from Shakespeare's Tempest

If a lion could speak, we would not understand him.
— Wittgenstein

If you couldn't pick pieces of meaning out of the world in advance, before
you learned a language, then language couldn't be learnt
— Chomsky

Language-like perception and cognition....
preceded and set the stage for language-like production.
— Seyfarth and Cheney

It's not just the species that makes the niche:
it's the niche that also makes the species
— Derek Bickerton

Have you ever tried learning a foreign language after the age of 21? If you have, you might be familiar with the experience of, at first, understanding far more than you're able to express in the new language. Related to this, you might also have had the rather unpleasant experience of native speakers thinking that you understood far less than you actually did. Without the ability to express yourself adequately, you weren't able to correct this annoying misconception on their part, causing you not a little frustration and even at times angst. You might even have reflected for a moment that the native speakers of your new language believed that you were in some way "dumber" than they were. Indeed, in many languages people who do not speak or understand the same language as the native group are often negatively labeled. For example, in Slavic languages, Germans are referred to as "Nemci" which means "dumb" in both senses of the word: not able to speak and, by implication, not exceptionally bright. For the ancient Greeks, those peoples who could not speak Greek were defined by the incomprehensibility of their own languages which sounded to the Greek ear as a cacophonous repetition of the sound "Bar...Bar" which led to foreign language speakers being designated "Barbarians" carrying all the usual negative connotations of that word.

As we shall see, this common prejudice against those who cannot linguistically express themselves extends not only to humans but to animals too. Ever since Descartes declared animals to be some kind of "soulless automatons" people have had a strong tendency to discount their abilities to think, communicate, and even feel. This way of thinking began to change however in the nineteenth century in part because of the work of Charles Darwin.

Famously, Darwin had written that "there is no fundamental difference between man and the higher mammals in their mental faculties ... The difference in mind between man and the higher animals, great as it is, certainly is one of degree and not of kind". (Darwin 2011) Indeed, modern research has in part vindicated Darwin's earlier insight. Today we now know that animals understand a lot more than they are able to express. Dogs, monkeys, apes, dolphins, birds, even insects, are thinking beings and to a certain if relatively limited extent communicating beings. There are many similarities between their cognition and our own. Upon first reflection this should not be so surprising when we think about the basic fact that we all inhabit the same world confronted by similar challenges related to survival and reproduction. Our common world woven together by causal laws and our innate drive to survive and spread our genes is what, ultimately, unites all living things so it should really come as no great surprise that there would be, at least, some commonalities in our various modes of cognition. Thinking is designed to solve existential problems in this world for beings designed to survive and reproduce within it. We will explore these and other ideas more fully in the following discussion about language, mind, and behavior.

The famous Ukranian-American Evolutionary biologist Theodosius Dobzhansky once said that "nothing in biology makes sense except in the light of evolution". The same, I feel, can be said about human language: "Nothing about human language makes sense except in the light of evolution".

Unquestionably, human language is complex. A complex communication tool reflecting a complex brain. Indeed, it has often been said that the human brain is the most complex object in the known universe, so it is not surprising that human language, too, could easily be considered the most complex means of communicating known to exist. While rates of evolution vary depending on the species-specific trait under discussion, evolution can happen very fast under the right environmental conditions. As the linguists Steven Pinker and Paul Bloom and others have rightly pointed out "tiny selective advantages are sufficient for evolutionary change". Somewhat astoundingly, "a variation that produces on average 1% more offspring than its alternative allele would increase in frequency from 0.1% to 99.9% of the population in a little more than 4,000 generations. Even in long-lived humans this fits comfortably into the evolutionary timetable." As an example of this, "a mathematical model has shown that a mouse like animal subject to selection pressure for increased size could in just 12,000 generations evolve to be as big as an elephant. Evolution, then, does not necessarily require vast amounts of time to effect significant genotypical and phenotypical change." (see Pinker and Bloom 1990)

Similarly, complex organs such as the human eye or brain or complex abilities such as human language can equally be explained by the workings of natural selection. Over time, slight morphological or behavioral advantages become ever bigger advantages gradually changing bodily organs to become better adapted to their environment granting their possessor ever more selective advantages. As Richard Dawkins once put it, "1 percent of an eye is better than 0%". You can do more, perhaps much more, with some vision than absolutely none. Even slight sensitivity to areas of relative darkness and light could conceivably open up new opportunities for survival and reproduction. Change is cumulative, transitional forms happen (even if their existence might be brief and thus notoriously hard to find in the fossil record), and complex organs such as the human eye and brain are the result of the blind tinkering of natural selection which admits of no foresight.

The origins of human language should be no exception to these general processes of evolution. It should be a product of natural selection. It most certainly did not arise, all at once, through a "Prometheus" gene that magically conferred a complex behavior like human language. Such an idea would be as absurd as if we imagined that the Elephant's trunk or Peacock's tail emerged all of a sudden, fully formed. (Pinker, 1994) No, human language took some time to develop and went through many stages, even if perhaps some of them were briefer than others, because under strong selection pressure for rapid development. What exactly those stages and pressures were are, not surprisingly, hotly contested.

There have been many theories of human language development throughout the ages. Many of these could be divided into two distinct groups which either viewed language as a "vehicle for thought" (the rationalists) or as primarily a public tool designed to enhance social communication (the social theorists). I take a middle ground in this debate. I agree with the social theorists that language development was strongly influenced by communicative needs and probably required a certain level of sociality, although that, by itself, was not enough. At the same time, I believe that individuals, irrespective of the nature of their social ties or the generalized social world in which they live, would have had some selective advantage in developing internal forms of communication, a so called I-language. Relating to oneself is just as important as relating to others. The development of the one does not necessarily exclude the other, in fact they mutually enhance each another as George Mead once famously explained in his theory of the social self. (Mead 2011)

Among the more recent influential theories of the evolution of human language are the "gestural theory" and the "singing theory". In a nutshell, the gestural theory of language suggests that because bipedalism (which freed our hands) preceded a significant increase in brain size and that "the modern human hand evolved before the modern human vocal tract" that it was more likely that early humans used gestural signals to communicate with one another. This theory also purports to have a neurological basis in what is known as "the mirror neuron system" which helps explain the ability of humans to recognize "significant instrumental gestures". And finally, the ability of some chimpanzees to learn and to effectively use a rudimentary sign system is given as support for the theory that a gestural communication system could have arisen early in human evolution. (See Fitch 2010 for a good overview of both theories)

Our second theory has speculative roots that stretch all the way back to Darwin. It bases its premises on the observation that many species, in particular birds, use song to communicate and successfully reproduce. This avian singing ability has been developed and enhanced in some species of birds through sexual selection meaning that the females of the species have selected their mates over time according to their preferred characteristics, in this case the power to produce a repertoire of intricate song. For some proponents of this theory, something similar occurred early in human evolution. A musical protolanguage preceded modern human language. According to Steven Mithen's "hmmmm" theory, this protolanguage was h (holistic: not composed of segmented elements) m (manipulative: influencing the emotional states of oneself and others) m (multimodal: using both sound and movement) m (musical: temporally controlled, rhythmic and melodic) and m (mimetic: utilizing sound symbolism and gesture). Mithen further explains that music and language are both human universals. They are both hierarchical, combinatorial, and recursive systems of communication able to generate an infinite number of expressions from a finite set of elements. (Mithen 2007)

I find both these theories fascinating and worthy of reflection even if I do not fully agree with them.

While I think it is plausible that early humans used gestures to communicate that doesn't necessarily mean that language itself emerged *from* a prior cognitive-behavioral system based on gestural communication. Gestures surely aided communication just as it does today but it is a much more daunting argument to say that it is the very origin of language. After all, many animals vocalize and communicate their intentions very nicely without using any gestural signals at all. Even if early humans did not possess the modern physiology necessary to produce modern sounds that does not automatically mean that they couldn't produce sounds that carried various meanings that in turn affected behavior. Language could have developed through a dialectical combination of increasingly more precise referential vocalizations and increased overall cognitive development without passing through a gestural phase at all.

Similar objections can be raised for the hypothesis that early man passed through a "singing phase" that preceded language. Although it is conceivable that early humans had the capability to produce song, particularly to attract mates, it is a skill that could have developed in parallel to speaking not prior to it. Also, the astounding ease with which children pick up their first language is not the same as regards their singing ability. Singing well seems to be a much rarer gift among humans than is language acquisition. If singing preceded language, should we not expect children to be able to be proficient signers early in their development? While it cannot be ruled out that humans started out as "ape-singers" and that language gradually "segmentized" afterwards, it seems unduly complicated and whimsically romantic.

Perhaps what is needed here is a fundamental change of perspective on the issue. And that is exactly what Dorothy Cheney and Robert Seyfarth provide in their highly provocative book *Baboon Metaphysics*. (Seyfarth and Cheney 2008)

Basing their insights on the prior work of such thinkers as Nicholas Humphrey, Jerry Fodor, and Robin Dunbar, the authors develop a highly persuasive account of the origins of language. (Fodor 1975) (Humphrey 1976) (Dunbar 2018)

Firmly in the social theorist camp, they strongly argue that cognition preceded language. That understanding came before expression. And that complex sociality formed the basis for thinking which in turn later formed the basis for language.

They support their views through their close field observations of Baboon social life inspired by Darwin's famous line: "He who understands baboon would do more towards metaphysics than Locke".

And what they set out to understand is what thinking is when it lacks both language and a theory of mind. And what they found out is that thinking is more than able to occur very well without these two human behavioral/cognitive attributes.

Their "language of thought" hypothesis, based on Jerry Fodor's famous book of the same name, is "that knowledge of objects, events, and conceptual and causal relations preceded language, and that language evolved later as a means to express this knowledge.". Cognition first, language second. Thus, syntax as a concept arose first long before it was expressed in language. If true, this deflates Derek Bickerton's idea of a "proto-language" made up of single words which gradually developed syntactic features. (Bickerton 2014) According to Cheney and Seyfarth, grammar began to take hold of the early human mind before it was effectively uttered by our lips. It was the grammar of social relationships.

In their own words "language-like perception and cognition thus preceded and set the stage for language-like production ... long before our ancestors spoke in sentences, they had a language of thought in which they represented the world — and the meaning of call sequences — in terms of actors, actions, and those who are acted upon." And what conditioned, developed, and refined this language of thought was sociality: "long before they could engage in the computations that underlie modern grammar, they performed the computations needed to understand their societies."

The social struggle for rank, food, sex underlay cognitive development, even in baboons and other creatures such as hyenas. "Baboons teach us that it is possible to have a complex society based on cognitive processes that are both computational and representational without either language or a theory of mind."

Concepts (of a sort) can exist without words; computation can occur without grammar. Along with many other species of animals, baboons provide us with a natural experiment that allows us to ask "What is thought — what can it possibly be — without language and a theory of mind?

Thus, it is the complexity of social life which is prior to language and gives rise to it. It develops cognition though developing the categories of cognition: objects, actions, and the relations between them. Sociality prepared early man for language production through the complexity of social interactions and the calculations necessary to successfully navigate them. With this view, a gestural theory or a singing theory becomes unnecessary since all you need is the "social ape". Complex sociality leads to complex cognition which prepares the ground for linguistic categories that can be later used productively.

Yet at the very end of their book, Cheney and Seyfarth reveal that their "social hypothesis theory" is really a tripartite one. They write of the speculation that innovation and technology, not the demands of social life, have driven the evolution of large brains in primates ... The ability to reflect actively upon one's own thoughts and beliefs permits the sort of introspection and mental time traveling essential not only for manipulating other individuals but also for manipulating things. The inventor of a tool must be able to imagine the tool's function in advance of its use and plan its manufacture accordingly. Furthermore, a tool's propagation requires that others recognize its use and understand that they may have to seek assistance from a knowledgeable tutor if they are to use it effectively. Like speech, tool manufacture and teaching have obvious adaptive values, but they require as a necessary precursor the ability to represent both another individual's and one's own thoughts and beliefs ... Although innovation, tool use, and technological invention may have played a crucial role in the evolution of ape and human brains, these skills were probably built upon mental computations that had their origins and foundations in social interactions.

To now succinctly spell out their equation of language evolution: Cheney and Seyfarth believe that complex sociality, such as we are able to observe among baboons today, laid the cognitive foundations for language long before its vocal production. Once language began to be actively produced it helped to give rise to a theory of mind which, in combination with increasing tool use and its manufacture led to a dialectical deepening and expansion of all of the following five processes: sociality, cognition, language production, theory of mind, and better tools through active learning. This is a powerfully persuasive theory. I know of no other that is more convincing.

But nevertheless, I have some questions.

First the obvious. If complex sociality explains the rise of language why didn't other highly social animals develop if not something like human language, then some other intermediate stage? Second, not all intelligent animals are social, even among the great apes we have the orangutan for example.

These two observations have led me to some tentative conclusions. Even without a highly complex social existence, like that of Orangutans, it is highly advantageous to be able to clearly recognize objects/actors, the differences between objects, and their various possible relationships. In essence, just living requires thinking. There are no animals that do not think. That should be obvious. Thinking by itself, without the slightest hint of productive language, procures essential advantages without which animals could not survive. Hence, not only are there no Cartesian automatons out there in the world, there are no, in principle, "dumb" animals either.

Hence, from my point of view, the challenge for cognition is not necessarily sociality, although that might indeed be necessary for language development as Cheney and Seyfarth suggest that it is, but rather it might be the greater challenge of understanding general causality, the way the world works. All living things are caught in the earthly web of causality. There is more than enough incentive and possible benefit available to each and every individual to try to better understand it.

In conclusion, I would say that Cheney and Seyfarth are probably close to the truth when they postulate that complex sociality is both necessary and must proceed language development and that tool use and tool making combined with increasing skill in using a theory of mind was essential to furthering that process. However, it might still be the case that these were all necessary but not sufficient causes. Perhaps the missing piece of the puzzle is indeed random mutation. Or some other unknown process lost to us because behavioral and thus unable to be fossilized and to enlighten us further. Nevertheless, I still think that Cheney's and Seyfarth's work have brought us much closer to the truth concerning the origins of human language.

Perhaps adding some of the ideas of the neuroanthropologist Terrence Deacon could help fill out the evolutionary picture provided by *Baboon Metaphysics?*

According to Deacon, language and language use is primarily about creating and using symbols. (Deacon 1998) That much is uncontroversial. Where his ideas get interesting is that he views the mental power which he calls symbolization (creating words, naming things, language in effect) as *the* selection pressure which reorganized both our brains and our bodies. As he says:

> The remarkable expansion of the brain that took place in human evolution, and indirectly produced prefrontal expansion, was not the cause of symbolic language but a consequence of it....the computational demands of symbolization not only are the major source of the selection pressures that could have produced the peculiar restructuring of our brains, they are likely also the indirect source for the selection pressures that initiated and drove the prolonged evolution of an entire suite of capacities and propensities that now constitute our language "instinct."

Thus, the co-evolution of brain and language is the answer to not only why we speak but why we think the way we do.

For Deacon, language/symbolization was *the* skill/trick that made us human. Language slowly (or rapidly?) colonized our minds and made us better able to survive and reproduce. The better we got at using it the more it changed us in order to be even better users of language. In a way, language changed us to better accommodate itself; it needed more efficient, fluent language users. In the end, it was a dialectical bargain: the more language became a part of us the more successful we became as a species; increasing vocabulary meant greater memory, better syntax meant better logic, the need for clearer pronunciation meant physiological changes. Increased vocabulary, better syntax, and clearer pronunciation meant increased opportunities for status, power, resources, sex and, finally, the accumulation and transmission of culture; indeed, symbolization is what made culture possible. And it might have all happened as early as Homo Erectus 2mya. As Deacon points out:

The near synchrony in human prehistory of the first increase in brain size, the first appearance of stone tools for hunting and butchery, and a considerable reduction in sexual dimorphism is not a coincidence. These changes are interdependent.

Language, the power of symbolization, is a special mental symbiont. As it thrived, so did we. It acted as a natural ratchet leveraging behavioral, cognitive, and, eventually, cultural transmission and complexity almost as if all of this were in its own interest. It can be viewed as a special multi-layered modularly distributed cognitive software that ultimately made us who we are today.

Merging the last two theories and my own contributions together I think we are now able to tell an even more powerful story about language evolution. First came what I call "the challenge of the world": figuring out general causality, how things work, picking out objects, discerning relationships among things and actors. This is something all living creatures must master on some level. Second, for some animals, a complex social life emerged demanding more complex computations and higher levels of both specific and general understanding. Complex sociality in combination with "the challenge of the world" built up cognition to a level that it was "pre-adapted" to language production once or if it came. The grammar of causality and sociality was thus already written into our minds, all that was needed was one more ability: symbolization. With cognition already pre-adapted to think in terms of actions, actors, objects, and relationships between them symbolization could now merge and unify these abilities into a higher synthesis of both verbal production and understanding. And of course, with the ability to symbolize, we could now symbolize ourselves and others. We could now picture other minds as well as our own adding another level of computation that was able to access the older cognitive abilities that were stimulated and developed by both the physical and the social world. World, social life, theory of mind-symbolization, language production all in that order. And where do tools come in? Mixing the thoughts of Cheney, Seyfarth, and Deacon together, tools appear on the scene once a basic ability to symbolize and, perhaps, maintain a simple theory of mind is available. If so, that could mean that even the Australopithecines had reached this cognitive threshold as evidenced by their primitive tool use as far back as 3.4 mya. (McPherron et al 2010) Time enough for the quintessential human skill of language to evolve. Indeed, one of the major consequences of accepting this way of looking at language evolution is that it lends itself to the idea that the origins of language are actually very old, predating the beginning of Homo, and in some basic profound sense even quite possibly predating the Australopithecines. Just ask the baboons.

If the origins of language are indeed far more ancient than is generally assumed then there should be some clear genetic traces of its venerable evolutionary lineage. And while the technical ability to search for "language genes" is rather new there are already some tantalizing clues in this regard.

Perhaps the most talked about "language gene" in recent years is the FOXP2 gene.

What, to my mind, is immediately striking about this gene is that it is highly conserved which is to say that it is very old and found in many species. This is exactly what you would expect if our preferred theories in this chapter were in any important sense close to the actual truth of language evolution. The FOXP2 gene while important for smooth human language functioning is also involved in the vocal learning of birds. This implies that at least one physical building block of human language predates the very existence of the great apes.

Thus, it should come as no surprise that the FOXP2 gene has been thought to have been carried around by Homo Erectus and probably the australopithecines as well. While we will never know exactly how it expressed itself in these early human ancestors, if our theory is at least partially correct, it might well have played an important part in early human communication.

It should be noted that in humans, deleterious mutations in the FOXP2 gene result in severe speech problems expressed as "an inability to work the lower face muscles with precision". In addition to this physical problem, there are also more general difficulties with the processing of the grammatical and linguistic aspects of speech. (Hurford 2011)

While the FOXP2 gene is certainly not "*the* language gene", it is nevertheless a tantalizing piece of the genetic puzzle that might surely one day contain other genes that will help to explain the regulation, control, and development of human language ability.

This chapter on language was the first in a triad of human abilities that significantly altered the fortunes of the global ape. The other two are religion and the advent of modern science and technology. All three of these conceptual and behavioral breakthroughs thoroughly transformed individual thinking and sociality while significantly adding to their powers. In terms of survival and reproduction, they contributed to the unprecedented global success of the human race. At least up until now.

Chapter Nine: The Religious Ape: Homo Religiosus

Man is by his constitution a religious animal.
— Edmund Burke

*In all its aspects and at every moment of history,
social life is only possible thanks to a vast symbolism*
— Emile Durkheim

Men create the gods after their own image.
— Aristotle

*Philosophy will clip an Angel's wings. /
Conquer all mysteries by rule and line, /
Emptythe haunted air, and gnomed mine, /
Unweave a rainbow*
— Keats

*We are all atheists about most of the gods
that humanity has ever believed in.
Some of us just go one god further.*
— Richard Dawkins

*The human mind is the result of a long series of
interactions with other animals.*
— Paul Shepard

Animals live in a world that children seem to climb right into
— Rosemary Wells

Until one has loved an animal, a part of one's soul remains unawakened
— Anatole France

Not how the world is, but that it is, is the mystery.
— Ludwig Wittgenstein

Only a God can save us now
— Martin Heidegger

E. O. Wilson wrote a beautiful book towards the end of the Twentieth Century (that may hopefully set the spiritual tone for the Twenty-First) called Biophilia. (Wilson 1984) Here he defined the main idea and title of his book as "the innate tendency to focus on life and lifelike processes." Among his many poetical expositions of his idea this one is perhaps among the most striking: From infancy we concentrate happily on ourselves and other organisms. We learn to distinguish life from the inanimate and move toward it like moths to a porch light. Novelty and diversity are particularly esteemed; the mere mention of the word extraterrestrial evokes reveries about still unexplored life, displacing the old and once potent exotic that drew earlier generations to remote islands and jungled interiors. That much is immediately clear, but a great deal more needs to be added. I will make the case that to explore and affiliate with life is a deep and complicated process in mental development. To an extent still undervalued in philosophy and religion, our existence depends on this propensity, our spirit is woven from it, hope rises on its currents.

The idea that we possess a strong innate inclination, interest, affinity for nature is not strictly a scientific proposition but nor is it difficult to imagine and tentatively affirm. Humans have exhibited a strong attraction to nature (if expressed in varying ways) both individually and culturally from at least the Cave-Paintings of Lascaux to present-day concerns of climate change and species loss.

Our ancient relationship with nature has shaped our minds as well as our bodies.

In the course of our evolution, we have developed something known as "folk-biology" which can be generally defined as how humans classify and reason about the organic world.

All known cultures appear to entertain notions of:

"(I) biological species, at least those "nondimensional" species (i.e., coexisting in the same locality over a few observed generations) of vertebrates and flowering plants that are manifest and phenomenally salient for human beings, (ii) sequential patterns of naming (e.g., "oak," "shingle oak," "spotted shingle oak"), (iii) taxa construction by means of an appreciation of overall patterns of morphological regularity (variously termed "habitus," "facies," or "aspect"), (iv) overarching animal "life-form" groupings that more or less correspond to modern zoological classes (e.g., bird, fish), and (v) overarching plant "life-form" groupings that have no place in modern botanical taxonomy but are nonetheless of obvious ecological significance (e.g., tree, grass)." (Atran 1993)

According to the cultural Anthropologist Scott Atran, we reason about nature and the objects to be found in nature in certain specific ways. We do not use a "general" "all-purpose" cognitive ability to order, define, understand animals, trees, and other natural objects, rather we are evolutionarily primed to conceive, interpret, and "see" the natural world in specifically universal trans-cultural ways. As Atran notes

"it is logically impossible that humans are able to conceptually generalize from limited experience without pre-existing structures that govern the projection of finite instances to their infinitely extendable classes." (Atran 1993)

We have been cognitively pre-formed by evolution to see the natural world in ways that enhance both our survival and reproduction. It is a process which began long before there were humans and extends back all the way to the first land vertebrates, and perhaps much earlier.

Interesting and salient examples of folk-biology at work and as such strong evidence for the evolutionary preparedness of the human mind to receive and interpret organic information in specific ways are to be found in some recent psychological studies of young children's developmental perceptions of animals.

In one study,

Thirty-two preschool children were given opportunities to ask questions about unfamiliar artifacts and animals. The children asked ambiguous questions such as "What is it?"about artifacts and animals alike. However, they were more likely to ask about the functions of artifacts, but about category membership, food choices, and typical locations of animals. They never asked questions about either artifacts or animals that would be considered inappropriate by adults. The results indicate that children hold different expectations about the types of information important for categorizing living and artifact kinds. Young children conceive of artifacts in terms of functions, but conceive of animals in terms of biologically appropriate characteristics. Such results speak to debates about the role of function in children's biological reasoning and to accounts of children's artifact concepts (Greif 2006)

Indeed,

> Children as young as 3 years old have intuitions about essential properties of living kinds and can distinguish them from artifacts ... Three-year-olds also understand that traits of biological entities serve the purpose of enhancing survival, and traits of artifacts serve the social purposes of benefiting people...they did not indiscriminately impute design and function to biological kinds ... (they) appear to understand that different kinds of abstract relations are essential to the domains of artifacts and animals, and their questions reveal a deep-seated conceptual contrast between animals and artifacts ... (they) were more likely to ask where animals typically were found than where artifacts typically were found. This question, although certainly sensible to ask about artifacts, does not strike children as conceptually important to learning about novel artifacts. Children also asked about properties that could pertain only to animals, such as eating habits and reproduction (Greif 2006)

Another psychological study of children was based on the assumption that:

> Natural selection is likely to have shaped developmental systems for rapid acquisition of knowledge about environmental dangers, including dangerous animals. However, learning about dangerous animals through direct encounters can be costly and potentially fatal. In social species such as humans, the presence of stored information about danger in the minds of conspecifics might favor the evolution of prepared social learning mechanisms that cause children to preferentially attend to and remember culturally transmitted information about
> danger. (Barrett 2012)

The experimenters in this study attempted to show that children from two very different cultures exhibit prepared social learning about dangerous animals: city-dwelling children from Los Angeles, who face relatively little danger from animals, and Shuar children from the Amazon region of Ecuador, to whom dangerous animals pose a much greater threat. Both populations exhibited similar prepared learning effects. Danger information was learned in a single trial without feedback, immediately entered long-term memory, and was recalled with only minor attenuation a week later, while other information presented at the same time (animal names and diets) was immediately forgotten. (Barrett 2012)

These experimental results suggest that:

> From the moment of birth, organisms face the problem of learning the fitness relevances of the diverse kinds of objects in their environments. They have to figure out what to eat and what not to eat, where to go and where not to go, which things might hurt them, and which are a source of protection. Because the fitness consequences of these decisions can be very large — sometimes, a matter of life and death — natural selection shapes the developmental systems that build these skills in childhood, selecting amongst various possible developmental designs based on their fitness consequences and the cost-benefit tradeoffs of each. (Barrett 2012)

Specifically,

> "dangerous animals have been present in ancestral environments stretching back in time to well before we were human. Second, opportunities to learn about dangerous animals through individual experience would have been extremely costly, especially in children, whose lack of expertise and physical ability would have rendered direct encounters with animals very risky. Third, valuable information about local dangers was stored in the minds of more experienced conspecifics who not only had their lifetimes to learn what was dangerous but also had access to the accumulated knowledge of the group. Social learning is likely to have been particularly important given the broad range of environments that humans inhabited over evolutionary time. While it is possible for evolution to create perceptual templates for certain kinds of dangerous animals, like snakes and spiders, that are highly recurrent over space and time, the variability of other animals that posed dangers to humans, from hippos to platypi, suggests that learning would have been crucial for adjusting to local dangers. And while there are reasons to suspect that a mechanism for prepared social learning of animal danger has a long evolutionary history and is phylogenetically widespread, the increasing reliance of humans on culture as a means of leveraging the accumulated expertise of others suggests that, if anything, the importance of social learning in the domain of danger is likely to have increased in the recent evolutionary past." (Barrett 2012)

Put in other words, human minds may be evolutionarily pre-prepared to readily conceive and apprehend of dangers in the natural world, but what particular kinds of local dangers, the specific content, will have to be filled out by culturally transmitted learning. We are born to be alert to natural dangers, but there is much local variation and consequent social learning involved.

However, perhaps most surprising of all in this second study is that the danger learning effects in the American children so nearly approximated those of the Shuar, given that the information was likely to have zero fitness value to children growing up in LA. This supports the view that human children are evolutionarily prepared to rapidly learn about dangers of a sort that was common in ancestral environments — dangerous animals — even when the threat from dangerous animals is very small in their present-day environments (Barrett 2012)

Evidence for "stone age" minds housed beneath kids' L.A. Baseball caps? Perhaps.

Our third study concerns children's strong interest in live animals. It is based on the theoretical assumption "that humans may have a natural affinity for animals that is evident very early in life". (LoBue 2012)

> These researchers experiments purported to show that "when confronted with a choice between live animals and attractive toys children interacted with the animals more often than with the toys. Further, they behaved differently towards the animals than the toys, talking about the animals more than the toys and asking more questions about them. The parents of the children also spent more time interacting with the animals, directing their children's attention more towards the animals than the toys. This research supports the idea that humans have an affinity for animals that draws their attention to animals, even when attractive toys are present." (LoBue 2012)

Also,

> "when presented with pairs of realistic videos — one of a moving animal and the other of a moving artefact, 4- to 12-month-old infants look significantly longer at the animals." (LoBue 2012)

All of our three studies seem to show some evidence for not only "folk-biology" but for specific types of unlearned cognitive abilities as regards the perception, classification, and understanding of animals that can be, nevertheless, subsequently modified by the culture in which one is born in and the individual people that one learns from. Not surprisingly, these findings, yet again, underlie a basic theme of this book which is that man is a bio-cultural animal.

Yet following the cognitive and social consequences of these studies further points us even deeper into the unique relationship between animals and humans. As Gail Melson has said:

> evolutionary biology has been prompting psychologists to ask about the evolutionary basis for human behavior. The coevolution of modern humans, not just alongside but interdependently with animal and plant species, makes it probable that built into the human psyche are interest in, use of, and feelings about animals. From this perspective, interspecies relations may be just as fundamental a building-block of human development as intraspecies ties. (Melson 2005)

Expanding on E. O. Wilson's Biophilia hypothesis she goes on to say:

> "Biophilia depicts children as born assuming a connection with other living things. The emotions and personalities of animals, real and symbolic, are immediate to children in the same way that the emotions and personalities of people are. Because of this, animals enter the drama of a child's life in direct and powerful ways. Children readily access animals as material in the development of a sense of self. Every human child begins life situated in what adults call "the animal world."" (Melson 2005)
> "And importantly based on the legacy of our coevolution with animal species, that life begins with an openness toward animals as creatures in equal standing with us, then animals become the essential first vocabulary for understanding ourselves and other humans. As children develop into adolescence and adulthood, this vocabulary, encoded in metaphors and folktales, retains its symbolic power." (Melson 2005)

Paul Sheppard significantly adds to this perspective when he writes:

> animals have a critical role in the shaping of personal identity and social consciousness. Among the first inhabitants of the mind's eye, they are basic

to the development of speech and thought. Later, they play a key role in the passage to adulthood. Because of their participation in each stage of consciousness, they are indispensable to our becoming human in the fullest sense. (Cited in Melson 2005)

To sum up then, some current research clearly seems to suggest the crucial role played by animals in human cognition and mental and spiritual development. We are not only "biophilic" we are what I would call "theriophilic" or "animal lovers". We are ontologically bound to animals. Our very way of being is, in part, a product of our evolutionary co-relationship with them. We saw and experienced the world through a specific bio-cultural combination of their eyes and our own.

Not only do children afford us with insights into the fundamental nature of human-animal relationships, but so does an investigation of the lives, customs, and beliefs of extant hunter-gatherers.

Starting with the natural conditions of the ancient past we should remind ourselves that

> "It is difficult to picture the close association that must have existed between...early hunter-gatherer societies and all the other animals within the environment." (Cited in Melson 2005)

Indeed, even earlier, perhaps for millions of years, much of the life of our species was about animals. How we hunted or scavenged them or how they hunted or scavenged us. Much later, when we had finally developed a theory of mind and symbolization, our special relationship revolved around questions like "What are they thinking/planning?" and what we might have thought about it. What and why they did when they did it and what they might eventually do? They were our next door " alien neighbors": necessary, ubiquitous, strange and yet familiar, an ideal source for endless conversations and tall story making; direct experience and imagination could come up with an infinite variety of possible, if not probable, interactions, powers, and shapes and forms: in short animals were symbolically transformed into the living "neighborhood gods".

Thus, early hunter-gatherers lived in much closer proximity to animals and had more frequent encounters with them. The world before agriculture was sparsely populated and rich in fauna and flora. We probably would be astounded by the tapestry of life that was available 30, 20, or even 10 thousand years ago. That world is now beyond our experience. It has been lost, perhaps forever.

But the next best (only?) thing are the anthropological records of the remaining hunter-gatherers on our planet.

Our story might perhaps start like this:

> "The brain evolved into its present form over a period of about two million years, from the time of Homo habilis to the late stone age sapiens during which people existed in hunter-gatherer bands in intimate contact with the natural environment. Snakes mattered. The smell of water, the hum of a bee, the directional bend of a plant stalk mattered." (Wilson 1984)

And the story might have continued something like this: "animal signs were the beginning of abstraction and symbolizing in a drama we primates already "knew" was social at heart: gestures, expressions, innuendos. In less than three million years, all these categories of the self and society were shaped by the traits of animals observed, the dangerous, competitive, beautiful, tasty, scrounging Others. The human hunter or hunted shared recollections through stories, song, and performance, nouning and verbing the Others and, by indirection and insight, themselves" (Shepard 1997)

Not a small part was also played by the exigencies of the hunt:

> "The human mind came into existence tracking, which for us creates a land of named places and fosters narration, the tale of adventure." (Shepard 1997)

And this:

> "During the evolution of mankind, for hundreds of thousands of years the most important form of the quest has been hunting the first examples of ta-

les within the quest pattern may well have been hunting tales, with combat tales following closely." (Burkert 1996)

And the practice of hunting was evolutionarily intertwined with developing a Theory of Mind for Animals:

> "Our evolutionary heritage of attunement to animals led early humans to place themselves imaginatively within animal skins and animal minds. Humans have always invested animals with moral urgency and emotional power.
> The fusion of social and natural-history thinking allows humans to think about animals as if they were people, as well as put themselves imaginatively into animal minds and bodies." (Melson 2005)

And perhaps most importantly for our purposes in this chapter:

> animals are frequently attributed with human type minds by hunter-gatherers (Mithen 1998)

Thus, beginning in the distant past, hunter-gatherer interactions with animals, especially during hunts, helped shape the human mind and, later, human culture particularly through the ability to both impute and read the anthropomorphized intentions of animal. We watched, observed, and thought about animals long before we were fully human. Once we developed a workable theory of mind for ourselves, we easily and naturally transferred that ability onto animals. Yet we did not regard animals as completely distinct from ourselves and thus attributed human like intentions to them. This, I will argue, was the royal road to religion, the Arts and the Immortal Gods.

> "The earliest and most pervasive human system of spiritual beliefs — found throughout the world in all hunter-gatherer societies and in many agricultural ones as well — was animism. Central to animism is the belief that animals have spirits or souls, which can cause illness and even death when offended or can help and protect as "guardian spirits." The spiritual leader, or shaman, through ritual, out-of-body trance states can contact these animal spirits. The shaman then talks to the animals in their languages, recovering a primordial but lost human ability. He (most shamans are males) can even transform himself into an animal. Shamanistic healing powers derived from this fusion of human with guardian animal spirit, or

animal "familiar." Vestiges of animism infused the premodern world." (Melson 2005)

If the theory I am proposing here is true then animism/shamanism as the "first religion" makes a lot of sense. The story goes something like this. Humans lived with animals since before they were human. They observed, hunted, and ate them. They watched them closely and tried to learn all about them. This behavior might have even bordered on the obsessive since their survival depended on it. Once humans developed the ability to both use a theory of mind and symbolization, they applied these two abilities to their relationships with animals. They imputed human like intentions to animals. Attempted to read their minds. And created stories in the process. They built a "mental" relationship with them. It was imaginary of course, but to them it was very real.

With imagined human like intentions and self-evident non-human powers it was a short cognitive step for our ancestors to create a new category of being for them: gods. Creatures with human like minds but distinctly non-human powers. Yet, since these existentially important beings were supposed to have human like intentions and thus minds, someone, an inter-species specialist in Theory of Mind, might be able to communicate with them to better discern their suspected but difficult to perceive wants and needs. This kind of "ToM specialist" we usually refer to as a "Shaman". He was the designated person who could move between interspecial minds, communicate with them and even share in their animal powers: by fully entering into their imagined minds, he could "become" one of them. Thus, religion and the "proto-priest" were both born simultaneously through the belief in anthropomorphized animal minds and non-human but coveted animal powers that could be shared and entered into through a special interpreter. Like the Hebrew God in The Garden of Eden, the first Gods walked the Earth alongside man and communicated either their pleasure or vexation in a special Realm of Shared Minds.

Even today among the San of Africa "trance-induced transformation — "tranceformation" — into a lion, antelope or giraffe, in which transformation can be at its most real to the person undergoing it and most direct and discernible to those who watch it unfolding" is still a very convincing and palpable experience. (Guenther 2019)

San cosmology is one in which "ontological boundaries between human and non-human are porous." (Guenther 2019)

Animals are front and centre also in San myth and cosmology. Animal stories are generated through the hunt, which provides an inexhaustible supply of narrative to San story tellers, who, in retelling the hunt and the animals encountered, through exciting or dangerous hunting endeavors or because of uncanny, "counter-intuitive" behavior on the animal's part rendering it beguiling and "attention-demanding" and transporting it into the realm of legend and myth. (Guenther 2019)

A culturally spectacular example of how an animal theory of mind, the human penchant for storytelling, and tens of thousands of years of obsessive animal observation can come together are the paleolithic cave paintings of Europe, in particular the Chauvet and Lascaux caves.

> "The new locus classicus for the contemplation of animals in primeval religion has become the Chauvet Cave, discovered in the Ardèche region in Southern France in 1995 by three local speleologists, whose initial response to what they saw within was to kneel. The Chauvet paintings represent the oldest collection of created animal images in the world, with most of the paintings radiocarbon-dated to 31,000 BCE. These fluid, astonishing images of lions, bears, horses, rhinos, aurochs, wooly mammoths and even an owl thus belong squarely in the Aurignacean period, upsetting for good the art historical chronology of Henri Breuil that had dated such perspectival ability millennia later. The iconography and archaeology of the cave testify to an extraordinarily complex relationship between animals and human beings. The existential nature of that relationship cannot be ignored, but neither can it be satisfactorily interpreted. Theories of hunting magic do not entirely help us here; these murals show hunting as well as hunted animals. The cave contains a high percentage of depictions of carnivorous predators, as well as animals that, as far as we know, were never hunted." (Patton 2009)

"We know that the Chauvet artists hunted animals. But did they love them? Fear them? Worship them? Do these murals belong to the realm of religion? If, following Geertz and Zuesse, we accept a broad definition of religion as systematic thought that orients human existential experience to metaphysical powers through external, culturally accepted forms, I think there can be no doubt on this point. The cave offers us a cognitive, spiritual map of part of the observable world: a world lost to us, but peopled by animal powers — or "powerful animals." What exactly the relationship was between the images of animals and the living, breathing animals known to the Aurignacean groups of ancient southern France remains a matter of (re-) constructive theology. As archaeologist and cognitive theorist Colin Renfrew asks of prehistoric peoples, whose ideologies are known to us only through fragmented material artifacts, "What did they think?" Animals and human thought belong together, for the latter seems to require the former." (Patton 2009)

"Upper Palaeolithic artists depicted mostly animals and geometric 'signs'. From among the available animals around them, the image-makers chose to represent the big herbivores which they hunted, especially horses, bison and aurochs, ibex and all varieties of deer. Aurignacians (as at the Chauvet Cave) seem to have favoured the most fearsome species: woolly rhinoceroses, cave lions, mammoths and cave bears. In all periods, birds and fish are only occasionally featured. Some creatures are very rare, like snakes, wolves, foxes and insects. Some animals are 'monsters' that have no counterpart in nature. The choices made have nothing to do with the relative proportions of animal species in the neighbourhood. Significantly, anthropomorphic images are rare, and usually appear deliberately sketchy or as caricatures." (Clottes and Hinnells 2009)

"The sun, stars and moon were never drawn, nor the ground line. No mountains, no huts, no natural landscapes, and very few recognizable representations of tools, weapons or personal adornment. Generally, the images were painted or engraved without any obvious reference to one another: explicit 'scenes' are exceptional. Clearly, Upper Paleolithic art was not intended to give an accurate account of the world outside the caves. Rather, it concerned beliefs entertained by the authors of the images. The image-makers were dealing with specific kinds of interactions between selected parts of the material and the supernatural worlds and with how they could take advantage of forces deriving from those interactions." (Clottes and Hinnells 2009)

"The spiritual/religious nature and function of these caves is, I think, indisputable. Even after the passing of 40 thousand years a team of highly trained specialists felt compelled to kneel inside the Chauvet cave overwhelmed by what they saw. In effect, the cave was able to trigger a typical religious reflex even in people who were well prepared for the kinds of images that they had fortuitously discovered. "(Patton 2009)

Another interesting fact,

"is that many of the animals depicted were neither hunted and thus presumably not eaten. This seems to rule out the construction of a sort of "wish-map" for projecting future desires for a better hunt or greater bounties of edible animals. The relationship between the creators of the caves, like Chauvet, to the animals that they depicted was not primarily one of consumption. They did not paint these animals in order to somehow better eat them." (Patton 2009)

The fact that the majority of the animals that they painted were of the more aesthetically imposing variety some of which were hunted others which were not seems to suggest that the paleolithic painters were impressed with the animals as they were and not for their potential uses. Even to us, these animals express an oftentimes sublime beauty and primal power. They inspire a kind of awe.

The lack of human figures and natural objects like the sun, moon, or stars strongly suggest that the caves were specifically created to direct and channel a powerful, emotional focus on animals. These caves were not primarily about the people who made the art (who were perfectly capable of drawing their likenesses if they had chosen to). It was about the animals, their power, beauty, and, as I am arguing, their imagined human-like intentions and mysterious origins.

Occasionally, human-animal hybrids (therianthropes) are depicted in the caves. Hybrids like the Sorcerer from Trois Freres, the bird-headed man from Lascaux, the bison man from Chauvet or the fish-humans found at Lepenski Vir on the Danube. (Patton 2009) While such figures have been interpreted as evidence for some sort of Shamanism, we can't be sure. What I think we can be surer of is that these paleolithic people believed that animals and humans shared something in common which allowed for humans to successfully take their form and by extension enter into their minds. It is highly unlikely that a human would assume to be able to take a form of something that was completely alien to him. At the very least, they must have believed that animals were similar enough to people that they could effectively interchange bodies and, probably, spirits. And that crucial point of similarity was probably a belief in a similarity of minds. In the paleolithic world, and even later, the human animal ontological divide was porous and, in principle, interchangeable. This may have required the services of an "animal theory of mind specialist" a shaman as Mircea Eliade argued over a half-century ago. (Eliade 2004) It would make sense that some people would be more "gifted" in entering the role or, as they believed, the minds (spirits) of animals. At the very least, it is not an illogical assumption. Long before Aesop's fables, people believed animals could communicate with us and even teach humans about their shared world.

Following the thread of my theoretical argument, it is my reasoned opinion that we can consider these cave paintings as primitive "theory of mind temples". Places where paleolithic man would have gone to in order to focus his mind upon the minds of those animals which he assumed to possess human-like minds and intentions as well as superhuman powers. Here, he sought to better divine animals' intentions, ultimate nature, and perhaps connection to other worlds whose messengers they might well have seemed to be. It was through imagining animal minds that the portal to great art which was directly connected to religious thinking and feeling and indeed simultaneously sprang up with it (as Hegel taught us) was opened. Religious awe served to open up our minds aesthetically, encouraging us to better and more reverently represent both the animal visions we saw in our minds and the stories we told about them. Caves like Chauvet and Lascaux, just like Notre Dame and the the Pyramids of Egypt much later, were cultural attempts to immortalize particular (in this case Animal) Gods through the creation of artifacts of man-made beauty. Indeed, it was these animals' impressive natural beauty and power that was the first logical bridge to the representation, celebration, and preservation of beauty as a concept in and of itself. Thus, Aristotle was wrong. Men did not create their first Gods after their own image. Instead, it was in direct dialectical confrontation with the animal that paleolithic man first met Religion and Art.

In his work *Totemism,* Claude Lévi-Strauss made a celebrated remark, explaining why certain animals but not others are chosen as totemic signifiers. "Natural species," he wrote, "are chosen not because they are 'good to eat' but because they are 'good to think.'" By this he meant that certain animals can "stand for" social arrangements, kinship relations, and modalities of thinking and interpretation. We can extend this notion of animals as a kind of cognitive language to the sphere of religion. (Patton 2009)

I do not deny Strauss' insight that thinking about and observing animals could not have had some impact on the development of our social arrangements and, in particular, on the creation of a "cognitive language" available for the construction of religion. However, I think the story is more complex than that and that it is ultimately tied to the theoretical insights of Cheney and Seyfarth and my own that we talked about in the previous chapter.

To quickly recap what was said earlier: All animals face what I have called "the challenge of the world". They have to make sense of causality and they have to effectively use what they understand about the world for their survival and reproduction. They have to have some understanding on some level no matter how basic of how things actually work in our world. Other animals, such as baboons as we have seen, are able to develop a complex and cognitively challenging social life which creates a kind of mental "social grammar". Cheney and Seyfarth have argued that this "social grammar" predates linguistic grammar and pre-prepared the ground for it. That before grammatical syntax came "social syntax". I have modified their theory to say that some animals as well as human ancestors as ancient as the Australopithecines were equipped with not only a "social grammar" but a more ancient "causal grammar" as well. Working in unison together these two types of grammar prepared our ancestors for language. But before that could happen two other steps had to occur. The first was the development of a theory of mind, followed closely or nearly simultaneously by the ability to symbolize. Thus, the evolutionary sequence of necessary mental events for the functional rise and use of language were: Causal "grammar", Social "grammar", a theory of mind closely followed or perhaps simultaneous to an ability to symbolize. With the last two mental abilities in place language could begin to effectively emerge.

Following the emergence of language, perhaps closely, was the advent of religious feeling and its symbolization by and through language. It seems logical that religious symbolization necessarily followed the emergence of language. You first needed the ability to meaningfully talk with others about what you believed in.

Turning Levi-Strauss' thesis on its head now and following Cheney and Seyfarth, I believe that humans did not learn their sociality in any meaningful way by observing animals. Strauss got it backwards. It wasn't nature in general or animals in particular that was our social guide and teacher but our previously evolved social grammar that helped to order and bring the natural world into our social orbit. We sought to imaginatively include the natural world into the human social world by extending our mind reading abilities to animals and not the other way around as Strauss would have had it.

Thus, our most fundamental religious move was that we attempted to extend our ability to read each other's minds to animals. We believed animals had human like minds and intentions if endowed with special powers which we admiringly coveted for ourselves. It is not so far-fetched to believe that the people who painted the caves of Lascaux and Chauvet believed themselves to be living in a world rich in signification. Man's special power of symbolization extended, as it does today, to everything in his world. In the Paleolithic world this meant the impressive backdrop of nature and the main intrinsically mysterious players inhabiting that backdrop: animals.

If, as Max Weber famously wrote, modern man lives increasingly in a world of "disenchantment" (Entzauberung), Paleolithic man, on the contrary, lived in an enchanted world filled with signification and meaning. (Weber 2020) For Paleolithic man, things didn't just happen, they always "meant" something. Often many things at once probably. Without modern categories of logic and the methods and practices of science, paleolithic man's imagination (and not only his) reigned supreme and unchallenged. There was no limit to the variety of stories that he could come up with to explain the relationships between men and nature or anything else. His was a "narratological" world while ours is a "scientific" world. Thus, man's natural state of mind, for good or bad, is perhaps more on the side of the poets rather than the physicists. Not surprisingly, the beginning and sustaining of modern science required very special conditions while the emergence of religions seem to be ubiquitous and spontaneous to this very day.

For Paleolithic man there was not two separate worlds, the animal and the human, but one world inhabited by a myriad of existentially interconnected beings. Animals were the First Gods and Nature was the first cosmos. As we gradually left nature and eventually built cities and empires and vast civilizations like the Hellenistic and Roman, we increasingly left behind the wild godlike animals and our natural home creating in its stead a new urban civilization inhabited by men and women. Not surprisingly the culturally parallel process of the moral deification of Man over animals and over nature in general turned the sacrificial Lamb into the sacrificial Man while leaving a distant animist trace in the hooves and horns of the Christian devil. From animals as gods to Cartesian automatons is a long-complicated journey about natural to man-made environments and actors.

Where did paleolithic man's self-conception begin and end? With himself? With himself and animals? How far out did our minds attempt to extend into the natural world? I would say that we probably conceived of ourselves holistically and that we exhibited "cognitive fluidity" not just within our own minds as Steve Mithen has ably described it but outside of our minds: between species and the natural world itself. The Paleolithic "I" was not just submerged within a tight knit social "we" but in nature's "others" as well.

Did paleolithic man have a concept for "nature"? I doubt it. For he was already and always within nature. Since he was so thoroughly inside it, he could not name it and examine it from the outside as modern man does. Just as Ancient Hebrew had no word for religion, I would be surprised if Paleolithic man had a word for nature. Paleolithic man was natural in so far as he did not know it and exactly because he did not know it, just as dolphins do not probably "know" that they are creatures who live in "the sea". They are surrounded by it. They are born into it. While completely tangible to the senses, it is conceptually invisible to the mind. For Paleolithic man, nature was completely seamlessly present. There were no conceptual ontological boundaries over which he could peek over. He was totally "in" there was as yet no "outside".

Paleolithic Man had not yet built a home for himself outside and above nature. He was a participant observer and not yet a removed observer. There was no possible cognitive distance between him and nature. Every flower told a story. Every rainfall was a sign. Every animal behavior a potential communication. Paleolithic man lived fully in nature and did not know it, we know much more about nature than he did but cannot fully experience it with the same existential depth and naive wonder. Our two minds look out across from two very different points in biocultural time each more than partially incomprehensible to the other.

I have told a story about what I think are the origins of religion. I do not discount the notion that religion has been supported by economic, political, cultural, and social motives and forces. Indeed, I most certainly believe this to be true. I also do not doubt that psychological phenomena, in particular, the belief to attribute agency to things that are not actually agents "like the rustling of leaves" and a frame of mind that seeks out teleological explanations for all sorts of objects in the world have not played a role in religion's development. It seems more than reasonable that they have. (Boyer 2002) (Dennett 2007) What I do dispute though is that all these factors are sufficient reasons to explain the deep origins of religion.

As I hope by now, it should be clear that I believe religion to have arisen as a result of human beings' imaginative attempt to extend their social way of being onto the natural world and in particular to animals. Equipped with their ability to mind read and symbolize, Paleolithic man extended these abilities to imagined anthropomorphized animal minds. They attempted to read animal minds just as they would their own and to attribute meaning to them. They recognized the similarities between themselves as well as the differences and wished to take part in the presumed superhuman powers of the latter (exceptional speed and strength for example). They were moved by the awe and sense of beauty that these animals evoked which in turn led them to first presumably create stories (narratives) and later cave art as a reaction to that awe-inspiring beauty. Thus, the birth of Physical Art and religion were the simultaneous result of a human theory of mind and symbolic abilities applied to imaginatively anthropomorphized animal minds.

My theory has some formal properties concerning all religions as well, particularly the crucial emotional experience of what Freud called that "oceanic feeling" or religious ecstasy often brought about especially through the spiritual/mental unification with the object/being of worship. As I have been arguing, Paleolithic man believed that his gods (animals) were able to share in the functional properties of his mind and therefore themselves possessed human like minds that could be entered into and communicated with. These first Gods not only had anthropomorphized minds but possessed coveted powers like speed, strength, and beauty which paleolithic man wanted to either possess or at least temporarily partake in. Something similar happens in all religions. The worshipper believes that the sacral object or being possesses a human like mind with which a two-way communication channel can be established "God(s) hear/understand me". These Gods have a whole range of various coveted super-human powers ranging from rain-making, bodily protection, health-enhancement, spiritual forgiveness, ever-lasting life, or moral redemption etc. The worshiper seeks to mentally enter into the sacred object/being through a mix of ritual and meditation thereby focusing/synchronizing both mind and body. Such focus, when completely successful in its spiritual aims, can result in a feeling of complete unification with the sacred object/being leading to the mystical experience of religious ecstasy. Such mental experiences can and have fundamentally changed peoples' beliefs, personalities, and entire lives. In this way, religion becomes a potent historical, cultural, and social force.

In conclusion, we didn't evolve to be religious or come to possess a "God gene" or "God Center" in the brain but we did evolve to communicate meaning to the world and through it to ourselves. Religion will probably exist for as long as man is struck by the wonder of what "is" and that "it is" at all. It is this sense of wonder tied to man's nearly infinite imagination and urgent need to communicate meaning both to himself and others of his kind which will probably continue to offer a much longer life to religion than was ever dreamt of by eighteenth and nineteenth century European intellectuals. Stories are what humans do. And religion(s) is one, perhaps the greatest, of these stories.

In the beginning, all was perceived as enchanted, as mystical. Yet, now that we live in a scientific civilization surrounded by wondrous often incomprehensible tech, I am not surprised that in this environment people "believe in" and "tell stories" about science and technology. It is where they live. It is where they are immersed. It is the water in which they swim. UFOs, for example, are the new "anthropomorphized animals" or "gods" of our technological-scientific world. We seek to tell new stories and to give new meanings about our scientific-technological civilization which is just now beginning to reach for the stars. As we reach for the stars, we imagine "others" who reach back, doing what we do only better and with more technological (supernatural?) powers. Our massive, mighty spacecraft are the aurochs of our time. They roam space with an initially loud roar. They have become fit, for some, as semi-conscious modern objects of worship. They are the beasts that roam the stars. We easily imagine an environment where there are more of them somewhere beyond the horizon, ready to pierce the place we inhabit and to communicate with us. To tell their stories and to impart their gifts. No, it is no surprise to me that UFOs are the new religion. We imagine them to share similar minds and intentions like us and yet to possess coveted special powers, very like the animals of paleolithic man. Yet this is also very much a new world and these our new stories.

Chapter Ten: The Shifting Sands of Science and Technology

Knowledge must continually be renewed by ceaseless effort, if it is not to be lost. It resembles a statue of marble which stands in the desert and is continually threatened with burial by the shifting sand. The hands of service must ever be at work, in order that the marble continue to lastingly shine in the sun. To these serving hands mine shall also belong.
— Einstein

Science is organized knowledge. Wisdom is organized life.
— Kant

Science has made us gods even before we are worthy of being men.
— Jean Rostand

*New philosophy calls all in doubt
The Element of fire is quite put out;
The Sunne is lost, and th'earth, and no mans wit
Can well direct him, where to looke for it.
And freely men confesse, that this world's spent,
When in the Planets, and the Firmament
They seeke so many new; they see that this
Is crumbled out againe to his Atomis.
'Tis all in pieces, all cohaerence gone;
All just supply, and all Relation:
Prince, Subject, Father, Sonne, are things forgot,
For every man alone thinkes he hath got
To be a Phoenix, and that then can bee
None of that kinde, of which he is, but hee.*
— John Donne

*Human knowledge and human power meet in one;
for where the cause is not known the effect cannot be produced.
Nature to be commanded must be obeyed.*
— Francis Bacon

> *Among the asserters of free reason's claim*
> *Our nation's not the least in worth or fame*
> *The world to Bacon does not only owe*
> *Its present knowledge, but its future too.*
> — John Dryden

> *Science is the last step in man's mental development and it may be regarded as the highest and most characteristic attainment of human culture.*
> — Ernst Cassirer

Science and technology are not the same things. Very generally speaking, technology is about "doing" while science is about "knowing". More specifically, technology " is a way of controlling the world, a set of tools that we can use to make things happen as we wish." Science, on the other hand, "is a way of understanding the world (including both the methods used to acquire knowledge, and also the facts and theories that make up our current worldview)." (Derry 2002) Over time, the two became ever more intertwined and co-dependent on each another.

Humans are not the only species to use tools but they are the only species to have invented and used science. In the wild, Chimpanzees have been observed expertly using stones (to crack open delicious nuts) while crows have been documented using twigs to obtain food. So, in this respect at least, we are not completely unique in the animal kingdom.

The earliest known use of stone tools is reported to have occurred at Lomekwi Kenya 3.3 million years ago. However, "the systematic production of sharp-edged stone tools" otherwise known as "Oldowan" tools appear in the fossil record no earlier than approximately 2.5 million years ago. (McPherron et al 2010) In both cases, these finds seem to indicate that tool use might have started before the hominin lineage "Homo" even arose.

Since tool use seems to have probably been known to Homo erectus and even before him, it would be interesting and worthwhile to ask in what ways it might have had an impact on the development of human cognitive abilities. It just so happens that the cognitive archaeologist, Lambros Malafouris, has offered us an interesting theory in this regard. (Malafouris 2013)

According to Malafouris, "human cognitive and emotional states or processes literally comprise elements in their surrounding material environment." Thus, "our ways of thinking are not merely causally dependent upon but constituted by extracranial bodily processes and material artifacts."

In simple terms, what these ideas suggest is that the tools that we fashion, use, and think about have a direct impact on both our current cognitive processes and on our cognitive evolution in general. If true, this would mean that the creation of tools and their use has had a direct and important impact on how the human brain developed over the last 2.5 or even 3.3 million years.

Thus, humans "became the only species to transform its biology by manufacturing a distinctive, collective, self-aware cognitive realm of social interaction and material engagement." Similar to the cognitive-material dialectical processes involved in our increasing use of symbolization, language, and even perhaps religion: as we made tools, tools made us. As we sharpened and shaped tools, so too did our minds further sharpen and shape themselves. As we opened up new landscapes of action and activity, so too did we open up new cognitive spaces that reflected and enhanced our new environmental realities and technical possibilities. The ever-growing practical power and skill of our hands and the artifacts they produced helped to create the cognitive conditions for the directional expansive power and skill of our minds. As Jonathan Kingdom has argued, humans became "artifacts of their own artifacts". (Malafouris 2013)

While the creation and use of tools is old, older perhaps than the species Homo, the rise of science is relatively new in the history of our species. Arguably, very unlike religion, it successfully arose but twice: in Ancient Greece with Thales of Miletus in the sixth century before Christ and in Northern Europe during the sixteenth and seventeenth century.

The difference between the ease and ubiquity with which religion(s) arise compared with the project of science bears some thought and reflection.

According to the cognitive philosopher, Robert McCauley, religions are "natural" bio-cultural outcomes of human thought and behavior while science is anything but. (McCauley 2000)

> "Scientific theories typically challenge existing, unexamined views about the nature of the world, and the forms of thought that are required for a critical assessment of such dominant views mark science as unnatural. Second, an examination of the modes of thought and the resulting products of the practices associated with religion leads one to view religion, by contrast, as natural in the very respects that science is not. Religious thinking and practices make use of deeply embedded cognitive predispositions concerning explanation, such as the tendency to anthropomorphize, to find narrative explanations that are easy to memorize and transmit, and to employ ontological categories that are easy to recognize. These conclusions may help explain the persistence of religion as well as raise concerns about the future pursuit of science.
>
> Thus, neither the birth nor the persistence of religion critically depends on any special cultural conditions. (If the experience of the twentieth century is representative, religions persist, as often as not, even in the face of direct suppression.) At least in comparison to interest in scientific ideas, the appeal of religious ideas is in no small part a function of our cognitive predilections.
>
> In contrast to science, religion relies far more fundamentally on our standard cognitive equipment.
>
> Acquiring the knowledge necessary to participate in a religious system is much more like acquiring a natural language than it is like mastering the knowledge and skills necessary to do serious science. Acquiring religious knowledge often requires little, if any, explicit instruction.
>
> Humans are born into religious and linguistic communities. Like natural language, religion exploits cognitive dispositions, which seem to arise early in human development. Because so many pivotal religious conceptions have so little theoretical depth, possessing everyday concepts prepares people for the acquisition of religion in a way that it does not prepare them for the acquisition of science.
>
> Religion is easy to acquire. We are in some sense born to it. We have no trouble excepting and believing it. The same cannot be said for the acquisition of science. Science and the scientific mind set is hard to acquire. It takes years of training and is largely counter-intuitive. It is no surprise then that the number of scientists in the world are far less than the number of those involved in organized religion. It seems by no means clear then

that science "had to emerge" or become successfully adopted into human cultures and practices." (McCauley 2000)

Or is this a somewhat premature conjecture?

Can science be viewed as a logical discovery and response to what I have called "the challenge of the world"?

As I have said in previous chapters, animals have to, at least on some level, deal with and figure out causality: how the world works. All animals do this successfully or else they wouldn't be here. In some sense, science also is very much about figuring out causality and "how the world works". If this is true, then it would only be a matter of time (2 million years?) that a unique bio-cultural animal like us would figure out a way of computing the world through the scientific method. Science is the ultimate evolutionary response to the "challenge of the world" the human solution to the practical and cognitive riddles posed by causality.

We have been disposed to solve causal problems ever since we emerged from the sea, and even long before that. Science is the last, best response to that ancient struggle and story. If we believe this line of thinking, science might have eventually arisen elsewhere rather than in just ancient Greece and northern Europe given a bit more time. We, of course, will never know for sure. The main idea though is that a bio-cultural animal predisposed to figuring out causality will, with the slow accumulation and diversification of culture, eventually find its way to the cognitive niche that we call science.

In another sense, science could be interpreted as a new form of hunting, an ancient human activity to be sure, even if we're not exactly sure how ancient.

> "There is some experience of hunting wild animals in every human culture … Roman lawyers regarded vestigia, which originally meant the tracks left by an animal, as a form of evidence. The word 'investigate' has as its root meaning to follow tracks when hunting." (Wootton 2015)

Indeed, following and interpreting the evidence wherever it might lead is very much part of the scientific enterprise. Whether they follow the tracks left by disease or sub-atomic particles, scientists are still sharp-eyed and clear-minded "hunters" ever after the elusive quarry of the natural world: germs, quarks, photons, gravitons, dark matter, extra-terrestrial life etc.

Three other classical concepts besides "vestigia" have also helped to further develop the inherent possibilities of science: Kosmos, Empeiria, and Episteme.

Kosmos means "a well-ordered place". To the Ancient Greeks, the universe was a pleasing, well ordered creation. Most importantly, it was an order that could be discovered and understood by human reason. Through the use of our mental faculties, the microcosm (man) could understand the macrocosm (the universe). This is indeed a fundamentally necessary belief for any kind of scientific project.

The other two concepts, Empeiria and Episteme define each other in opposition.

> "Empeiria is a "knack or skill acquired through practice" while Episteme is "being able to give reasons as to why something was the case".
> The person having empeiria might be able to manipulate the world, but he would not be able to explain why what he was doing should work. A typical example for the Greeks was the difference between someone who knew a few folk remedies for disease, and a doctor who knew the nature of the body and could explain why, how, and in what circumstances those folk remedies would be effective. Plato in particular was keen on this distinction, and contrasted what someone who had a basic empirical or practical acquaintance with a subject was capable of with the theoretical and synoptic knowledge an expert might be expected to have." (Gregory 1999)

These three ideas: Kosmos, Empeiria, and Episteme are foundational to science and were first expressed by the Ancient Greeks. We owe them a deep debt of gratitude (a sentiment which is increasingly uncommon to express today especially in this regard).

> "If you are a relativist, if you believe that science makes no real progress, or you believe that the methods and contents of science are no better or worse than any other belief system, then you are likely to believe that all societies have had science (where science is only a world view) or that science only began when the term science was coined. One of the great achievements of Greek philosophy was to reject such relativism. To para-

phrase Plato in his Theaetetus, you cannot believe that no theory is better than any other theory, because that entails holding that theory itself is better than others which deny that theory. He also points out that if relativism were true, there would be no real knowledge, no real progress, no real expertise. If you share the Greek optimism that we can generate knowledge and make real progress though, then you ought to locate the origins of science with them." (Gregory 1999)

Another time and place of scientific (re)birth was the England of the early seventeenth century symbolized, in part, by the profound visions if not practical inventions of one man, Francis Bacon.

The world that Bacon was born into and lived all his life and its implications for the development of his thought has been masterfully described thus:

> Those who criticize the aim of mastering nature to which Bacon's science aspired either forget or are ignorant of what his world was like. In that world, human beings were extremely liable to disease, physical suffering, and early death. Average life expectancy in sixteenth- and seventeenth-century Western Europe was probably not much over thirty years of age. Infant mortality was very great, averaging around 20 to 25 percent per thousand births. Populations were afflicted by recurrent bubonic and pneumonic plague and other epidemic diseases. Physicians were nearly helpless to diagnose or treat illness and to alleviate pain. Cities were unhealthy from poor sanitation and danger of infection. Food supply was precarious and regularly affected by scarcity and dearth due to periodic harvest failure. Local famine and starvation were not uncommon. Preindustrial economies were subject to widespread unemployment, underemployment, and chronic poverty. Heavy labor was essential to the performance of many different kinds of work. The gap in standards of life between rich and poor was enormous, and as a much as a third of the population may have lived at a subsistence level.
>
> Such was Bacon's world, which lasted well down into the eighteenth century and then began to change with accelerating rapidity into the very different modern world we have come to know. (Zagorin 1998)

The celebrated Israeli historian, Yuval Harari, has written similarly that the "Four Horsemen of the Apocalypse" regularly rode through the pre-industrial world sowing Death, Famine, Plague, and War beyond anything that today's average Western citizen could imagine. (Harari 2016) Thus, that Bacon dreamed of arriving at a better world sometime in the future where all these things would be absent should come as no great surprise.

As Luis Borges once pointed out, Bacon, unlike Shakespeare, was aware of both history and of progress. The Age of Discovery and the social, political, and moral impact of the compass, gunpowder, and the printing press had begun to turn history into an accelerating arrow going somewhere. Bacon envisioned that "somewhere" in grand fashion:

> "The prolongation of life, restitution of youth and retarding of age, the cure of incurable diseases, and the mitigation of pain, he mentioned such other things as the following: increasing human strength and activity; altering statures and features; enhancing the intellectual parts; creating new species; new instruments of destruction for war and new poisons; acceleration of natural processes; extracting foods form substances not in use; making new textiles and materials; producing artificial minerals and cements." (Zagorin 1998)

Bacon's imagination was centuries ahead of his time. In his preoccupation with human enhancement, we could, without exaggeration, call him the first "trans-humanist". He was not afraid, despite his allegiance to the basic tenets of Christianity, of giving man more than he was born with. It was not that Bacon wanted men to really become like gods, rather in what I call the "Baconian attitude" he envisioned science and technology in the practical service of humanity catering to its many needs. That basic attitude is still with us today, especially, for example, when we hear people complain of spending money on the space program instead of ameliorating hunger and poverty here on earth.

> "Bacon's central claim was thus that knowledge (at least, knowledge of the sort that he was advocating) was power: if you understood something, you acquired the capacity to control and reproduce nature's effects. Far from the products of human expertise being necessarily inferior to the products of nature, human beings were in principle capable of doing far more than nature ever did, of doing things 'of a kind that before their invention the least suspicion of them would scarcely have crossed anyone's mind, but a man would simply have dismissed them as impossible'. Where the goal of Greek philosophy had been contemplative understanding, that of Baconian

philosophy was a new technology. Bacon's ambitions for this new technology were remarkable: it was to be a form of 'magic'; that is, it was to do things which seemed impossible to those unacquainted with it (as guns seemed a form of magic to Native Americans)." (Wootton 2015)

Bacon was a late product of the vigor, exuberance, and curiosity of the Renaissance mind with all its precious glories and its bigoted faults. He expressed a new found confidence in what man could do and dared imagined a world in which man's fate would be in his own hands through the work of his own independent mind. This was nothing short of a cognitive-social revolution which dared to turn its back on venerable intellectual authorities like Aristotle and the Universal Church and trusted more in the verve of its own senses and the direct observations of things as they seemed to be. Indeed, the Baconian revolution was to set into motion a chain of revolutions extending at least into the Age of Enlightenment (many philosophers of which were critical admirers of Bacon) causing political, social, and moral upheaval.

With the advent of the Baconian vision of early modern science, for all of its methodological faults, Progress was born. The Algorithm of the Modern World came to be.

Science can indeed be viewed as an operational Algorithm that becomes more efficient and powerful over time; it optimizes itself by its very nature. Why? Because it not only questions the world, but it questions itself and its practitioners as well. No other social activity known to man does that. Asking organized questions in the intellectual form and social activity of the scientific method is the most powerful intellectual tool man has ever created. It has been solving the ancient problems of the "challenge of the world" in ways that have so far immensely enhanced our survival and reproduction.

At the start of the scientific revolution around 1600 there were a half a billion people. Today there are over 7 billion. Past successes do not guarantee future ones of course, as stock market brokers like to say, but, for now, we cannot be but impressed with the correlation between the rise of science and the absolute increase in the human population and its relative well-being when compared with previous historical epochs. Science and technology together help to feed, clothe, educate, make healthier, extend lifespans, reduce toil, and, arguably, make people significantly happier even. (Pinker 2018)

Taken together, they are *the* crowning success of mankind.

That we could also blow up the world or terminally poison it, however, is another argument entirely. Yes, we can build a world of peace and prosperity with the aid of modern science and technology. The obverse outcome of this power is that we can call forth a living hell as well. Which result we choose however is not up to science but to our much older traditions, values, and religions, that predate the scientific revolution. What we can, in principle, do in the world will not necessarily help us to decide what we should want or what grand narrative we would wish to weave for our ourselves and our future.

In Pierre Bourdieu's phrase science gives us "trans-historical truths". But these truths do not necessarily give us "trans-historical moral truths". There is no correlation, although there may be definite causation. How, for example, has the moral imagination of modern man been affected by the ongoing "Darwinian Revolution" to take but one prominent example. What has been the moral effect, if any, of quantum physics? Relativity theory?

For billions of people, I dare say: none whatsoever. But for those who set the tone and direction of our world culture and thus of that which will be left for those of the future to watch, read, and ponder quite a lot actually.

Whether or not we are living near the "End of Science" as one provocative book would have it or at the beginning of a quasi-mystical techno-religious moment known as the "Singularity" no one can really say. (Kurzweil 2005) (Horgan 2015) The truth may well turn out to be something in the middle. Much will be probably retained such as Quantum Physics, the theory of natural selection, Newtonian mechanics etc but as we slowly push out from our provincial spot on an outer-galactic arm and into and among the stars and even other galaxies there may well be "Baconian" surprises along the way. Quite unexpected, perhaps even wonderful.

Chapter Eleven: Moral and Unfree or On the Moral Graciousness of Fatalism

Time held me green and dying
Though I sang in my chains like the sea.
− Dylan Thomas "Fern Hill"

Fate show thy force, ourselves we do not owe
What is decree'd must be, and be this so
− Shakespeare from "Twelfth Night"

How stands our Global Ape when confronted with Nietzsche's concept of the Eternal Return? Can he withstand Eternity? Would he want to?

I often catch myself doing semi-conscious automatic things (such as needlessly refreshing my email web page, repeatedly touching my face, moving my body in certain specific ways) in short, a myriad of semi-conscious acts that I am but barely aware of and then only when I force myself to pay attention to them. I then asked myself how much of myself am I aware of. How much of myself is being "freely decided by myself"?

Well, upon cursory reflection, it seems to me that much of what is myself is not under my direct conscious control. I don't consciously control the natural growth of my nails or hair, the beating of my heart, the division of my cells, or the transport of oxygen throughout my body. These very important things all happen "automatically". But some people assert, in fact most people do, that I have an almost magical faculty called "free will" that allows me to choose what I will do and even exactly when I want to do it.

Now, some people suffer from compulsions such as incessantly checking doors to see if they are open or not. Many of these people report that they would consciously prefer not to be doing such things if they could, but they can't. They feel they are being compelled. Normally, we would say that such people so compelled are not exercising their free will at all. Yet, I wonder if all life does not simply comprise what amounts to a series of compulsions? A compulsion to drink, to eat, to sleep, to quarrel etc. And that these processes/acts are all not under what we would prefer to term "our conscious control". For instance, the fact that I wanted to take a sandwich out of the refrigerator today and did? Was that a "freely" taken decision of mine or did my body, that is to say, everything that I am decide for me before I was even aware that I was going to get up and retrieve a sandwich? To be sure, I may have the subjective feeling that "I decided" to take this action. I feel that it was most certainly "me" and "my free will" that were the main actors in all this. But can I be certain that there is an "I" which exercises "free will" over my "decisions" or could I just be an existential passenger on a train of life which is taking me for a predetermined ride and that all my notions of "self" "free will" and "decisions" are mere words referring to just so many ghosts?

In a profound sense, the question of the ultimate reality of free will was succinctly put by Schopenhauer when he asked "Can you want, what you want?". In other words, in what sense are your actions and desires consciously your own? Schopenhauer also pointed out that true freedom of the will could only exist absent any and all necessity. That is to say, it could only exist if it was caused by itself and nothing else outside of it.

Yet, you still say, that we, all of us in fact, "feel" free. I openly admit that it may indeed seem so to us. But what I would also add is that what we are probably feeling is our physical-mental power to do things, not our free will to do them. We cognitively confuse the two things. And from our power and ability to do things we conclude that we do them freely. That our power to act springs freely from a mysterious source we call free will, rather than necessity. But indeed, what we really are feeling is the power of necessity working through us, not at all by us.

So in order for us to ascertain whether or not we have free will, we would have to explain how it would be possible for me to do something, in principle, without something else having made me do it in a material world. That is the challenge for those who, often spiritedly, uphold numerous philosophical versions of free will under the academic heading of "libertarianism".

Libertarians, being philosophers, have come up with a variety of clever arguments. One of the most famous among them perhaps is that of the "torn argument". Simply put, we are sometimes, maybe every day, torn between two or more choices. Yet, if the choice selected turns out to be random, we have no free will. And again, which is what we will be arguing, if the choice selected will be ultimately the one with the most "causal force" behind it, then once again it was fully determined. For what does it mean to have two or more choices before one? The fact that you are cognitively aware of one or more choices is itself determined by you being an intelligent, rational animal evolved to think about prior causes and their possible outcomes. But the decision you ultimately make will be the result of all that you are/consist of up to that point in time. All of the innumerable causal forces that have impelled you up to the very moment of your choice in what seemed to you a "torn" moment was in actuality nothing of the sort. You may often cognitively register many a possibility before you which causes you different levels of anxiety depending on its importance to your future thriving, but what you ultimately choose will either be random or, more likely in our view, predetermined.

Evolution might itself be another word for biological determinism. True that that was most certainly *not* the view of some notable scientists such as Stephen Jay Gould and John Maynard Smith who made much of contingency. But it *is*, in modified form, the idea held by equally prestigious life scientists such as Simon Conway Morris. For example, according to him, life's genetic code, if it was either random or contingent, would almost never have been able to come into being. Rather, under the conditions of the early earth, it seems that the primordial amino acid soup that then existed *had to* give rise to the kind of optimal genetic code that it did. (Morris 2004) Life is material. Consciousness, if it is anything, is material. Decisions therefore result from material causes. Reject materialism and it is hard to see with what a scientific mind could actually work with except perhaps with speculations based on the quantum world which, even then, seem to present us with the problem of randomness. And what is random is also not under conscious control.

To help us think more clearly about "free will" we might start with the not very controversial observation that human beings take part in at least three levels of reality. The physical. The biological. And the cultural. Perhaps a thought experiment will better explain what I mean.

First, conjure up the image of the Empire State building. Now imagine someone standing near the top floor next to a window. This person now opens the window and jumps. According to well understood physical laws we will be able to be fairly certain about the exact speed and the final force with which she will hit the ground. At no point does she have the free will to stop what is going to happen to her. She is just as much a physical object as is any stone under the same circumstances. Indeed, she will hit the ground as is often colloquially said "like a rock". After all, she is part of the physical universe and subject to its laws, any exercise of her "free will" will not prevent the sequence of events that will inevitably occur once she jumps out of that window.

At around the moment when she hits the ground from that height and with that speed she will surely die. This is a result of her biological inheritance. No act of free will on her part will change that. She is a certain kind of biological creature created by evolutionary processes that will not help her to survive such a fall. She does not possess enormous wings and thus cannot fly or glide for instance. She is a large land-based creature, and like her ancient arboreal ancestors, will cease to live if she happens to suffer a great fall, such as from the top of the Empire State building. She carries within her a biological inheritance that has its limits which unfortunately cannot be crossed at the moment of her untimely demise. A very different result might well have occurred if a small insect had jumped out of that very same window instead of a full grown modern human female.

Now imagine if you will a different human female who is anatomically modern but living a hundred thousand years ago near the horn of Africa. This hypothetical ancient female may resemble the unfortunate woman who recently jumped down from the Empire State building in many respects but in at least three ways she is vastly different. First, she lives near the horn of Africa, for the moment this is not so important. Secondly, and far more significant, she lived one hundred thousand years ago. And thirdly, she possesses a very different type of culture and technology. This ancient woman would not be able through any act of her presupposed free will to either imagine or physically create, either alone or with others of her group, something like the Empire State building. She is temporally, spatially, socially, and culturally locked where she is as regards some of the possible exercises of what is commonly referred to as her free will. She immutably exists at the dawn of humankind. At a time and place that could not through any creative act of human free will *then* have known or utilized anything about cars, planes, trains, steel buildings and/or philosophical musings about the existence or non-existence of free will.

In such ways then, human beings and their exercise of their alleged free will are, at the very least, constrained by the physical, the biological, the temporal, the spatial, the social, the cultural/technological, and some would add the Divine (but we'll leave that one out for this essay).

I mentioned stones. Spinoza once famously said that if a stone flying through the air suddenly acquired consciousness it would think that it was the one causing itself to fly! (de Spinoza 2005) But following this thought a bit further, are human beings, viewed in a certain way, not much more than a complex set of stones (elements) mixed with a certain amount of water (if often an extremely vociferous prideful mix)? Over 99% of the human body is composed of oxygen, carbon, hydrogen, nitrogen, calcium, phosphorus, potassium, sulfur, sodium, chlorine, and magnesium. Each of these elements taken by themselves possesses no known aspects of "free will" but assembled into a human being we are expected to believe that the phenomenon of "free will" now occurs on a massively regular basis? How do such elements combine to produce "free will" then? Is it located in the human brain? Is it immaterial even? In choosing between the two, perhaps the human brain would be a good place to start.

The brain is organic and subject to the fundamental laws of physics and those of biology. Whatever decisions are made inside the brain they are surely made according to these rules. The question then becomes are they made in some sense independently of these laws or not? Is "free will" an emergent property that magically springs forth in the human brain, a property that clearly does not exist for its independent elements?

What is a "decision"? Where is it "taken" from? From what magical well does "free will" spring? At what point does the past become wondrously canceled, material causes serendipitously suspended, and the future magically unbounded? What kind of substance is free will? How can free will be an "uncaused" thing? From our fatalistic point of view, free will is nothing more and nothing less than a magical concept on par with the soul, ghosts, and witches. It functions, like the concept of the soul once did, by ennobling us. It even thereby gives us a myriad of reasons to live. It makes us feel special. For all these purposes and more, it is thus very hard to give up. It is an idea that does a lot of regulatory heavy lifting within our private and public lives. Yet, nevertheless, every decision is ultimately a neurological biochemical expression based on a previous neurological biochemical expression and so forth. One may recall the famous Libet experiments where subjects were recorded to have "made" decisions before they were aware of consciously making them, in this case when to flex their wrists. Or to cite a more recent if similar experiment by Haynes which showed that people selected which button to press, the left one or the right one that they were alternately holding in their hands, a full seven to ten seconds before they were themselves aware of their own choice. (Harris 2012)

Moreover, it is interesting to note how many thinkers, both ordinary and extraordinary, are loathe to give up the notion of free will because it is "intrinsically good". I, on the other hand, am arguing that there is nothing at all wrong with giving up this idea especially if it is quite possibly completely wrong. I think one of the reasons that people resist the idea of the non-existence of free will is fear of a loss of control. The ability to control oneself in particular and society in general. But giving up the concept of free will does not mean you lose control of yourself, since after all you have been necessarily built as a "survival machine" as someone once memorably put it.

Indeed, I suspect that those who cling to the idea of free will do so from a strong attachment to the idea of human beings as something noble and special. After all, the idea of freedom, with so much historical blood spent in its name, has thereby bestowed upon itself a secular aura of divinity. Freedom is the supreme goddess of the West and she reigns closely alongside that other goddess of the West, justice. We cherish the idea that we are free to follow our inner nature, not that our inner nature forces us precisely to be and to do as we must. More than this, our societies have been built around themselves the notion that good and evil are freely chosen and thus merit the full ferocity of collective punishment against the one who has chosen wrongly. This being so, I think the original various blood lusts of the ancient human community to both protect itself and regulate its existence stands behind much of the often-desperate drive to preserve the notional existence of free will. We must feel ourselves completely justified in judging who is evil and who is good, who, in the extreme case, lives and who dies. Free will helps us feel morally cleansed that we belong to the "just". It is an idea that ritually absolves us from collective guilt. Condemnation of the "evil" or "unclean" one is not our fault, after all he or she brought his or her own punishment upon their own head. Therefore, we are not willful executioners, for free will exists which allows for the existence of good and evil. The various cultural narratives that weave the cautionary tales of the protagonists known as Good and evil who are sprung from our free will, immediately call out for punishment and or reward upon their birth. I find it interesting, in this regard, that in the bible one of the first men, Cain, is clearly marked by God for killing his brother, Abel, but not immediately killed for his crime. Was God here acknowledging the necessity of the crime, its inevitability? The story of Cain viewed as a necessary outcome of human behavior that must in some way be accepted, because under certain conditions it is natural?

People need to regulate their social lives. Punishment is one very effective way to do it. Could free will be just a parasitic moral notion helping to resolve the social dynamics of humankind? We must postulate a metaphysical mechanism that allows us to explain the *rightness* of collective punishment. We must be absolved from naming the one that must be destroyed. The primitive community might even require some basic notion of free will to survive and prosper. It must understand itself as a collection of people that could individually, at any time, choose to obey or not, the communal law. Thus, it would appear that only someone who is in some sense "evil" could "willfully" contradict the collective good. Perhaps this is the way it began. But that was the beginning. Today we may not need the notion of "free will" at all to arbitrate among ourselves and, in the worst-case scenario, fatally settle scores with a righteous conscience.

Yet, after all this, what you in actuality are giving up in giving up free will is a certain way of interpreting yourself and your actions. You most certainly will continue to *feel* that you are in control of yourself but that is an apparently useful illusion to help you survive and flourish. However, even if you were completely convinced that you have no free will that would not, necessarily, negate your inborn will to live, both because it is so strong *and* that there is no *urgent* reason to collapse on the couch and wither away and die with this new found certain knowledge about yourself. Knowing you are and will be the result of both prior and future causes does not *negate* your existence, it simply helps to explain it, to illuminate it. You still will always *act as if* things are up to you even if you *now know* that both philosophically and naturalistically, they are not.

Possessing a certain knowledge of necessity must not extinguish the joy of living unless, of course, you are so constituted that the idea of necessitous causality leads you to be terminally depressed. If, after all, I am not the true agent of myself in a deep mystical sense, I am still the causal being that I am who is the direct result of evolution and can accept myself as such and live as I was meant to live: as a person in pursuit of those things which generally make people happy. Now those things were certainly prescribed before my existence, but it is also in the nature of causality that things are in flux and thus change, always step wise of course, for nature never "jumps". The infinite complex causal interplay of both life and the universe is the guarantor of change, it is never the death of hope.

Real change is inevitable and definitely not precluded by causality and we as causal beings will affect change according to both our nature and the planes of causality within and through which we move and that move through us: the physical, biological, and in our special case, the cultural/technological as we illustrated above through our two hypothetical women. We would not exist if we were not adapted to our world and that world adapted us to seek out more pleasure and to avoid more pain aided by our natural/cultural capacities of rationality and intelligence. We will, because of our nature, seek out a felicitous average of pleasure over the total span of our lives. If due to constraints either within us or outside of us or a combination of both we will not do so, we will soon perish and such tendencies may on average perish with us according to the logic of natural selection. For what does not further life, under prevailing circumstances, is soon removed from the vital circulation of biological existence. What does not increase a being's power to the necessary point of ensuring its survival will not itself persist. In this Spinoza meets Darwin.

As beings that are born into the world and survive and are happy in doing so, we have much to hope for. Our natures are not thereby fixed, but they are surely not infinitely malleable, for they will always obey some kind of necessary laws, even if we go about radically changing ourselves as we may indeed soon do through new technologies such as genetic engineering and artificial intelligence. But whatever technologies we use they will, like everything else in the cosmos, be constrained by necessity. Necessity is the reigning goddess of existence from which nothing can escape.

Thus, our decisions spring from the deep well of the past that extends beyond our births, our parents, the very point of origin of our species to the beginning of the cosmos itself. That we cannot practically be aware of the long convergent causal chains that led up to our seemingly "free decision" to study medicine and not law this summer is beside the point. In principle, those long multiple convergent causal chains are always there. We are not, as the existentialists would have it, always on the way to making something of ourselves for ourselves are already made and all our future decisions are predeterminately baked in. Even our very possible belief in some form of "soft existentialism" will, in itself, help to determine our lives. No belief and no action no matter how radically conceived can free us from the past and thus tear asunder the inevitable fabric of the future. We are condemned to be unfree but that does not mean we are condemned to be ignorant. Evolution both cultural and genetic, has given us the power to reason and to explore both ourselves and the world around us more fully than any other being that we currently know of. We are biological expressions of causality. Just as we are physical expressions of it. Just as we are spatial and temporal expressions of the very same logic. Just as we are even cultural expressions of it. We are overdetermined. There is no need to add "the magical" property of free will. Prior causation can explain all that we are or ever will be. Free will is a needless "Ptolemaic ring" added to all that is obviously apparent and explainable without it. We cling to this "ring" because we desperately want (and perhaps need) to believe in some special human-given relative degree of freedom and moral uniqueness. But desperate belief is not an argument, no matter how cleverly drawn up. No, then, we are not free but we are intelligent and curious by nature and that might, in the end, be all that we really need to lead meaningful and, yes, even moral lives.

Following Schopenhauer's thoughts on free will, we should ask ourselves does not everything that exists have a certain nature? (Schopenhauer 2014) Can there ever be existence of a thing without some sort of essence? How can something exist and not "be" something? Thus, if free will exists, it too must be possessed of a definite essence, it must "be" something. And what is this essence? Is it not something like a scale of justice that before it is used does not move but when it does it does so only when something is placed in either its left or right scale? And what is after all placed there if not matter and the causes that follow from it? The more overwhelming the material's force the more certain the decision; yes or no, left or right, up or down, life or death.

From this way of thinking, so Schopenhauer, it follows that given the same person under the same set of circumstances there can only be *one* possible action, not, therefore, a *choice* between some actions and not others. Thus, it follows that if we were to run the tape of existence backwards to its very beginning it would unfold exactly as it did the first time. This is the idea of *quidquid fit necessario fit*: that whatever happens, happens necessarily. Thus, we should never, in all seriousness, entertain the commonly expressed thought that "if only" I could go back in time I would do things differently. My dear reader, as we will argue, no not ever. You always do what you must give the exact same circumstances. In fact, if you think about it, wishing to change things in the past happens because you now have extra *additional* causal information. So, your imagination can simulate your past state armed with this new causal information and, of course, with your future knowledge you could now choose differently because the situation would *not* be the same, you would now have future knowledge of future states which you would have carried into the past. However, there is some good news in all of this is: and that is that you are absolutely justified to leave *all* feelings of regret, remorse, even melancholy and nostalgia behind you. *It's never your fault.* And this entails the first, perhaps for many, radical moral law of fatalism.

Following up on this idea, we could say, along with Schopenhauer, that we know ourselves, what we are, through our acts such that actions flow from "being": *operari sequitur esse*. However, thinking a bit more upon this I'm not so sure. For instance, someone could give a bouquet to someone else which is usually interpreted as a sign of friendship or even love but harbor the most intense dislike for that person without ever letting on externally. In this way, our subjective states can remain perfectly hidden from others while our acts may convey a perfectly false picture of who we really are at least inwardly. These thoughts also bring us to quarrel with Aristotle. Is it really through acts/habits that we become who we are? Is it through acts of courage that we become/are courageous? Is it through teaching that I become a teacher? Perhaps in part. Habituation has effects on subjective states surely. But at what point can we discern between the possible dissimulation of outward acts and the nature of a person's true being? Much of the dramatic tension in Shakespeare; Iago, Macbeth, Richard the III and other literary figures are based on this awareness/acting out of seeming versus being. It is also the very heart of the teachings of Machiavelli.

Should we perhaps now turn our attention to Hobbes' modern formulation of the problem? He certainly has some interesting things to say. For instance, Hobbes, like us, believes that everything is causally determined. However, he also believes that if someone is not thwarted in his or her desires, then, in this sense and only in this sense, could they be appropriately called free. Thus, for Hobbes, the unfettered ability to satisfy our desires is the only freedom that we can truly speak of. This is of course the metaphysical foundation of much of our liberal society. A society where the obstruction of our desires or the interference with life projects tied to our identity (a modern word for nature or essence perhaps?) is not tolerated in so far as it does not prevent others in realizing the very same kinds of life projects.

Let us walk a while longer with Hobbes. Modern man speaks of his right to happiness. For us, his conception of happiness is causally over-determined. We seek what we call happiness because we are bound to do it. We can do no other. And our happiness, following Hobbes and Spinoza also, are tied to those things which increase our individual power(s), sense of well-being, and, ultimately, survival. Indeed, it could not be in any other way. Modern man is determined to seek happiness, and modern liberal society is determined to not stand in his way. It grants him the "freedom" to be what he already is and to do what he must.

But this inception of political freedom only comes at a necessary point in history. A point where the state, science, and conceptions of man begin to coalesce around new ideas of power and of knowledge. The birth of every idea, too, has definite causes. And the birth of Hobbesian "freedom" is certainly no exception to that.

Implicitly, then, the liberal state acknowledges the "essences" of men or to put it in another way their self-conceptions and the life projects tied to them. Their "being" is a given as is their future development from whatever necessary starting point. Everyone is a destiny that must be fulfilled. Now, whoever lived under a totalitarian regime also fulfilled their destiny, but perhaps not as pleasantly as someone who lived comfortably in London in 2023. Each individual, whether someone in Stalinist Moscow or someone in Post-Modernist London lived out their destiny to the full. The only difference was under what historically determined formulation of social-political freedom. Interestingly enough both historical possibilities were, in part, actually two sides of Hobbes' thought; the Absolutist, Leviathan state or an ineradicable natural right of man (in this case the right to one's own preservation of life under any political circumstances).

Locke too offers us an intriguing way of looking at the problem of free will. He imagines that a man wakes up in a room that is locked from the outside. The man decides to stay inside the room. This example is often brought up as an instance where constraints did not affect decisions. A more modern version of this sort of thing, are so called "Frankfurt Cases" where for example a device is implanted in a would-be terrorist's brain (unbeknownst to her) to ensure that she carries out a bombing attack on an elite university. If she chooses to not carry out the attack, the device will impel her to do it, while if she does carry out the attack the device will remain inactive. In this case, the terrorist carries out the attack and the device remains inactivated.

Yet, do these clever thought experiments really reveal that people are capable of making free decisions under constraints? I think not. And simply because the terrorist, continuing with our latest example, was under all sorts of constraints besides the cautionary one of the devices pre-implanted in her brain. The terrorist has a history: genetic, psychological, cultural, experiential which led her to make the decision she did. Indeed, we are always impelled by multiple constraints, causes. When our terrorist set off the bomb she did so as an expression of multiple convergent chains of causality. Her every act was/is over-determined. The "constraints" are always far too many (infinite?), the fall-back device in her brain was only one of them.

More seriously, imagine a world that was *not* determined. How would it operate? Perhaps anything would be possible. There would be no universal laws. There would be no causality. In short, there would either be absolute material chaos or maybe, very quickly, nothing at all. Indeed, I find it much *harder* to conceive of a world that is *not* deterministic than one that *is*. Life, consciousness, existence itself might very well depend on natural deterministic laws.

And then there are those who, from time to time, like to invoke some aspects of the radical indeterminacy of the quantum world. Some have even speculated that the key to the "hard problem" of consciousness as well as free will are to be found here. That the "randomness" of quantum phenomena explains the operative reality and functioning of free will. However, others point out the simple fact that if something is "random" it is not thereby under our control. So that even if we were to discount the fascinating problem of how quantum mechanics effects the "big" world we would still be left with how if free will is random it thereby reflects "my" decision. Of course, it doesn't; precisely because it is random.

Furthermore, think of modern science and everyday life. Are not both strongly grounded in our ability to make accurate predictions? Would both science and our everyday lives be possible without a deterministic universe offering us the very real likelihood to anticipate the future outcomes of, say for example, our industry, sun, medicine, and all the quotidian cycles of daily life? Perhaps, really, we should be immensely thankful that the world is deterministic rather than lamenting the loss of the prospect of a world where "uncaused" decision making would be possible.

Yet knowledge itself, when it is possessed, becomes a cause in and of itself. Thus, the more we know of ourselves and the world around us, the more the scope of our ability to affect future causes grow. By knowing the world, we increase our possible arc of action. This is of course not the same thing as the exercise of a free will, but it is the next best thing. In the human expansion of knowledge, in the minute investigation of causation we find our powers increasing with ourselves becoming a new source of that much greater future causes. In this way, Kant's famous "Dare to know!" takes on a new and perhaps unexpected meaning.

We are existential beings. We are essential beings. The one presupposes the other. We are, so that we become. In our becoming is all that we must be. We are necessary but we also possess through our evolutionary history the ability for self-reflection and reason. This allows us the illumination of our own history and probable future. Probable because we are not able to calculate all the causal variables going forward, we are not an infinite calculating machine, but nevertheless with increasing knowledge we can see ever farther into our own future states of being. In fact, we might say that the relative level of civilization that humanity has attained is always equal to the levels of causality it has absolutely understood. This relative level, particularly in the last fifty years, seems to be undergoing an exponential increase.

Do worms have free will? Do rocks (Spinoza?)? Do animals in general? We too are of course driven by instincts, indeed we perhaps have many more of them, or at least different ones than many other animals, for example our famed "language instinct". Evolution has supplied us with many psychological instincts and dispositions many of which can be found in the "lower animals" and some which are peculiar only to us. We are as much driven by our biology as any other living thing. That we fancy ourselves "reasoning animals" is to obscure the fact that our reasons are, ultimately, biologically-culturally based material motives. For indeed, if man is distinguished from the animals at all, it is in the necessary evolutionary interplay between his genetic and cultural inheritance.

Does reason have anything to do with freedom? Evolution has made us rational animals because we developed that way by genetic, environmental, and cultural causes. The daily reasons that we come up with for ourselves are determined exactly by those same causes which gave rise to our capacity for reason in the first place.

Most startling perhaps in all this is that the future turns out to be as fixed a proposition as the past, in a sense all is past, all "is" already has been. Thus, every fine new building you past is in some sense already in ruins, every future planet we encounter teeming with life already a dead planet, and every stirring contemporary deed already the stuff of ancient legend and song. Within such a vision, forwards and backwards even life and death tend to lose their absolute orientation and meaning.

In our lives, we merely feel ourselves as the ones who are participating or deciding in the course of our existence but it is just a subjective feeling, an illusion. Participation in a sense is lived *through* us, not *by* us.

Possibly, in the end, the laying to rest of the notion of "free will" is just another step in the historical progression of the "Copernican/Darwinian Revolution". The feeling of the uniqueness of man is to be overcome if he is ever to see himself, his fellow man, and the world around him more clearly.

Under this view, it makes as much sense to punish a man for murder as it does to whip a stone for having rolled down a hill. In both cases it could have been in no other way. Stones roll down hills, some men murder. Both are caused events with not the slightest choice involved. People do not *choose to be* serial killers, they *become* serial killers through specific sets of causes: genetic, cultural, or psychological usually all three. They do not choose to kill; they kill because they must.

If true, this might well mean that so much of our present liberal society is complete gobbledygook. That our political systems based on particular notions of freedom are inherently false. That even our justice system based on notions of free will is also fundamentally false. We are determined beings who, at most, *feel* themselves to be free. We are all caused objects that have the subjective illusion of being potentially uncaused. We believe that our future is open, although it is most assuredly closed. It is our fondest, last illusion. It is the final grandest piece of pride in the modern psychological edifice of man. Men desires to be free, but that in itself has causes; psychological, economic, and historical. It is indeed a motivating dream that, itself, has become a historical cause in the demiurgic development of mankind.

Nietzsche, borrowing from Indian philosophy among other sources, confronted the moral challenge of determinism in a characteristically extreme fashion. He dared us to imagine that we are beings that are not only locked in a predetermined word, but one that repeats itself infinitely in an "eternal return". (Nietzsche 1974) From this metaphysical idea, Nietzsche asked of us to be able, at every moment in our lives, to completely and utterly affirm our actions in a subjective manner. As he would put it, for us to say absolutely "Yes" to life and ourselves for all eternity. A tremendous affirmation of all of existence no matter its presumably endless repetition. For Nietzsche, endless repetition does not give rise to a feeling of absurdity, as it would for a Camus, but is rather an existential opportunity for joyous proclamation.

This grand poetic vision is tied to Nietzsche's idea of *amor fati* (the loving of one's fate). This is not just the understanding of universal necessity, not just its matter-of-fact acceptance, but loving one's fate with all one's subjective might. In a sense, it is rather an inverse existentialism that says "love what you must be and love what you cannot change; you are what you are". To be in love with our unfreedom. One problem of course is that whether you are able to love or not love your fate is, by this theory's very premises, not at all up to you. Whether or not you are a fatalistic optimist who rejoices in the unfolding of one's being in time and space or a morose fatalistic pessimist who complains at every turn of events is not for you to decide. There can be no decision here, thus no independent moral declarations affirmative or otherwise.

Yet in one sense perhaps Nietzsche was on to something. What is "is", that much is uncontroversial. How should we subjectively evaluate the "is"? Thinking about the fate of ourselves is certainly one way. If ours is a fate that unfolds in suffering, we shall, quite naturally, be inclined to deprecate our existence, even to curse it. Pain for us is evil. The loss of our power(s) is bad. It would take a sublime form of character to see in our individual suffering any natural kind of redemption. Indeed, just in this, lies the genius of many, if not all, religions (and perhaps Marxism too?). The promise of redemption from necessity. Freedom from inevitable pain caused by the inescapable causal nature of the world. No wonder then that the promises of religion take place in another world, for they surely could not take place in this one. In this world, we either have the strength of character to "sing in our chains like the sea" or we do not. The Nietzschean tone of Dylan Thomas' famous poem "Fern Hill" that we started out with has not escaped us.

But being free from ultimate responsibility for our actions does not necessarily make us non-moral. Rather, it opens up possibilities for a new morality. A more scientific sort of morality. Perhaps even a more rational, sublime one. Morality becomes an investigation of causes. *Why* a person *became* a serial killer, rather than why and how he should be punished. If we understand how someone becomes a serial killer, perhaps we can take steps to prevent someone else, in future, from becoming a serial killer. In the extreme Utopian case of this way of thinking, if we understand why someone becomes a criminal, we can perhaps be in a better position to eliminate criminality all together one day. In giving up the notion of free will we do not give up morality. What we give up is the ancient fetish of collectively meting out punishment and what we gain is a focus on a deeper understanding of our world and ourselves. We free ourselves from guilt and self-recrimination while we fill ourselves with new forms of enlightenment and of mercy. We open ourselves up to what I call the "moral graciousness of fatalism". Through our intelligence and our reason, we strive to do great things and make things better for ourselves; indeed, all of our presupposed knowledge of causal determinism does not prevent us from such acts. Rather, it provides us a with a deep sense of cosmic mercy. For when what we call evil (which is usually what is inimical to our material interests among which are survival and prosperity in the broadest of senses), is committed we can perceive it not through the terrible moral lens of reflexive communal punishment (in the extreme case the meting out of death) but as a challenge to our intellect to understand and unravel the skein of past consequences that led to whatever was the unfortunate result under consideration. Thus, such a moral concept of fatalism lies beyond traditional notions of good and evil but, to achieve some kind of semblance of morality, it must become one with the understanding and reason.

Some ideas lend themselves to mystical visions, as was famously the case for Plato in his allegory of the cave, perhaps the most celebrated allegory in all of Western civilization. When I meditate on the problem of free will and fatalism I often visualize and almost even hear the various rushing streams, sometimes slight other times wide, deep, and powerful, of causality. I almost seem to perceive how whatever seems to unfold both inside and outside of myself has been impelled by these vast waters of fate. Another thought which often moves me in an admittedly mystical way is the thought that if I'm right and fatalism is the correct existential situation for all things, human and non-human both, then it was inevitable that the universe was to achieve present consciousness of itself and its own past and future existence. That in a sense, humans are the universe investigating itself while simultaneously creating layers of novel ways of being: culture, morality, technology, all of which necessary potential lay dormant for billions of years. If true, this is a profound thought leading to awe. For if fatalism is true, teleology must also be true. This is to say that if everything is determined from the very beginning of material existence then so are its ultimate purposes or ends. Yet, there may be a multitude of ultimate purposes, not just human ones. However, humans special and particular way of being seems to have an innate potential to change, to some extent, the nature of the physical universe; it already has profoundly changed the material nature of this planet. The more we know about material causes the more we seem to be practicing a kind of modern alchemy that seeks to transform the whole world. An ever-deepening knowledge of causes is the true alchemy. It might very well be the elixir of life and transformer of worlds

Indeed, just as much as it was for Socrates, "Know Thyself!" is the fatalist's moral credo and yet perhaps it must become more than this: "Know the causes that led to yourself and others and the world around you!". Free yourself of the blindness of hate, while not necessarily relinquishing the benevolence of love. There is no contradiction in this. For in a predetermined world, there is no need for a rational being to feel anger either towards oneself or others, although one's genetic endowment will probably make you feel it anyway, but there is every reason for a rational being to feel pity, love, understanding, and mercy for a world and the beings in it that share with you and every one of us the same inexorable path of existence. For Essence here not only precedes Existence, it is Existence. So yes, we are saying that free will, contingency, even reason when construed to be in some form causally independent are common illusions with which we comfort ourselves as individuals and with which we provide often specious reasons for the actions we take in our collective life. As a recent popular book would have it, human beings and the societies they build follow a blueprint. (Christakis 2019) This blueprint allows for variation but is not infinitely malleable. It most certainly is based on what went before and will slowly change, step wise, necessarily following a long causal chain into the future. Hopefully, this extended causal chain which we call the "future" will be guided by more fundamental knowledge of itself rather than by wishful ignorance. By more cold facts than cherished ancient beliefs. For, ultimately, we are the necessary unfolding of material essence as is the very world itself. Yet, although we often pose as the mad clowns of either chance or necessity; it is to existence as it is that we are firmly bound. Indeed, we may at times wistfully grimace as if we were free, but, nevertheless, we continuously and oftentimes nervously dance the jig of eternity.

Chapter Twelve: The Global Ape: Between Transcendence and Extinction

When looms weave by themselves, man's slavery will end.
— Aristotle

The future influences the present just as much as the past.
— Nietzsche

The future ain't what it used to be.
— Yogi Bera

There is no such thing as a human nature independent of culture.
— Clifford Geertz

The greatest invention of the nineteenth century
was the invention of the method of invention.
— Alfred North Whitehead

All the labours of the ages, all the devotion, all the inspiration,
all the noonday brightness of human genius, are destined to extinction. ...
The whole temple of Man's achievements must inevitably be buried
beneath the debris of a universe in ruins
— Bertrand Russell

Our souls have been corrupted just as our sciences
and our arts have progressed
— Rousseau

A garden shall arise, in loveliness, surpassing fabled Eden
— Shelly

"Where is Everybody?"
    This question was famously asked by the physicist Enrico Fermi in 1950 over a casual lunch.

What he meant by this question was that given the vast number of stars in the universe and an equally vast sum of planets, life and, in particular, technological civilizations should have arisen many times over and might have been able to visit our own planet at least once or even repeatedly. Yet, as far as Fermi and everybody else knew, there were no credible signs that such an event had ever taken place.

Fast forward to the twenty-first century and we find extensive infrared surveys of at least 100,000 galaxies in search of "techno-signatures" that would serve as evidence for "large scale macroengineering" and thus the probable existence of advanced extraterrestrial civilizations. Unfortunately (or fortunately?) nothing that would indicate a non-natural origin was ever found. The universe continues to be a "silent" place. (Last 2020)

How can we account for this silence? Innumerable explanations have been offered. We're not looking with the right instruments or methods, we're somehow being denied access to them, they're hiding, they destroyed themselves, or, even, Extraterrestrials are so far advanced and so different from us that we wouldn't know that we were looking straight at them even if they were literally right in front of us ... and many, many more of such like apologetic argumentation and reasoning.

However, there *is* a powerful and convincing alternative to all this speculation and that is: The Rare Earth Hypothesis. (Ward and Brownlee 2007)

According to this hypothesis simple life is indeed ubiquitous throughout the universe most likely in the form of bacteria. Yet, the existence of multi-cellular life (complex animals) is highly improbable. The reason given for this conclusion is that bacterial life requires far fewer evolutionary steps and necessary initial and ongoing (highly improbable) physical conditions for its emergence and successful continuation.

If this is true, then the Rare Earth Hypothesis explains not only the Fermi Paradox but the Great Filter as well.

The Great Filter Argument suggests that there is some stage in life's evolutionary development that renders the existence of space exploring civilizations highly unlikely. If this is the case, then the question for us and our future is: is this stage something that lies ahead of us or far behind us? Happily, according to the Rare Earth Hypothesis, it is something that very definitely lies far behind us with the successful rise of multi-cellular life. The ability to create and sustain multi-cellular life is *the Great Filter*. If true, this should give us at least some renewed confidence in ourselves and in our future.

Yet the Rare Earth Hypothesis offers us much more than "just" confidence in our future. It reawakens old ideas of the "specialness" of Earth if not necessarily its "centrality". For if it is true that the rise of multi-cellular life is extremely improbable then we are indeed "special" in the universe. Every life form, every species would be, in this sense, something not only valuable in its own right but "cosmologically" priceless. It would suggest that the extinguishing of species on this planet would not just be a loss for us, but an irretrievable cosmic catastrophe. Accepting the Rare Earth Hypothesis transforms us once again into a "unique" planet and a miraculously fragile one at that.

In a sense, with the Rare Earth Hypothesis we have come full circle from the intellectual revolution begun by Copernicus in the Sixteenth century. Here, Copernicus "de-throned" the Earth from its spiritual position at the center of the Cosmos thus beginning a long intellectual series of the diminishment of Man and His Place in the Universe with scientific discoveries and conceptual revolutions from the likes of Darwin and Freud to name but a few. Yet, now, employing the highest level of current scientific understanding and fact, the authors of the Rare Earth Hypothesis have "re-centered" the Earth and its numerous and diverse denizens to a position of the highest bio-cosmic importance, if only in terms of uniqueness and the very improbability of its existence.

The Rare Earth Hypothesis reveals a universe probably teeming with bacterial life but devoid of animals and higher technological civilizations. We may, indeed we shall, search for sentient life but we will continue frustrated, perplexed, even discouraged. Perhaps though, in time, we will come to realize the astounding news inherent in the Rare Earth Hypothesis which is that what we already have is incredibly precious and, in some sense, unrepeatable. That we are indeed the stewards of a "paradise" in a lonely cosmos and that we search in vain for something else that could match its beauty, richness, and potential.

This is not to say that Man should not explore and go forth among the stars. But it does mean that he should value and never lose sight of what he has left behind during his perhaps quixotic quest for stimulating extraterrestrial conversation. In the end, he may find that ET will have turned out to be "only" us after all.

But what of the contemporary "stewards" of this planet: us?

Whether or not we have the right to manipulate, control, modulate, decide over the present and future state of this planet and most, if not exactly all, of its inhabitants is one question. The fact that we *do* have this power though is apparent and inescapable. So, the practical and urgent question becomes: What should we do with it? How should we act? What should we aim for? Where are we going?

The answer, in its extreme form, is that we are headed either towards self-extinction or self-transcendence.

Those who argue for the former point out the various possibly near-future risks increasingly inherent in our scientific-industrial civilization. (Bostrom and Cirkovic 2011) They cite our ability to unleash biological, technological, and ecological plagues upon ourselves and our planet. They see ourselves as "dark magicians" who call forth powers that they cannot control. They have a severely qualified faith in man's powers of restraint and reason. In this scenario deadly swift bio-engineered viruses, unstoppable nanobots, accidental nuclear war, uncontrollable AI, and environmental collapse play the ancient part of the grim horsemen of the apocalypse. Here, our civilization rises to its own ruin. We develop ourselves into a technologically engineered oblivion. It is the technically amplified vision of Rousseau who famously wrote: Our souls have been corrupted just as our sciences and our arts have progressed. Our intelligence and our culture become the twin compelling lights leading us to our inevitable doom.

At the other extreme, we find those who are almost dizzy with excitement about the promise of technology and the future development of mankind. Here we find visionaries who see the destiny of humanity as one of self-transcendence; of an almost Nietzschean transformation of body, mind, and soul: the creation of the Trans or Post Human. (Kurzweil 2000) (Bostrom 2008)

The Trans/Post Human will be the next step in human evolution or rather the first step in human self-directed evolution. It is the place where human culture and biology meet in an explosive technological singularity. Where technology fully enters the human and the human fully enters technology. It is a millenarian faith in the power of technology to bring immortality, god-like strength, beauty and intelligence to our mortal existence: behold "Der Übermensch" 2.0.

Some of our most intelligent and creative minds believe in the eventual possibility of this scenario. They believe in the therapeutic and amplifying powers of genetic engineering, artificial intelligence, fusion power, asteroid mining, nanomedicine, and climate control technology to name but a few of their favorites. Seen collectively, they are the widely grinning face of the great-great-great-grand children of the Enlightenment. They have a boundless faith in man's ability to create the world that he wants to ultimately live and thrive in. They, too, have an unlimited (Protestant?) belief in the human ability for self-perfection and societal optimization. They celebrate, often in "Dionysian" prose, a new festival of the "Supreme Being" which in this case is Man himself. Homo transcendens.

The truth perhaps, as it often does, might lie somewhere in the middle.

There will most certainly be dramatic change as well as catastrophes avoided. Man's adaptability, ingenuity, imagination, reason, and, perhaps most important of all, accumulated cultural knowledge will mitigate and limit both the worst and the best of all possible outcomes. It is likely humanity will learn to better control its environment, create new sources of clean energy, colonize other planets, more effectively cure disease, and increase overall happiness both for itself and even other species. Whether or not the wilder predictions of the trans/post humanists or the technological pessimists will come to pass may in part depend on how the irrational side of man's character plays out in combination with his new found powers. As E. O. Wilson once wrote: we are creatures with "stone age emotions, medieval institutions, and godlike technology". Following him, our ultimate fate may depend on whether or not we are able to emotionally mature, rethink our institutions, and responsibly contain our technologies. So far, so good I would say. We have come a long way from our Australopithecine origins and we have endured much along the way: fierce climate changes, diseases, wars, civilizational collapses, racism, misogyny, and genocide to name but a few of our greatest historical challenges.

To conclude on a mystical note, perhaps our greatest challenge, as it is the greatest challenge for all that exists, is the challenge of the laws of thermodynamics and in particular the ever-growing entropy in the universe. This was something which occupied the mind of Bertrand Russell when he wrote: All the labours of the ages, all the devotion, all the inspiration, all the noonday brightness of human genius, are destined to extinction. The whole temple of Man's achievements must inevitably be buried beneath the debris of a universe in ruins. For some modern mystics, this is exactly the ultimate "reason" why humanity exists, why intelligence arose, why civilization and technology reach for more and better solutions. For these mystics, humanity will prove not only to be the guardians of this planet but of the universe as a whole. Its sacred mission to solve the riddle of what now appears to be the inevitable destiny of the universe: heat death. Admittedly, it is an improbable and unlikely vision, but there is something grand about it nonetheless. Perhaps it is the stirrings of a new religion. Or just a worthy suggestion for a noble and open-ended future of Man.

Bibliography

Adorno, Theodor, and Max Horkheimer. *Dialectic of Enlightenment*. Verso, 2016.

Alexander, R. D. *Darwinism and Human Affairs*. University of Washington Press, 1979.

Arendt, Hannah. *The Origins of Totalitarianism*. Mariner Books, 1973.

Atran, Scott. *Cognitive Foundations of Natural History: Towards an Anthropology of Science*. Cambridge University Press, 1993.

Avineri, Shlomo. *Hegel's Theory of the Modern State*. Cambridge University Press, 1974.

Axelrod, Robert. *On the Evolution of Cooperation*. Basic Books, 2006.

Barrett, Clark H., and James Broesch. "Prepared Social Learning about Dangerous Animals in Children." *Evolution and Human Behavior*, vol. 33, no. 5, 2012, doi:10.1016/j.evolhumbehav.2012.01.003.

Bartov, Omer. *Mirrors of Destruction: War, Genocide, and Modern Identity*. Oxford University Press, 2000.

Bauman, Zygmunt. *Liquid Modernity*. Polity, 2000.

—. *Modernity and the Holocaust*. Cornell University Press, 2001.

Benitez-Burraco, Antonio, et al. "Editorial: Self-Domestication and Human Evolution." *Frontiers in Psychology*, vol. 11, Aug. 2020, doi:10.3389/fpsyg.2020.02007.

Berghahn, Volker R. *Europe in The Era of Two World Wars: From Militarism and Genocide to Civil Society 1900 1950*. Princeton University Press, 2006.

Bickerton, Derek. *More than Nature Needs: Language, Mind, and Evolution*. Harvard University Press, 2014.

Boehm, Christopher. *Hierarchy in the Forest*. Harvard University Press, 2001.

Bostrom. "Why I Want to Be a Posthuman When I Grow Up." *Medical Enhancement and Posthumanity*, Springer, 2008.

Bostrom, Nick, and Milan M. Cirkovic. *Global Catastrophic Risks*. Oxford University Press, 2011.

Bowles, Samuel, and Herbert Gintis. *A Cooperative Species*. Princeton University Press, 2013.

Boyd, Robert, and Joan B. Silk. *How Humans Evolved*. W. W. Norton & Company, 2012.

Boyer, Pascal. *Religion Explained: The Evolutionary Origins of Religious Thought*. Basic Books, 2002.

Bruford, W. H. *The German Tradition of Self-Cultivation: "Bildung" from Humboldt to Thomas Mann.* Cambridge University Press, 2010.

Burckhardt, Jacob. *Judgements on History and Historians.* Translated by Harry Zohn, Routledge Classics, 2012.

Burkert, Walter. *Creation of the Sacred: Tracks of Biology in Early Religions.* Harvard University Press, 1996.

Carneiro, Robert L. *The Evolutioin of the Human Mind.* Eliot Werner, 2010.

Chomsky, Noam. *Hegemony or Survival: America's Quest for Global Dominance.* Holt Paperbacks, 2004.

Christakis, Nicholas A. *Blueprint: The Evolutionary Origins of a Good Society.* Little, Brown Spark, 2019.

Clottes, Jean, and John R. Hinnells. "Paleolithic Art and Religion." *The Penguin Handbook of Ancient Religions*, Perseus Books, 2009.

Cochran, Gregory, and Henry Harpending. *The 10,000 Year Explosion: How Civilization Accelerated Human Evolution.* Basic Books, 2010.

Cummins, Denise. "Dominance Hierarchies and the Evolution of Human Reasoning." *Minds and Machines*, vol. 6, no. 4, 1996, doi:10.1007/bf00389654.

Dahrendorf, Ralf. *Society and Democracy in Germany.* W. W. Norton & Company, 1979.

Damasio, Antonio. *The Strange Order of Things.* Vintage, 2018.

Darwin, Charles. *On The Origin of Species.* Penguin Classics, 2009.

—. *The Descent of Man.* CreateSpace, 2011.

Davis, Nicola. "End of Neanderthals Linked to Flip of Earth's Magnetic Poles, Study Suggests." *The Guardian*, 18 Feb. 2021.

Dawkins, Richard. *The Selfish Gene.* Oxford University Press, 2006.

de Spinoza, Benedict. *Ethics.* Translated by Edwin Curley, Penguin Classics, 2005.

de Tocqueville, Alexis. *The Ancien Régime and the Revolution.* Translated by Gerald Bevan, Penguin Classics, 2008.

de Waal, Frans. *Our Inner Ape.* Riverhead Books, 2006.

—. *The Age of Empathy.* Crown, 2010.

Deacon, Terrence. *The Symbolic Species.* W. W. Norton & Company, 1998.

Dennett, Daniel. *Breaking the Spell: Religion as a Natural Phenomenon.* Penguin Books, 2007.

—. *Consciousness Explained.* Back Bay Books, 1992.

—. *Darwin's Dangerous Idea.* Penguin Books, 1996.

Depew, David J., and Bruce H. Weber, editors. *Evolution and Learning: The Baldwin Effect Reconsidered.* A Bradford Book, 2007.

Derry, Gregory N. *What Science Is and How It Works.* Princeton University Press, 2002.

Dugatkin, Lee Alan, and Lyudmila Trut. *How to Tame a Fox (and Build a Dog)*. University of Chicago Press, 2017.

Dunbar, Robin, et al. *Thinking Big: How the Evolution of Social Life Shaped the Human Mind*. Thames & Hudson, 2018.

Eliade, Mircea. *Shamanism: Archaic Techniques of Ecstasy*. Princeton University Press, 2004.

Elias, Norbert. *The Civilizing Process: Sociogenetic and Psychogenetic Investigations*. Translated by Edmund Jephcott, Blackwell Publishing, 2000.

Evans, Dylan. *Emotion: A Very Short Introduction*. Oxford University Press, 2010.

Ferguson, Niall. *Civilization: The West and the Rest*. Penguin Books, 2012.

—. *Empire: How Britain Made the Modern World*. Penguin Books, 2012.

Fischer, Fritz. *Griff Nach Der Weltmacht. Die Kriegszielpolitik Des Kaiserlichen Deutschland 1914/1918*. Droste, 1961.

Fitch, W. Tecumseh. *The Evolution of Language*. Cambridge University Press, 2010.

Fodor, Jerry A. *The Language of Thought*. Crowell, 1975.

Fredrickson, George M. *Racism: A Short History*. Princeton University Press, 2002.

Freud, Sigmund. *Beyond the Pleasure Principle*. Translated by James Strachey, W. W. Norton & Company, 1990.

—. *Totem and Taboo*. Routledge, 2012.

Fry, Douglas P. *War, Peace, and Human Nature*. Oxford University Press, 2015.

Fukuyama, Francis. *Identity: Contemporary Identity Politics and the Struggle for Recognition*. Profile Books, 2018.

—. *The Origins of Political Order*. Profile Books, 2019.

Gat, Azar. *War in Human Civilization*. Oxford University Press, 2008.

Gellately, Robert. *The Specter of Genocide: Mass Murder in Historical Perspective*. Cambridge University Press, 2010.

Gentile, Emilio. *The Sacralization of Politics in Fascist Italy,*. Translated by Keith Botsford, Harvard University Press, 1996.

Gregory, Andrew. *Eureka: The Birth of Science*. Icon Books, 1999.

Greif, Marissa L., et al. "What Do Children Want to Know about Animals and Artifacts? Domain-Specific Requests for Information." *Psychological Science*, vol. 17, no. 6, 2006, doi:10.2307/40064392.

Guenther, Mathias. *Human-Animal Relationships in San and Hunter-Gatherer Cosmology*. Palgrave Macmillan, 2019.

Haidt, Jonathan. *The Righteous Mind*. Vintage, 2013.

Harari, Yuval Noah. *Homo Deus: A Brief History of Tomorrow*. Vintage Digital, 2016.

Hardt, Michael, and Antonio Negri. *Empire*. Harvard University Press, 2001.

Hare, Brian, et al. "The Self-Domestication Hypothesis: Evolution of Bonobo Psychology Is Due to Selection against Aggression." *Animal Behavior*, vol. 83, 2012, pp. 573–85.

Harris, Sam. *Free Will*. Free Press, 2012.

Hegel, G. W. F. *Hegel's Philosophy of Right*. Translated by T. M. Knox, Oxford University Press, 1967.

—. *The Phenomenology of Spirit*. Translated by A. V. Miller, Oxford University Press, 1977.

—. *The Philosophy of History*. Translated by J. Sibree, Dover Publications, 2004.

Heidegger, Martin. *The Question Concerning Technology and Other Essays*. Translated by William Lovitt, Harper Torchbooks, 1977.

Henrich, Joseph. *The Secret of Our Success*. Princeton University Press, 2015.

Herf, Jeffrey. *Reactionary Modernism: Technology, Culture, and Politics in Weimar and the Third Reich*. Cambridge University Press, 1986.

Herman, Arthur. *The Idea of Decline in Western History*. Free Press, 2007.

Hobbes, Thomas. *Levianthan*. Penguin Classics, 1982.

Hobson, J. A. *Imperialism: A Study*. Cosimo Classics, 2005.

Holland, John H. *Complexity: A Very Short Introduction*. Oxford University Press, 2014.

Horgan, John. *The End Of Science: Facing The Limits Of Knowledge In The Twilight Of The Scientific Age*. Basic Books, 2015.

—. *The End of War*. McSweeney's Publishing, 2014.

Hume, David. *A Treatise of Human Nature*. Penguin Classics, 1984.

Humphrey, Nicholas. "The Social Function of Intellect." *Growing Points in Ethology*, Cambridge University Press, 1976.

Hurford, James R. *The Origins of Grammar: Language in the Light of Evolution II*. Oxford University Press, 2011.

Husserl, Edmund. *The Crisis of European Sciences and Transcendental Phenomenology: An Introduction to Phenomenological Philosophy*. Translated by David Carr, Northwestern University Press, 1970.

Huxley, Thomas Henry. *Evolution and Ethics*. Princeton University Press, 2009.

Jones, Adam. *Genocide: A Comprehensive Introduction*. 3rd ed., Routledge, 2017.

Jones, Peter. *The 1848 Revolutions*. Routledge, 1991

Kallis, Aristotle. *Genocide and Fascism: The Eliminationist Drive in Fascist Europe*. Routledge, 2009.

Kant, Immanuel. *Basic Writings of Kant*. Modern Library, 2001.

Kee, Alistair. *Masters of Suspicion: Feuerbach, Marx, Nietzsche, and Freud*. SCM Press, 2011.

Keeley, Lawrence H. *War before Civilization*. Oxford University Press, 1997.

Kojeve, Alexander. *Introduction to the Reading of Hegel: Lectures on the Phenomenology of Spirit*. Translated by James H. Nichols, Cornell University Press, 1980.

Kropotkin, Peter. *Mutual Aid*. Dover Publications, 2006.

Kurzweil, Ray. *The Age of Spiritual Machines: When Computers Exceed Human Intelligence*. Penguin Books, 2000.

—. *The Singularity Is Near: When Humans Transcend Biology*. Penguin Books, 2005.

Last, Cadell. *Global Brain Singularity*. Springer, 2020.

Le Blanc, Steven. *Constant Battles: Why We Fight*. St. Martin's Griffin, 2004.

LoBue, Vanessa, et al. "Young Children's Interest in Live Animals." *British Journal of Developmental Psychology*, 2012, doi:10.1111/j.2044-835x.2012.02078.x.

Locke, John. *The First & Second Treatises of Government*. CreateSpace, 2016.

Lorenz, Konrad. *On Aggression*. Translated by Majorie Kerr Wilson, Mariner Books, 1974.

Lucretius. *On the Nature of Things*. Translated by Smith, Martin Ferguson, Hackett, 2001.

MacMillan, Margaret. *War: How Conflict Shaped Us*. Random House, 2020.

Malafouris, Lambros. *How Things Shape the Mind: A Theory of Material Engagement*. The MIT Press, 2013.

Marcuse, Herbert. *Eros and Civilization*. Beacon Press, 1974.

—. *One-Dimensional Man*. Routledge, 2013.

McCauley, R. N. "The Naturalness of Religion and the Unnaturalness of Science." *Explanation and Cognition*, The MIT Press, 2000, pp. 61–85.

McPherron, Shannon P., et al. "Evidence for Stone-Tool-Assisted Consumption of Animal Tissues before 3.39 Million Years Ago at Dikika, Ethiopia." *Nature*, 2010, doi:10.1038/nature09248.

Mead, George H. *G.H. Mead: A Reader*. Edited by Filipe Carreira da Silva, Routledge, 2011.

Melson, Gail F. *Why the Wild Things Are: Animals in the Lives of Children*. Harvard University Press, 2005.

Menschenfreund, Yaki. "The Holocaust and The Trial of Modernity." *Azure*, no. 39, 2010.

Mithen, Steven. *The Prehistory of the Mind: A Search for the Origins of Art, Religion and Science*. Orion Pub Co, 1998.

—. *The Singing Neanderthals: The Origins of Music, Language, Mind, and Body*. Harvard University Press, 2007.

Moore, G. E. *Principia Ethica*. Jovian Press, 2017.

Morris, Desmond. *The Naked Ape*. Delta, 1999.

Morris, Ian. *War! What Is It Good For?* Farrar, Straus and Giroux, 2014.

Morris, Simon Conway. *Life's Solution (Inevitable Humans in a Lonely Universe)*. Cambridge University Press, 2004.

Mukherjee, Siddhartha. *The Gene An Intimate History*. Vintage Digital, 2016.

Nietzsche, Friedrich. *The Gay Science*. Translated by Walter Kaufmann, Vintage, 1974.

Orwell, George. *A Collection of Essays*. Mariner Books, 1971.

Patton, Kimberley. "Traditional Views of Animals in Religion." *A Communion of Subjects: Animals in Religion, Science, and Ethics*, Columbia University Press, 2009.

Peterson, Dale, and Richard Wrangham. *Demonic Males: Apes and the Origins of Human Violence*. Mariner Books, 2003.

Pinker, Steven. *Enlightenment Now: The Case for Reason, Science, Humanism, and Progress*. Penguin Books, 2018.

—. *The Better Angels of Our Nature: The Decline of Violence In History And Its Causes*. Penguin Books, 2011.

—. *The Language Instinct*. William Morrow, 1994.

Pinker, Steven, and Paul Bloom. "Natural Language and Natural Selection." *Behavioral and Brain Sciences*, vol. 13, no. 4, 1990.

Pope, Alexander. *An Essay on Man and Other Poems*. Dover Publications, 1994.

Power, Samantha. *A Problem from Hell: America and The Age of Genocide*. Perseus Books, 2002.

Rattansi, Ali. *Racism: A Short Introduction*. Oxford University Press, 2007.

Richards, Robert J. *Was Hitler a Darwinian?* University of Chicago Press, 2013.

Richmond, Oliver. *Peace: A Very Short Introduction*. Oxford University Press, 2014.

Rosling, Hans. *Factfulness*. Sceptre, 2018.

Roth, John K. *Genocide and Human Rights: A Philosophical Guide*. Palgrave Macmillan, 2005.

Rousseau, Jean-Jacques. *A Discourse on Inequality*. Translated by Maurice Cranston, Penguin Classics, 1984.

—. *On the Social Contract*. Translated by Donald A. Cress, Hackett, 1988.

Sartre, Jean Paul. *Being and Nothingness,*. Washington Square Press, 1993.

Schopenhauer, Arthur. *Über Die Freiheit Des Menschlichen Willens / Über Die Grundlagen Der Moral*. Marix Verlag, 2014.

Schutt, Bill. *Cannibalism: A Perfectly Natural History*. Algonquin Books, 2018.

Segerstrale, Ullica. *Nature's Oracle: The Life and Work of W. D. Hamilton*. Oxford University Press, 2013.

Seyfarth, Robert M., and Dorothy L. Cheney. *Baboon Metaphysics: The Evolution of a Social Mind*. University of Chicago Press, 2008.

Shakespeare, William. *Henry V*. Penguin Classics, 2017.

—. *Julius Caesar*. Dover Publications, 2009.

Shepard, Paul. *The Others: How Animals Made Us Human*. Island Press, 1997.

Sidanius, Jim, and Felicia Pratto. *Social Dominance: An Intergroup Theory of Social Hierarchy and Oppression*. Cambridge University Press, 2001.

Singer, Peter. *A Darwinian Left: Politics, Evolution, and Cooperation*. Yale University Press, 2000.

—. *Marx: A Very Short Introduction*. Oxford University Press, 2001.

—. *The Expanding Circle*. Princeton University Press, 2011.

Smith, Maynard, and Eörs Szathmáry. *The Major Transitions in Evolution*. Oxford University Press, 1998.

Sombart, Werner. *Der Bourgeois*. Duncker & Humblot, 1913.

Spengler, Oswald. *The Decline of the West*. Translated by Arthur Helps, Oxford University Press, 1991.

Stone, Dan. *Histories of The Holocaust*. Oxford University Press, 2010.

Taguieff, Pierre-Andre. *La Force Du Prejuge': Essai Sur Le Racisme et Ses Doubles*. Gallimard, 1987.

Taylor, Richard. *Good and Evil: A New Direction*. Prometheus Books, 1984.

Thayer, Bradley A. *Darwin and International Relations: On the Evolutionary Origins of War and Ethnic Conflict*. University Press of Kentucky, 2009.

Tomasello, Michael. *A Natural History of Human Morality*. Harvard University Press, 2018.

Turner, Jonathan. *On Human Nature*. Routledge, 2020.

van Vugt, Mark, and Anjana Ahuja. *Selected: Why Some People Lead, Why Others Follow, and Why It Matters*. Profile Books, 2010.

Wade, Nicholas. *A Troublesome Inheritance: Genes, Race, and Human History*. Penguin Books, 2015.

Ward, Peter D., and Donald Brownlee. *Rare Earth: Why Complex Life Is Uncommon in the Universe*. Copernicus, 2007.

Weber, Max. *Charisma and Disenchantment: The Vocation Lectures*. Translated by Damion Searls, NYRB Classics, 2020.

—. *The Protestant Ethic and the Spirit of Capitalism: And Other Writings*. Translated by Peter Baehr, Penguin Classics, 2002.

Weitz, Eric D. *A Century of Genocide: Utopias of Race and Nation*. Princeton University Press, 2015.

Wilson, David Sloan. *This View of Life: Completing The Darwinian Revolution*. Pantheon, 2019.

Wilson, David Sloan, and E. O. Wilson. "Survival of the Selfless." *The New Scientist*, Oct. 2007.

Wilson, E. O. *Biophilia*. Harvard University Press, 1984.

—. *The Social Conquest of Earth*. Liveright, 2013.

Wootton, David. *The Invention of Science: A New History of the Scientific Revolution*. Harper, 2015.

Wrangham, Richard. *Catching Fire: How Cooking Made Us Human*. Basic Books, 2009.

—. *The Goodness Paradox*. Vintage, 2019.

Zagorin, Perez. *Francis Bacon*. Princeton University Press, 1998.

***ibidem**.eu*